*The Script of Decadence*

# The Script
# of Decadence

*Essays on the*
*Fictions of Flaubert*
*and the Poetics*
*of Romanticism*

Eugenio Donato

*New York   Oxford*
Oxford University Press
*1993*

Oxford University Press

Oxford   New York   Toronto
Delhi   Bombay   Calcutta   Madras   Karachi
Kuala Lumpur   Singapore   Hong Kong   Tokyo
Nairobi   Dar es Salaam   Cape Town
Melbourne   Auckland   Madrid

and associated companies in
Berlin   Ibadan

Library of Congress Cataloging-in-Publication Data
Donato, Eugenio.
The script of decadence : essays on the fictions of Flaubert
and the poetics of Romanticism / Eugenio Donato.
p. cm.   ISBN 0-19-505724-4
1. Flaubert, Gustave, 1821–1880—Criticism and interpretation.
2. Decadence (Literary movement)
3. Romanticism.
4. Poetics.
I. Title.   PQ2249.D56
1993   843'.8—dc20   90-19590

9 8 7 6 5 4 3 2 1

Printed in the United States of America
on acid-free paper

# Contents

1 "A mere labyrinth of letters": Flaubert and the Quest for Fiction—A Montage 3

2 Flaubert and the Question of History: The Orient 35

3 The Museum's Furnace: Notes Toward a Contextual Reading of *Bouvard and Pécuchet* 56

4 Gnostic Fictions: A Reading of the Episode of the Heretics in *The Temptation of Saint Anthony* 80

5 Who Signs "Flaubert"? 100

6 Lancelot Brown, Rousseau, and the Enlightenment's Rhetoric of Nature 114

7 Divine Agonies: Of Representation and Narrative in Romantic Poetics 130

8 The Ruins of Memory: Archaeological Fragments and Textual Artifacts 168

9 Bodies: On the Limits of Representation in Romantic Poetics 191

*The Script of Decadence*

*We are Alexandrians still, and we may as well
be proud of it, for it is central to our profession.*
  Harold Bloom

*In the* Affendämmerung, *or the twilight of
  the apes
What is more fitting than that man should
  for reassurance turn to japes?*
. . . . . . . . . . . . . . . . . . . . . . . . . . . . . . . . . . . . . . . . . . .
*I'm all for Daniel. In this age penumbral
Let the timbrel resound in the tumbrel.*
  Ogden Nash

# 1 "A mere labyrinth of letters": Flaubert and the Quest for Fiction— a Montage

## I

*The universe (which others call the library)* . . . Jorge Luis Borges

*Je crèverai entre deux périodes.* Flaubert

Hegel's *Phenomenology of Spirit* and *Encyclopedia of the Philosophical Sciences,* Novalis's *Encyclopedia,* Mallarmé's *Livre,* and Borges's "Library of Babel" all name the different moments—under barely differing metaphors for the certitude, nostalgia, or nightmare of the same concept—of a unified, self-generated, total discourse joining in a circular movement the absolute Origin and End of a linear order. The concept of a unified, global knowledge which is not simply an indiscriminate accumulation (for example, Diderot's *Encyclopédie*), but a Total Order which accounts for all past, present, future, artistic, philosophic, and religious endeavors— this concept belongs to Hegel. Hegel's *Phenomenology* was to mark the advent of the Totalizing End of History, *Geist*'s revelation of and to itself in Absolute

3

Knowledge, and the true authorial Voice of the *Encyclopedia*. Such a history is above all rational: "The sole thought which philosophy brings to the treatment of history is the simple concept of *Reason:* that Reason is the law of the world and that, therefore, in world history, things have come about rationally."[1]

Novalis also entertained the dream of a self-generated *Encyclopedia*. Novalis's project runs parallel to Hegel's but is exemplary in that it remains incomplete and fragmentary for intrinsic and not accidental reasons. For Novalis:

Everything must be encyclopedized.

It must be possible to put into table any possible history of *literature*, of art and of the *world*.

My book must become a scientific bible—a model real and ideal—and the seed for all books.

Properly speaking, the description of the Bible is my enterprise—or, to state it even better, the theory of the Bible—art and theory of the Bible. (Manner of elevating a book to the level of the Bible.) Fully complete, the Bible is a *perfect library*—well-ordered. The schema of the Bible is at the same time the schema of the library— the authentic schema—indicating at the same time its own genesis—its own use, etc.[2]

Novalis's project not only shows the theological nature of the enterprise but connects it directly with the Bible on the one hand and with the idea of an Ideal Library on the other. Such an Ideal Library, the concretization of the Ideal Encyclopedia, would not simply be the random depository of as many books as possible, but would display them in such a way that their spacing would manifest a totally rational order. As such, the library is an institution that attempts to generate a lay equivalent of the divine Book. In the nineteenth century the "Encyclopedia Libraries" came to be conceived as the primary conceptual tool by means of which men were to decipher the world, yet the decipherment itself has a preordained place in the library. The "Book-Encyclopedia-Library" then becomes what Borges was to describe ironically in another context as "the inconceivable museum of platonic archetypes, intelligible essences and universals."

Yet, as Derrida has shown, Novalis's *Encyclopedia* is inscribed in a system of representation which it does not master. Hence, Novalis's project of totalization is doomed to remain a project.[3] For our purposes let us take the fragmentary nature of the *Encyclopedia* as emblematic of a cleft in the plenitude of Hegel.

Mallarmé's *Livre* in many respects echoes Hegel's *Encyclopedia:*

The Book where spirit lives satisfied . . . unpersonified, the volume, inasmuch as one separates oneself from it as author, does not require any approach by the reader. As such, among human accessories, it exists by itself: made yet already there [il a lieu tout seul: fait, étant]. The buried meaning moves of its own accord, disposing the pages in chorus.[4]

Yet, like Novalis's *Encyclopedia*, Mallarmé's *Livre* remains in fragments.[5] His oft-quoted declaration that "everything in

Une préface . . . énoncerait au futur ("vous allez lire ceci") le sens ou le contenu conceptuels . . . de ce qui aurait déjà été écrit.

Jacques Derrida

Le temps est le temps de la préface, l'espace—dont le temps aura été la vérité—est l'espace de la préface. Celle-ci occuperait donc en totalité le lieu et la durée du livre.

Jacques Derrida

Le livre ne commence ni ne finit, tout au plus il en fait semblant.                    Mallarmé

Commencer et finir sont des actes décisifs et dérisoires.

Roland Barthes

the world exists to end in a book"[6] perhaps marks the reason for the necessary failure of both enterprises within the text as representation. The "world" as "thing," "meaning," or "signified" logically and temporally predates its metaphoric transcription in the *Book,* and the *Book* as totalization is always on the horizon as a never present future. As Derrida has so convincingly argued, the time of the text is the time of a continuous *preface* which is always written after that which the text represents in a book yet to come. The temporality that Derrida ascribes to the text is similar, in this respect, to that which, for Frank Kermode, characterizes fiction. In Kermode's words: "Men, like poets, rush 'into the middest,' in *media res,* where they also die in *mediis rebus.*" And of course, since "men die because they cannot join the beginning and the end," they invent fictions: "to make sense of their span they need fictive concords with origins and ends, such as give meaning to lives and to poems."[7]

Fiction, as Kermode would have it, is nothing but the imposing of artificial, absolute origins and ends on that which is, by definition, without beginning or end. Hegel then believed in a supreme and absolute fiction, whereas Mallarmé, at the opposite extreme, did not think any such absolute fiction possible. Between these two extremes, fictions remain the representations of texts which never quite coincide with them.

Of course some fictions, with the summoning of a monstrous imagination, will attempt to join opposites, to juxtapose fiction with the impossibility of fiction. Take, for example, Borges's "Library of Babel." Its halls which contain

everything: the minutely detailed history of the future, the archangels' autobiographies, the faithful catalogue of the Library, thousands and thousands of false catalogues, the demonstration of the fallacy of those catalogues, the demonstration of the fallacy of the true catalogue, the Gnostic Gospel of Basilides, the commentary on that gospel, the commentary on the commentary on that gospel, the true story of your death, the translation of every book in all languages, the interpolations of every book in all books[8]

are nothing but the fictional nightmare of the Hegelian *Logos*. It is against such a background of absolute or impossible fictions, and of their teratogenic mixture, that we might best try to understand Flaubert's fictional enterprise.

## II

*Je lis des catalogues de livres que j'annote.*
    Flaubert

*Je suis un homme-plume. Je sens par elle, à cause d'elle, par rapport à elle et beaucoup plus avec elle.* Flaubert

*Avant-hier, dans la forêt de Touques, un charmant endroit près d'une fontaine, j'ai trouvé des bouts de cigares éteints avec des bribes de pâtés. On avait été là—en partie! J'ai écrit cela dans Novembre, il y a onze ans! C'était alors purement imaginé,*

It has often been said that Flaubert's fictional enterprise, despite its aesthetics and metaphysics, is sustained by an ambivalent relation to the concepts of Book, Encyclopedia, and Library. For Hugh Kenner, Flaubert "is the great student of cultural feedback, writing books about what

*et l'autre jour ça a été éprouvé.*
*Tant ce qu'on invente est vrai,*
*sois-en sûre.* . . . *Ma pauvre Bo-*
*vary sans doute souffre et pleure*
*dans vingt villages de France à*
*la fois, à cette heure même.*

Flaubert

books do to the readers of books";
"Emma Bovary herself would have been
impossible without books, quantities of
books, books of the very sort that
*Madame Bovary* itself approximates."[9]
For Foucault, *The Temptation of Saint
Anthony* is "the book of books: it composes in one 'volume' a series of elements
of language which have been constituted
from books already written and which are
by their rigorously documented character
the repetition of that which has already
been said."[10] *Bouvard and Pécuchet,*
which for Kenner is emblematic of "the
incompetence of fiction itself, which is
endlessly *arranging* things,"[11] represents
for Foucault a case where "the Library . . . is visible, catalogued, named
and analyzed. . . . It possesses its powers
by virtue of its very existence—through
the indefinite proliferation of printed paper. . . . The Bible has been transformed
into a bookstore."[12]

Flaubert's quest for fiction will thus
minimally coincide with a quest for the
form of the Book. Its requirement is simple: to find a finite condensed narrative
conforming to its subject matter. This simple requirement is stated by Bouvard and
Pécuchet when they decide to write a historical book: "one can take a subject, exhaust the sources, analyze it well, then
condense it in a narrative, which would be
a summary of facts, reflecting the entire
truth."[13] Yet such a task quickly turns out
to be intrinsically impossible. This impossibility exists on two levels: on the one
hand, the "reality" quickly fragments itself into an infinity of disconnected and
contradictory events; on the other hand,

the written representation is incapable of acceding to a completed form.

For Flaubert, who described it metaphorically as "a complicated organism" (798),[14] and a "heavy machine" (342), a Book exists as a privileged form, distinct and independent from any of its possible semantic representations. The first property of form is its unity: "beautiful fragments are nothing. Unity, unity, everything is there" (158). A Book, then, "is a totality where each part concurs in the whole, and not an assemblage of sentences which, no matter how well made, are of value only if individually isolated."[15] In a letter to George Sand, Flaubert compares the Book to a wall of the Acropolis: "I ask myself whether a book, independently of what it says, cannot produce the same effect. In the precision of its assembly, the rarity of its elements, the gloss of its surface, the harmony of its whole, is there not an intrinsic virtue, a kind of divine force, something eternal like a principle?" (1573). This form or principle is in fact deceptively simple and is nothing other than that of a straight line, like a wall: "Prose must stand straight, from beginning to end, like a wall carrying its ornamentation all the way to its foundations, and in its perspective it should form a long, unified line" (405). There is, however, a major difference: whereas the beginnings and ends of walls are clearly demarcated, the line which constitutes the architectonic of prose and of the Book can never be temporally or spatially terminated: "prose is a dog-gone thing! It is never finished!" (335); "this is what is diabolical about prose, it is never finished" (404). The in-

*Je ne crois seulement qu'à l'éternité d'une chose, c'est à celle de d'illusion, qui est la vraie vérité.*                    Flaubert

*O no, there is no end; the end is death and madness!*            Kidd

*. . . balivernes que j'aligne très sérieusement sur de beau papier blanc.*                        Flaubert

completion is intrinsic: there cannot be any privileged end point. The belief that an author can conclude is that of a fool: *"ineptitude consists in wanting to conclude. . . .* Yes, stupidity consists in wanting to conclude. We are but a thread and we want to know the web" (267).

The capacity to reach an end point does not belong to prose or literature. If literature could conclude, it would conform to reality and be able to postulate a truth-value. It cannot do so, however. Hence the contradictory requirement that the novelist must, on the one hand, reach for an impossible realism and, on the other, pursue a futile aestheticism. "Art in the last analysis cannot be more serious than a game of skittles" (292), a game which knows that, because of its inevitable cleavage from the reality that it pretends to portray, it is unable to attain any representational identity: "The first quality and end of art is illusion" (426).

God concludes, whereas artists pretend to while knowing all along that fictions are fictions precisely because they are unable to conclude: "One always falsifies reality when one wishes to bring it to a conclusion that belongs to God alone. And then, is it with fictions that one can manage to discover truth? . . . The frenzy to conclude is one of the most fatal and sterile manias peculiar to humanity" (765).

*Bouvard and Pécuchet* is the emblematic literary landmark of fiction's necessary incapacity to raise the description of reality to intelligibility, to find within representation an order which might somehow adequately correspond to what, by contrast, remains a world of human events submitted to chance—"suppose the flight of the King [Louis XVI] unhindered, Robespierre escaping or Bonaparte assassinated—chances which depended on a less scrupulous innkeeper, an open door, a sleeping sentry—and the course of the world was changed" (BP, 138); a world of dubious genealogies—"they even wished to learn Hebrew, which is the mother-language of Celtic, unless it is derived from it!" (BP, 131); of uncertain logic—"cause and effect are interchangeable" (BP, 86); of the earth's unfathomable depths—"geology is too restricted! . . . As for the rest, and the ocean-beds, we shall always be ignorant" (BP, 112). A century later, Bouvard and Pécuchet would have no doubt found solace in Borges's discovery of a "Samoyedic Lithuanian dialect of Guarani, with classical Arabian inflections."[16]

The failure of prose to reach an end point and the concomitant failure of fiction to accede to a privileged form is, in one respect, only the consequence of the incapacity of language to sustain a proper representation of the world. This incapacity of language is inscribed in each of its signifying modes. Language fails to sustain a stable semiology, a coherent rhetoric, a true philological history, or a structured grammar.

After their failure at agronomy and aboriculture, Bouvard and Pécuchet continue their "natural" quest, which follows an arbitrary alphabetical sequence, and move on to landscape architecture. What the two protagonists never realize, never recognize, is that their "natural" mistakes are, above all, linguistic mistakes.

*Le langage en tant que forme est devenu la passion de l'écrivain.*　　Roland Barthes

*Strings of letters and empty spaces, like a code that I've lost the key to.*　　John Barth

*Si les signes vous faschent, ô quant vous fascheront les choses signifiées.*      Rabelais

*. . . l'on meurt presque toujours dans l'incertitude de son propre nom, à moins d'être un sot.*      Flaubert

*Gardens were before Gardeners, and but some hours after the Earth.*      Browne

*La "nature" est un produit du Néolithique.*      Pouillon

Bouvard tries to grow "proper" nominal species of melons and plants. But because he plants the seeds too close to one another, through metonymic contamination they produce monstrous metaphors: "Actually, as he had grown different species next to one another, the sweet variety got mixed with the bitter, the big Portuguese with the great Mongolian, and the presence of tomatoes completing the anarchy, there resulted abominable hybrids of a pumpkin flavor" (BP, 48). "Proper" names are no more natural than "proper" species; both are the result of artificial differentiating grids. The failure of these adventures in arboriculture is in fact due to the failure of taxonomic nomenclature, that is, to a failure to match plants and names correspondingly: "They looked in their books for plants to buy, and, having chosen names which to them seemed wonderful, they wrote to a market-gardener at Falaise, who eagerly undertook to send them three hundred saplings for which he had no market" (BP, 55). Garden architecture, in turn, leads them to a rhetorical disaster.

The author [of *The Architect of the Garden*] divides gardens into an infinity of styles. There is, in the first place, the Melancholy or Romantic, which is distinguished by everlastings, ruins, tombs, and an "ex-voto to the Virgin, indicating the spot where a cavalier has fallen under an assassin's dagger." The Terrible is constructed with overhanging rocks, shattered trees and burnt-out cabins; the Exotic, by planting Peruvian torch-thistles to bring back memories to a settler or traveller. The Pensive must provide, like Ermenonville, a temple to philosophy (BP, 59–60).

*Je soutiens qu'il n'y a qu'un géomètre et un sot qui puissent parler sans figures.*      Rousseau

*What therefore is truth? A mobile army of metaphors, metonymies, anthropomorphisms; in short a sum of human relations which became poetically and rhetorically intensified, metamorphosed, adorned, and after long usage seems to a nation fixed, canonic, and binding; truths are illusions of which one has forgotten that they are illusions, worn-out metaphors which have become powerless to affect the senses; coins which have their obverse effaced, and now are no longer of account as coins, but merely as metal.*
Nietzsche

*Let it be as if. Let's make a philosophy of that as if.*
Laurence Sterne

Since our gardeners fail to recognize the artificial distinction of codes, they end up producing a new monstrosity: "In the half-light it was somehow terrible. The rock, like a mountain, took up the lawn, the tomb made a cube in the midst of the spinach, the Venetian bridge a circumflex accent over the kidney beans—and the cabin beyond, a great black smudge, for they had fired the thatched roof to make it more poetical" (BP, 65).

The ironic quest of Bouvard and Pécuchet stems from their incapacity to recognize that language is incapable of grasping the nature of things. After failing in their botanical endeavor, they pass on to science and then to history, always convinced that the web of language will be sufficient to help them come to terms with the world. In the same manner that, in their gardening, they ended up creating metaphoric monsters, their attempts to organize the world of events into a representational order culminate in a metaphoric breakdown of the semiological mechanism of signification—signifier and signified become indistinguishable and the sign qua sign collapses: "the world became a symbol. They sought, on the walls, a quantity of things that were not there, and ended by seeing them" (BP, 140–41). Thus they had to reach the conclusion ihat "syntax is a fantasy and grammar an illusion" (BP, 165).

## III

*What confusion in greater THEATRES from words of little meaning.*      Laurence Sterne

Flaubert's characters are in search of an

absolute, and their quest is mediated by the written word: literature for Emma Bovary, the Bible for Anthony, the Library for Bouvard and Pécuchet. Their ironic mistake is to believe in the absolutes implied by their enterprises. Art, Truth, and Knowledge are only teleological mirages. Take the Bible, Anthony's only and supreme book: it is not certain that it is unique, that it does not exist, like the treatises of Bouvard and Pécuchet, in many a different and contradictory version. When Anthony wants to dispel the ghosts of the heretics, they all at once brandish in the air their rolls of papyrus, tablets of wood, scrolls of leather, rolls of woven stuff bearing inscriptions; and elbowing and pushing each other, they all shout to Anthony:

THE CERINTHIANS "Behold the Gospel of the Hebrews!"

THE MARCIONITES "Behold the Gospel of the Lord!"

THE MARCOSIANS "The Gospel of Eve!"

THE EUCRATITES "The Gospel of Thomas!"

THE CAINITES "The Gospel of Judas!"

BASILIDES "The Treatise upon the Destiny of the Soul!"

MANES "The Prophecy of Barkouf!"[17]

If one took for granted the singularity of the Bible, the problem of interpreting it would not be very different from that encountered by Bouvard and Pécuchet when they attempt to interpret History:

ANTHONY: "It matters little! We must believe the Scriptures!"

HILARION: "Saint Paul, Origen, and many others did not understand the Scriptures in a literal sense: yet if Holy Writ can be explained by allegories it becomes the portion of a small number, and the evidence of the truth disappears. What must we do?" (TSA, 58)

Emma Bovary, Anthony, and Bouvard and Pécuchet are the shadows projected by the virtual end point of theology. If their reality dissolves in the labyrinths of the Library, it is because they are the creations of the author's original wandering in it. When Bouvard and Pécuchet decide that history is nothing but a bundle of contradictions, what follows is true of characters and author alike: "To judge it impartially, it would be necessary to have read all the histories, all the memoirs, all the newspapers and all the documents in manuscript, since from the least omission an error may ensue which will lead on to others *ad infinitum*. They renounced the undertaking" (BP, 139).

Impossible as it may seem, the task is as inevitable as it is necessary. Bouvard and Pécuchet, in attempting to totalize the Library, end up copying

*Words, displaced and mutilated words, words of others.*

Jorge Luis Borges

everything that came into their hands, . . . long enumerations . . . notes on authors already read, old papers bought by weight from the nearby paper factory.

But they felt the need to classify. . . . They then copied again in a big commercial register. Pleasure to be found in the material act of copying over.

Examples of all styles: agricultural, medical, theological, classical, romantic, circumlocutions. . . .

"What shall we do?" "One should not re-

*. . . if he is a man of the least spirit, he will bear fifty deviations from a straight line to make with this or that party as he goes along, which he can in no way avoid . . . he will moreover have various*
*Accounts to reconcile:*
*Anecdotes to pick up:*
*Inscriptions to make out:*
*Stories to weave in:*
*Traditions to sift:*
*Personages to call upon:*

*Panegyrics to paste up at . . . this door:*
*. . . To sum up all; there are archives at every stage to be look'd into, and rolls, records, documents, and endless genealogies . . . in short, there is no end of it.*        Laurence Sterne

*Il n'y en a plus, de ces artistes comme autrefois, de ceux dont la vie et l'esprit étaient l'instrument aveugle de l'appétit du Beau, organes de Dieu, par lesquels il se prouvait à lui-même. Pour ceux-là le monde n'était pas. . . . Ils regardaient la vie humaine avec un regard étonné, comme nous contemplons des fourmilières.*        Flaubert

flect! . . . Let us copy! The page must be filled, let the 'monument' complete itself. Equality in everything, good, evil, the beautiful and the ugly, the insignificant and the characteristic!"[18]

Bouvard and Pécuchet's wandering in the maze of the written word is a mirror image of Flaubert's undertaking where, in order to write *Bouvard and Pécuchet* (but the same would be true of *The Temptation of Saint Anthony* or *Salammbô*), he has to start where his characters end: "I am accumulating note upon note, book upon book" (551); "Do you know the number of volumes that I have had to absorb for my two fellows? More than 1500! My file is eight inches high" (1935); "As for myself, I have gotten indigestion from books. I burp *in-folio*" (537). Like his two antiheroes, Flaubert is lost in the web of the written word: "when I say soon, it is only by way of speaking, for the subject extends itself considerably, with each new reading a thousand others come forth! I, sir, am in a labyrinth!" (550); "reading is an abyss; one never gets out of it" (397).[19]

*Bouvard and Pécuchet* remains an unfinished book which tells of the impossibility of finishing books. One should not think that literature in any way provides an aesthetic alternative to the failure of metaphysics. The act of writing fiction is intrinsically isomorphic to totalizing the *Encyclopedia* or the Library: "To write one would have to know everything. As long as we remain petty scribblers [*écrivassiers*], we have a monstrous ignorance. . . . The books from which entire literatures derived, like Homer and Rabelais, are encyclopedias of their times.

Those good men knew everything; we know nothing" (466).

## IV

*Solvitur ambulando*

*La storia che volevo raccontare dunque è impossibile non solo raccontaria ma innanzitutto viveria.* Italo Calvino

*Peut-être qu'il n'y a pas de but.* Flaubert

Before trying to answer the question as to why the modern author's failure is inevitable, let us briefly explore his strategy. As we said, to write a successful fiction—that is, one that has representational access to truth and thus to "Beauty"—one must be able to conclude. But only God has that privilege, for only God can grasp form in its totality, since he alone perceives absolute Origins and Ends and the Order that they sustain. For our purposes, Borges's definition is as good as any: "What is a divine mind? . . . There is not a theologian who does not define it; I prefer an example. The steps a man takes from the day of his birth until that of his death trace in time an inconceivable figure. The Divine Mind intuitively grasps that form immediately."[20] The modern author, on the other hand, condemned to the infinite mediation of fragmentary texts, has to have recourse to a topographical strategy in order to see the form. Since the problem of seeing can be translated into a spatial metaphor of perspective, the act of writing can be described as a climb and a search for

*Quand je lis Shakespeare . . . il me semble que je suis sur une haute montagne; tout disparaît et tout apparaît. On n'est plus homme, on est oeil.* Flaubert

*Il me semble que je vais m'embarquer pour un très grand voyage, vers des régions inconnues, et que je n'en reviendrai pas.*
                                    Flaubert

*Le seul moyen de vivre en paix, c'est de se placer tout d'un bond au-dessus de l'humanité entière et de n'avoir avec elle rien de commun, qu'un rapport d'oeil.*          Flaubert

*Depuis le temps où j'écrivais en demandant à ma bonne les lettres qu'il fallait employer pour faire les mots des phrases que j'inventais, jusqu'à ce soir où l'encre sèche sur les ratures de mes pages, j'ai suivi une ligne droite, incessamment prolongée et tirée au cordeau à travers tout. J'ai toujours vu le but se reculer devant moi, d'années en années, de progrès en progrès. Que de fois je suis tombé à plat ventre au moment où il me semblait le toucher.*          Flaubert

elevation. The task of the author is to climb high enough to *see:*

Is not the artist's life, or rather the work of art to be achieved, like a great mountain to be scaled? . . . First, you glimpse a peak from below. Up in the heavens, it sparkles in its purity; its height is frightening but it beckons you for this very reason. You set out. Yet with each leveling of the path, the summit grows larger, the horizon recedes and one proceeds through precipices, vertigo and discouragements. . . . The Earth is lost forever, and the end will likely never be attained. . . . You are left with nothing but an indomitable desire to climb still higher, to be done with it, to die. Sometimes, however, a blast of the winds from heaven arrives and unveils to your dazzled eyes innumerable infinite and marvelous perspectives! One can make out men twenty thousand feet below, an Olympian air fills your giant lungs and you see yourself as a colossus having the whole world as a pedestal. Then the fog descends again, and you continue, fumblingly, gropingly, tearing your nails against the rockface and crying in solitude. Let us die in the snow, perish in the white agony of our desire, in the murmur of the torrents of Spirit [*l'Esprit*], our faces turned toward the sun![21]

The space of the act of writing is permeated with fog which blocks sight, hides direction, and changes the journey into endless and aimless wandering. It transforms the altitude of the mountains, which for the nineteenth century were a privileged place of health and permanence, into one of bleeding and death which is now coextensive with writing itself. It reduces the Voice of Hegel's *Geist* to a murmur and hides the Nietzschean sun, preventing

*We climb by the most dangerous paths, our eyes open, impervious to the risk, on the rooftops, on the cliffs, on the towers of fantasy, without the slightest vertigo, born as we are to climb—we sleep walkers of the day! We artists! We dissimulators of nature! We lunatics and seekers of God! We travellers in the silence of death, tireless travellers on heights.* Nietzsche

*Mais le sol tremble sous nous. Où prendre notre point d'appui, en admettant même que nous avons le levier. . . . Ce qui nous manque c'est le principe intrinsèque . . . c'est l'idée même du sujet. Nous prenons des notes, nous faisons des voyages; misère! nous devenons savants!* Flaubert

*Like all men of the Library, I have travelled in my youth; I have wandered in search of a book, perhaps the Catalogue of catalogues; now that my eyes can hardly decipher what I write, I am preparing to die just a few leagues from the hexagon in which I was born.* Jorge Luis Borges

it from defining a direction toward the End.

Nietzsche later will have his Zarathustra climb to the summit, look into the noon sun, and return. Having reached the End, and after reinscribing "Truth" into a "Fable—that is, into a fiction—Nietzsche will be able to reinstate origins through a movement opposed to that of Flaubert: "incipit Zarathustra." Flaubert's nihilism is perhaps more radical: the writer is doomed to remain in the fog of undifferentiation, in a middle ground which subverts aim, direction, and ultimately life. Not surprisingly, then, Flaubert, unable to have access to a supreme fiction and alone without origin or end, will write: "literally speaking, I don't know where I am" (270). Given the symmetry between Flaubert and his characters, it is not surprising to find Anthony perched on a plateau in the middle of the desert—another directionless, boundless, flattened, undifferentiated space. To the metaphor of writing corresponds that of crossing the desert: "I have undertaken an insane book. . . . I expect nothing more out of life than a string of papers to daub in black. It seems to me that I am crossing a solitude without end, to I know not where. And I am the one who is, all at once, the desert, the traveller and the camel" (1530).

Unable to gain access to the plenitude that eschatology alone can provide, the writer can only play at generating pseudofictions which pretend to describe events from a divinely elevated standpoint when in fact he has no elevation. His question—"when will facts be written about

BLAGUE, sb. [Fr.]: *Pretentious falsehood, "humbug."* 1837: Carlyle—Fr. Rev. . . . *The largest, most inspiring piece of blague manufactured for some centuries.* 1886: Huxley—Pall Mall G. . . *.It believes in shibboleths and sentimental blague.*

Oxford English Dictionary

*Un philosophe à l'écoute des sciences entend, aujourd'hui . . . une parole de mort. . . . Cette mort que notre savoir et nos pratiques portent dans le flanc depuis quatre siècles à peu près, qui en est, depuis hier, à son abominable gésine. Pas un savant qui ne le crie dans le désert.*

Michel Serres

from the point of view of a superior blague, that is to say, the way the good Lord sees them: from above?"—has to remain a rhetorical one.

Yet phrasing the problem in this way, one begs the real question: why is modern written prose denied a privileged position to which others had access in the past? For Flaubert, literature seems to be something of the past, perhaps of the future, but not available to his present.

The answer resides perhaps in the fact that, for Flaubert as for the later Nietzsche, God—God as Origin, Order, and End, God as Reason; in a word, God as grammar—is dead.

For Nietzsche this does not mean that God is not, but that he once was and is no more. Pseudofictions now tell about the time of an ambiguous crepuscular agony, of a Götterdämmerung, in between the bygone time of literature and the science to come.

## V

*Voilà des mondes qui disparaissent. . . . Si le nôtre, à son tour, faisait la cabriole, les citoyens des étoiles ne seraient pas plus émus que nous ne le sommes maintenant.*     Flaubert

*The Temptation of Saint Anthony,* with its three versions which span Flaubert's entire literary career, occupies a privileged position in the Flaubertian canon. The author himself underscored more than once the significance of the work—"St. Anthony is my lifetime's work" (1304)—and identified with its main character: "I am in the

Flaubert and the Quest for Fiction  □  21

L'Art, comme le Dieu des Juifs,
se repaît d'holocaustes. Allons!
déchire-toi, flagelle-toi, roule-toi
dans la cendre, avilis la matière,
crache sur ton corps, arrache ton
coeur! Tu seras seul, tes pieds
saigneront, un dégoût infernal
accompagnera tout ton voyage.
                                    Flaubert

L'équilibre final à la Fourier, à la
Boltzmann, implique l'oubli des
conditions initiales de la durée.
Quelle que soit l'origine de
l'histoire, sa fin est univoque,
déterminée, identique partout,
nécessaire. Equilibre universel,
distribution monotone, entropie
maximale. . . . Fatal, le monde
boltzmanien est sans mémoire
distinguée, il gomme, à mesure,
les stocks et les dif-
férences . . . soumis à cette loi
unique linéaire assignant pour
fin de l'histoire le peuplement
du lieu sans classe. Et qu'im-
porte la longueur du temps, il
suffit d'attendre et quoi qu'on
fasse.                    Michel Serres

The equalization of European
man is today the great irreversible process.            Nietzsche

. . . le monde va devenir bougre-
ment bête. D'ici à longtemps ce
sera bien ennuyeux. Nous
faisons bien de vivre maintenant.
Tu ne croirais pas que nous
causons beaucoup de l'avenir de
la société. Il est pour moi presque certain qu'elle sera, dans un
temps plus ou moins éloigné,
régie comme un collège. Les
pions feront la loi. Tout sera en
uniforme.                  Flaubert

place of St. Anthony . . . the *Temptation* has been for myself and not for the reader" (332). In a letter to George Sand, Flaubert himself stressed the importance of the episode of the death of the Gods. He wrote: "I am having the Gods speak in their death-throes; the subtitle of my book could be: *The Height of insanity*" (1204).

When Pécuchet, during his geological quest for origins, is threatened by an avalanche of pebbles after a conversation with Bouvard about volcanic catastrophes, he shouts in a gesture of stupid optimism: " 'Stop, stop! The period hasn't run its course yet.' . . . He made enormous bounds with his alpenstock, bellowing, 'The period hasn't run its course yet!' " (BP, 106) But for Flaubert's nihilistic (the word is his) pessimism, the period is in fact achieved: "The great period is accomplished! Men, animals, the gods, the bamboos, the oceans, the mountains, the sandgrains of the Ganges, together with the myriad myriads of the stars—all shall die" (TSA, 121).

This achievement of the period coincides, of course, with the death of the Gods: "We knew these things!—we knew them! There must come an end even for the Gods" (TSA, 143). This death must be a willed one; Gods and men cannot live together. The chosen disappearance of the former is in fact a rejection of the latter. In the words of an agonizing Jupiter: "I no longer desire to receive those [the souls] of men. Let the Earth keep them, and let them move upon the level of its baseness. Their hearts are now the hearts of slaves— they forget injuries, forget their ancestors, forget their oaths—and everywhere the stupidity of crowds, the mediocrity of individuals, the hideousness of races hold sway!" (TSA, 143) Jupiter's words find an echo in those of Flaubert who, in a letter to Louise Colet, writes:

> But mediocrity is infiltrating everything, even the stones are becoming stupid. . . . Should we perish by it (and we shall perish, though it matters little) we must by all means stem the flood of dung that is invading us. . . . We are all jokers and charlatans. Pose, pose and blague everywhere! . . . Our century is a century of whores and the least prostituted of all until now are the prostitutes themselves. (456)

We shall see later the function of prostitution. For the moment let us note that Flaubert adopts Jupiter's evaluation of humans. We come late in time, in an epoch when men have hearts of slaves, that is to say, when mastery and the differentiating elements between mastery and slavery have disappeared; when men live in forgetfulness of ethical values, that is, when the distinction between Good and Evil has been erased; when ancestors are forgotten, that is, when genealogical hierarchies are minimized; when differences between individuals are abolished in favor of crowds, in favor of the mediocre similarity of the individual members of hideous races which have lost their form.

It should be evident by now that, for Flaubert, the death of the Gods is nothing more nor less than the abolishment of differences and their general dissolution in the quicksands of similarity.

We understand better now the failure of the writer to reach the summit of the mountain. The mountain topographically

*Les mots Dieu, Sport, Académie, intégrité nationale, etc. . . . sont dans le même caca que le mot Poésie.*        René Magritte

*Qu'est-ce que ça fout à la masse, l'Art, la poésie, le style? Elle n'a pas besoin de tout ça. Faites-lui des vaudevilles, des traités sur le travail des prisons, sur les cités ouvrières et les intérêts matériels du moment, encore. Il y a conjuration permanente contre l'original, voilà ce qu'il faut se fourrer dans la cervelle.*        Flaubert

*Duration, identity with itself, being are inherent neither in that which is called subject nor in*

that which is called object. They are complexes of events apparently durable in comparison with other complexes—e.g., through the difference in tempo of the event (rest-motion, firm-loose): opposites that do not exist in themselves and that actually express only variations in degree that from a certain perspective appear to be opposites. There are no opposites.

Nietzsche

Je suis seul comme en plein désert.

Flaubert

MEDIOCRE:
1. adj: of middling quality; neither bad nor good; indifferent. Said chiefly of literary or artistic works, ability or knowledge, and hence of persons considered with reference to their mental power or skill.
2. sb., only plural: Mediocre persons.

MEDIOCRITY n.:
1. The quality or condition of being indeterminate between two extremes. . . . Also something (a quality, position, etc.) equally removed from two opposite extremes; a mean. . . .
2. A middle course in action; measured conduct or behavior; moderation, temperance.
3. The position of possessing attributes in a medium or moderate degree; moderate degree or rate, average quality or amount. . . .
5. The quality of being mediocre. . . .
6. A person of mediocre talents or ability.

Oxford English Dictionary

represents the greatest possible distance, that is, the maximum difference, or form. If the maximum difference is denied, the whole central part *flattens out* into a desert. The same can be said of the climatic conditions present in each topography. The mountain is cold and preserves each individual in its form; thus it preserves the differences between forms. Deserts, on the other hand, through their fiery heat—the ideal analyzer—decompose forms in order to reduce them to the undifferentiated similarity of their components.

Mediocrity, the sign of our times, which conditions the author's endeavors, is nothing but the property of being in the middle away from the ends: the indifference of middling qualities.

No doubt humanity does not stand up well against the state of undifferentiation to which it is doomed. It will try to re-create gods, religions, and Art. In the desert it will be reduced to worshiping idols.

The time is not far off when universal languors, beliefs in the end of the world and in the coming of the Messiah will return. But since the theological basis will be missing, where will this enthusiasm, unconscious of its own existence, find its foothold? Some will look for it in the flesh, others in ancient religions, others in Art; and humanity, like the Jewish tribe in the desert, will adore all sorts of idols. (341)

The dilemma of the writer is evident: he can strive with nostalgia for forms forbidden to him, or renounce art in favor of a science to come, since, for Flaubert, science thrives on the very nondifferentiation which torments art. In the words of his character Hilarion: "My kingdom is vast

*L'égalité c'est l'esclavage. Voilà pourquoi j'aime l'Art. C'est que là, au moins, tout est liberté dans le monde des fictions. On y assouvit tout, on y fait tout, on est à la fois son roi et son peuple, actif et passif, victime et prêtre.* Flaubert

*Si les sciences morales avaient, comme les mathématiques, deux ou trois lois primordiales a leur disposition, elles pourraient marcher de l'avant. Mais elles tâtonnent dans les ténèbres. . . . Le mot l'âme a fait dire presque autant de bêtises qu'il y a d'âmes! Quelle découverte ce serait qu'un axiome comme celui-ci: tel peuple étant donné, la vertu y est à la force comme trois est à quatre. . . . Autre loi mathématique à découvrir: combien faut-il connaître d'imbéciles au monde pour vous donner envie de se casser la gueule?*
Flaubert

as the universe; and my desire knows no limits. I go on forever—freeing minds, weighing worlds—without hatred, without fear, without pity, without love, and without God. Men call me SCIENCE!" (TSA, 156–57)

Art and Science, then, are the two impossible limit-points between which Flaubert's ironic, cloven text will oscillate.

## VI

*J'ai loué avec la démence et le fantastique comme Mithridate avec les poisons.* Flaubert

When the narrator of Borges's *The Immortal* reaches the City of the Immortals, he finds a place so monstrous, so unstructured by differences that it cannot even be linguistically represented: "I do not want to describe it; a chaos of heterogeneous words, the body of a tiger or bull in which teeth, organs and heads monstrously pullulate in mutual conjunction and hatred can (perhaps) be approximate images."[22] His reaction to this discovery passes through three distinct moments: " 'This palace is a fabrication of the gods,' I thought at the beginning. I explored the uninhabited interiors and corrected myself: 'The gods who built it have died.' I noted its peculiarities and said: 'The gods who built it were mad.' "[23]

Madness is the necessary limit-experience of radical nihilism. Nietzsche is, of course, exemplary here. Flaubert too is haunted by the experience of madness and, like Borges, he at one point in the *Temptation* has one of the characters exclaim: "The world is the work of a God in delirium!" The notion of a world created and dominated by a demented God does not ordinarily follow the proclamation of the death of God. The death of God has its own temporality, quite different from that implied by the eternal madness of God. The particular temporal mode of the death of God as something both accomplished and yet to be accomplished is best illustrated by its most famous version, namely section 125 of the third part of *The Joyful Wisdom.* The aphorism is appropriately entitled *The Madman,* and in it the burden of madness is shifted from God to man. The madman appears at noon holding a light, looking for God. Meeting an assembly of persons, many of whom are unbelievers, the madman answers their laughter with the narrative of God's death:

Where is God gone? . . . I mean to tell you! *We have killed him*—you and I! We are all his murderers! But how have we done it? How were we able to drink up the sea? Who gave us the sponge to wipe away the whole horizon? What did we do when we loosened this earth from its sun? Whither does it now move? Whither do we move? Away from all suns? Do we not dash on unceasingly? Backwards, sideways, forwards, in all directions? Is there still an above and below? Do we not stray, as through infinite nothingness? . . .[24]

We can easily imagine how Nietzsche's text is isotopic with Flaubert's. In Nietzsche too we have the death of God as an impossible narrative told in conjunction with an experience of madness, from a "desert" which has neither up nor down,

*. . . There is no help,*
*The bitter disposition of the time*
*Will have it so.*　　　Shakespeare

*On croit un peu trop générale-*
*ment que le soleil n'a d'autre*
*but ici-bas que de faire pousser*
*les choux. Il faut remplacer de*
*temps à autres le bon Dieu sur*
*son piédestal. Aussi se charge-t-*

*il de nous le rappeler en nous envoyant par-ci par-là quelque peste, choléra, bouleversement inattendu et autres manifestations de la Règle, à savoir le Mal-contingent qui n'est peut-être pas le Bien-nécessaire, mais qui est l'Etre enfin: chose que les hommes voués au néant comprennent peu.*   Flaubert

*Nature threw away the key; and woe to the fateful curiosity which might be able for a moment to look out and down through a crevice in the chamber of consciousness and discover that man, indifferent to his own ignorance, is resting on the pitiless, the greedy, the insatiable, the murderous, and, as it were, hanging in dreams on the back of a tiger.*   Nietzsche

through the "foggy" darkness of a world which is now detached from its sun. To accentuate the correspondence we may recall the devil's words to Anthony: "Ascend skyward forever and forever, yet thou wilt not attain the summit. Descend below the earth for billions of billions of centuries: never wilt thou reach the bottom. For there is no summit, there is no bottom; there is no Above, no Below—nor height, nor depth as signified by the terms of human utterance" (TSA, 161–62). Anthony's answer is also echoed in the words of the Madman: "A hideous cold freezes me, even to the depths of my soul! This is beyond the extreme of pain! It is like a death that is deeper than death!" (TSA, 163)

But let us return to the aphorism and to the problem of the temporality of God's death: " 'I come too early,' he then said; 'I am not yet at the right time. This prodigious event is still on its way, and is travelling—it has not yet reached men's ears. . . . Deeds need time, even after they are done, to be seen and heard.' "[25] The narration of the event is never temporally coextensive with the event itself, which is both before and after but not *now*. More precisely, as event it is always before, whereas the representational reading of the event is always yet to come.

The forms of fiction are thus the useless epigones of a past event which necessarily predates its conceptual representation—predates, that is, the reintegration of the absence of the event. For, as Derrida has reminded us, the body of the king is absent from the sarcophagus in the pyramid. Or, in the words of the Madman: "What are

The story I wanted to tell is the encounter of two individuals who don't exist, since they are definable only with regard to a past or a future, a past and a future whose reality is reciprocally doubted. Or else it's a story that cannot be separated from the story of all the rest of what exists, and therefore from the story of what doesn't exist and, not existing, causes what does exist to exist. Italo Calvino

This doctrinal item observed that the lottery is an interpolation of chance in the order of the world and that to accept errors is not to contradict chance—it is to corroborate it. Jorge Luis Borges

Ainsi le monde comme il est, le monde comme il vit, le monde absent des formalités abstraites, est-il d'un coup cette bibliothèque de Babel où les livres dispersés, disjectés, adoptent des formes reconnaissables, classables et réglées: ce qui est écrit dans ces tomes, c'est la pure multiplicité. Le secret des choses, c'est qu'il n'y a pas de secret. Michel Serres

these churches now if they are not the tombs and monuments of God?"[26]

In other words, the death of God marks the temporal/spatial moment of the oscillation of the limits of the Form of fiction, through which fiction attempts and fails to accede to the metaphysics of "Truth" and "Beauty."

It should be evident by now that, at least to my way of thinking, the world as governed or generated by a mad God does not belong to the same epistemological space as the death of God. God's madness is discontinuous with the diacritical "concepts" of Past and Future, Absence and Presence, which govern the limits of representation and fiction. God's madness points to reality as something unrepresentable, like the City of Immortals, or as something unaccountable, like the world of chance in "The Lottery in Babylon." In the case of Flaubert, God's madness is evident in the explosion of fictional representation into the chaotic linguistic labyrinth of the end of *Bouvard and Pécuchet,* and in the passage from the quest for narrative to the act of *copying:* the eternal reduplication of events unredeemable by form. At that juncture, madness, of course, spills over into the act of inscribing madness. Both the undertaking and the result are demented. If, as Flaubert says, in art and metaphysics one always navigates in madness, then the writing of "mad" texts like the *Temptation* or *Bouvard and Pécuchet* is equally demented: "One must be a madman and frenzied three times over to undertake that sort of book!" (1318).

## VII

*Le Saint-Esprit est féminin.*    Flaubert

Palabras *neighbour* Verges    Shakespeare

For Flaubert, as well as for his character Anthony, madness is an experience closely associated with eroticism. "Madness and lust are two things which I have so well fathomed, where I have so well navigated by my will that I shall never become (I hope) a madman nor a Sade" (406). It should follow, then, that if the experience of madness is closely related to narrative's quest for fiction, eroticism—under the various guises of prostitution, lust, or the Queen of Sheba—must of necessity be related to the same experience. At some point in his delirium Anthony sees Nebuchadnezzar, who "dreams of rebuilding the tower of Babel, and dethroning God" (TSA, 41). For an instant, the saint identifies with the character in the vision: "Anthony, from afar off, reads all these thoughts upon his brow. They penetrate his own brain, and he becomes Nebuchadnezzar. Immediately he is cloyed with orgiastic excesses" (TSA, 41). After regaining his consciousness he asks the question "why these things?" and answers, "they come from the rebellion of the flesh" (TSA, 42).

This relation has a converse. To the phantasmagoria of fiction generated by the desires of the flesh correspond the fantasies of desire generated by fiction. In fact, between *Madame Bovary,* read as a fiction which stages literature as a disease of desire, and *Bouvard and Pécuchet,* the two bachelors reduced to fantasizing phalluses everywhere, the second alternative seems to be more common.

Bouvard and Pécuchet's obsession is interesting inasmuch as it shows how close sexuality is to words: "Thus the tumulus signifies the female, as the upright stone is the male organ. . . . At one time towers, pyramids, candles, mile-posts, and even trees had the significance of phalluses—and for Bouvard and Pécuchet everything became a phallus" (BP, 130–31). In fact, then, sexuality is related to language by the very nature of the latter since sexuality can stand in a relation of sign, simile, or metaphor to words and things alike.

This leads to a contradictory exigency, for on the one hand language and fiction have to distance themselves from sexuality, yet sexuality cannot be done away with, since it has to be postulated as origin or end. For Flaubert, the unresolvable alternative is between writing and a life associated with desire. "When I do not hold a book or dream of writing one I am overtaken by such boredom that I want to scream. Life seems to me tolerable only if one can conjure it away [*la vie ne me semble tolérable que si on l'escamote*]. Otherwise one would have to surrender oneself to disorderly pleasures" (1385). Because "desire makes one live" (1716), "*so as not to live,* I immerse myself in Art as if mad. I intoxicate myself with ink as others do with wine" (629).

This ascetic quest will not dispel the creatures of desire who will haunt Flaubert/Anthony under various guises in the desert/library. Their names are well known: Annonaria, who returns three

---

*La Tentation de (saint) Flaubert*
Paul Valéry

*The Saint in whom God takes pleasure is the ideal castrate.*
Nietzsche

*COIT, COPULATION—Mots à éviter. Dire: "Ils avaient des rapports."*
Flaubert

*Le texte suspend le désir, nul n'a jamais écrit qu'en attendant de faire l'amour, et parce qu'il ne peut pas toujours faire l'amour.*
Michel Serres

times to torment the hermit, "that black child who appeared to me in the midst of the sands, who was very beautiful, and who told me that he was called the Spirit of Lust" (TSA, 24); Maximilla; Priscilla, who left her husband to follow a eunuch in the desert, the last of the prophetesses after whom "the end of the world shall come" (TSA, 72). The two most important ones remain the Queen of Sheba and Helen-Ennoia.

The Queen of Sheba, in fact, contains all possible creatures generated by desire's imagination. She is the world invested by the totality of desire; more precisely, she is desire made flesh. "All the women thou hast ever met—from the leman of the cross-roads, singing under the light of her lantern, even to the patrician lady scattering rose-petals abroad from her litter—all the forms thou hast ever obtained glimpses of—all the imaginations of thy desire—thou hast only to ask for them! I am not a woman: I am a world!" (TSA, 51)

Not surprisingly, she is a source for fiction: "I know a host of merry tales to tell, each more diverting than the other" (TSA, 47). Through her bird, Simorg-Anka, she is desire's totalization of all events recast in fictional representation—in a word, the writer's impossible dream of a total text: "He flies swiftly as Desire! He circles the world in his flight. At eve he returns; he perches at the foot of my couch and tells me all he has seen—the seas that passed far beneath him with all their fishes and ships, the great void deserts he has contemplated from the heights of the sky, the harvests that were bowing in the valleys,

Caïus César Caligula en est devenu amoureux, puisqu'il voulait
coucher avec la Lune!        Flaubert

No, the Moon is a desert, that
was the answer of the poet.
From that arid space originates
every tale, poem and every journey.                    Italo Calvino

Je n'ai jamais pu voir passer aux
feux du gaz une de ces femmes
décolletées, sous la pluie, sans
un battement de coeur, de
même que les robes des moines
avec leur cordelière à noeuds
me chatouillent l'âme en je ne
sais quels coins ascétiques et
profonds. Il se trouve, en cette
idée de la prostitution, un point
d'intersection si complexe, luxe,
amertume, néant des rapports
humains, frénésie du muscle et
sonnement d'or, qu'en y regar-
dant au fond le vertige vient, et
on apprend là tant de choses!
                        Flaubert

and the plants that were growing upon the walls of cities abandoned" (TSA, 50–51). In a letter to Bouilhet, Flaubert defined the form of the *Temptation* as that of a whirlwind, since the Queen of Sheba's imperative invitation to the saint to "inhale the perfume of my bosom, madden thyself with the beauty of my limbs: and thus, consumed by the fire of my eyes, clasped within my arms as in a whirlwind . . ." (TSA, 52) is nothing less than an invitation to possess the very form, that is, to possess the very fiction in which the Author/Saint is a character.

Helen also "discourses of marvellous things" (TSA, 93) and personifies the totality of desire, but in the form of unfulfilling availability: "She was that Helen of Troy, whose memory was cursed by the poet Stesichorus. She was Lucretia, the patrician woman violated by a king. She was Delilah, by whom Samson's locks were shorn. . . . She has loved adultery, idolatry, lying and foolishness. She has prostituted herself to all nations. She has sung at the corners of all crossroads. She has kissed the faces of all men" (TSA, 95).

We may now better understand Flaubert's reference to prostitution quoted earlier. Prostitution is the availability of desire, and if desire is available, then the form of fiction is also available. Unfortunately, they both belong to a bygone age. They are both myths of doomed practices:

I like prostitution. . . . During my first years in Paris, I used to sit in front of Tortoni's on hot summer evenings and watch the streetwalkers stroll by in the last rays of the sun. At such moments I used to gorge myself with biblical

Ah! quels vices j'aurais si je
n'écrivais! *Flaubert*

... renonçant à la jouissance, il
[l'écrivain de plaisir] a le droit et
le pouvoir de la dire: la lettre est
son plaisir, il est obsédé, comme
le sont tous ceux qui aiment le
langage ... tous les logophiles,
écrivains, épistoliers, lin-
guistes. . . . La critique porte
toujours sur des textes de plaisir,
jamais sur des textes de jouissance. . . . Avec l'écrivain de
jouissance (et son lecteur) commence le texte intenable, le texte
impossible. *Roland Barthes*

ERECTION.—Ne se dit qu'en
parlant des monuments. *Flaubert*

poetry. I thought of Isaiah, of "fornication in high places." ... My only complaint about prostitution is that it is a myth. ... The courtesan does not exist any more than the saint does. (394).

The writer will have to remain forever in a state of suspended and unfulfilled desire. Satisfaction—which Flaubert calls *fouterie*—is "a projection into infinity." Meanwhile the impotent writer continues, knowing full well his incapacity to reach a satisfactory end: "I apply myself to it, not because I am inspired in the least, but because I would like to see this. It is a sort of curiosity which one might qualify as a lustful desire without erection [*un désir lubrique sans érection*]" (547).

The best emblem Flaubert finds for his doomed activity is that of an incurable venereal disease: "Yes, literature bores me to a supreme degree! But it is not my fault; it has become with me a constitutional pox of which I am unable to rid myself" (551). And this, with its connotations of infection, violence, organic malady, and madness, is perhaps as good an emblem as any of fiction's hopeless quest for its ontology.

## Notes

1. G. W. F. Hegel, *Reason in History*, trans. Robert S. Hartman (1953; rpt. New York: Macmillan, 1985), p. 11.
2. Novalis, *L'Encyclopédie*, trans. Maurice de Gandillac (Paris: Editions de Minuit, 1966), fragments 1, 8, 11, 12. I follow this translation for my translation. Italics are in the original.
3. See Jacques Derrida, "Outwork," in *Dissemination*, trans. Barbara Johnson (Chicago: University of Chicago Press, 1981), pp. 1–59, especially pp. 50–59.
4. Stéphane Mallarmé, *Oeuvres complètes* (Paris: Gallimard, 1945), p. 372.

5. See Jacques Scherer, ed., *Le "Livre" de Mallarmé* (Paris: Gallimard, 1957).

6. Mallarmé, *Oeuvres complètes*, p. 378.

7. Frank Kermode, *The Sense of an Ending* (Oxford: Oxford University Press, 1966), p. 7.

8. Jorge Luis Borges, "The Library of Babel," trans. James E. Irby, in *Labyrinths*, ed. Donald A. Yates and James E. Irby (New York: New Directions, 1964), p. 54.

9. Hugh Kenner, *The Stoic Comedians* (1962; rpt. Berkeley: University of California Press, 1974), p. 22.

10. Michel Foucault, "La Bibliothèque fantastique," *Cahiers Renaud-Barrault* 59 (1967); rpt. in *Travail de Flaubert*, ed. Gérard Genette and Tzvetan Todorov (Paris: Editions du Seuil, 1983), p. 118.

11. Kenner, *The Stoic Comedians*, pp. 12–13.

12. Foucault, "La Bibliothèque fantastique," pp. 118–19.

13. Gustave Flaubert, *Bouvard and Pécuchet*, trans. T. W. Earp and G. W. Stonier (New York: New Directions, 1954), p. 142. Subsequent references will be identified in the text by the letters "BP" followed by the page number.

14. All references followed by a number refer to Geneviève Bollème's remarkable anthology of Flaubert's correspondence published under the title *Préface à la vie d'écrivain* (Paris: Editions du Seuil, 1963). As the title suggests, Flaubert's correspondence constitutes a parallel text to the novels, one in which Flaubert stages their genetic inscription.

15. Quoted by Henri Ronse in his edition of *La Tentation de Saint Antoine* (Paris: Gallimard, 1967).

16. Borges, "The Library of Babel," p. 54.

17. Gustave Flaubert, *The Temptation of Saint Anthony*, trans. Lafcadio Hearn (New York: Williams, Belasco and Meyers, 1930), p. 77. Subsequent references will be identified in the text by the letters "TSA" followed by the page number.

18. From the "Résumé sommaire" published in Gustave Flaubert, *Oeuvres complètes* (Paris: Club de l'Honnête Homme, 1971–75), 6: 759–61.

19. See also letter 584. The reader, in fact, is caught in a movement similar to that of the author and the characters. As Jean Seznec aptly put it: "In order to understand Flaubert at work . . . one must become ascetic along with him" (Jean Seznec, *Nouvelles études sur "La Tentation de Saint Antoine,"* London: Warburg Institute, 1949, p. 2). In this Author/Reader symmetry it would not be difficult to find a problematic isomorphic to that elaborated by Borges in "Pierre Menard, Author of the *Quixote*" (trans. James E. Irby in *Labyrinths*).

20. Borges, "The Mirror of Enigmas," trans. James E. Irby, in *Labyrinths*, p. 212 n.

21. Gustave Flaubert, *Oeuvres complètes de Gustave Flaubert: Correspondance* (Paris: Louis Conard, 1926–33), 3: 342–43.

22. Borges, "The Immortal," trans. James E. Irby, in *Labyrinths*, p. 111.

23. Ibid., p. 110.

24. Friedrich Nietzsche, *The Joyful Wisdom*, trans. Thomas Common (1909–11; rpt. New York: Russell and Russell, 1964), pp. 167–68.

25. Ibid., pp. 168–69.

26. Ibid., p. 169.

One of the most striking characteristics of Flaubert criticism is the uneven way in which it has treated the various works, practically dividing his writings in two. On the one hand there are the works which have attracted an inordinate amount of attention—*Madame Bovary* and *Sentimental Education,* which are supposed to illustrate, according to a myth initiated by the naturalists but rejected by Flaubert himself, the latter's "realism." On the other hand there are *Salammbô, The Temptation of Saint Anthony,* and *Bouvard and Pécuchet,* neglected in spite of Flaubert's conceiving *Salammbô* in dialectical opposition to *Madame Bovary,* his claim that the *Temptation* was his life's work, and finally, the importance he gave to *Bouvard and Pécuchet,* his unfinished last work. Among the many consequences of this division, not the least significant is the classification of *Salammbô* and the *Temptation* as Romantic works exemplifying Flaubert's hapless quest for a temporal as well as spatial exoticism. Such a classification makes Flaubert's so-called "realism" a self-fulfilling prophecy, for it generates an opposition whereby *Madame Bovary* and *Sentimental Education* are novels of a successfully mimetic "here and now," while the *Temptation* and *Salammbô* represent their author's misconceived quest for an exotic "there and then." It is through the explicit or implicit acceptance of this dichotomy that *Salammbô,* from Sainte-Beuve to Lukács and beyond, came to be treated as a "historical novel," and the problems of history with respect to Flaubert's texts came to be localized within that single work. I would argue, however, that the opposition between a Flaubert centered upon a contemporary reality and a Flaubert in quest of an exotic bygone Orient is untenable, and that if there is a problem of "history" with regard to *Salammbô,* that same problem touches Flaubert's total literary production.

In spite of their irreducibly divergent aesthetic and critical ideologies, the objections of Sainte-Beuve and Lukács to *Salammbô* are remarkably similar. Both reproach Flaubert's novel for being simultaneously *too* exotic and *too* contemporary. The reproach is always one of excess: on the one hand, Flaubert has chosen a subject that is too oriental and too archaeological; on the other, his main characters—and in particular the character of Salammbô—resemble too closely characters and heroines of contemporary romantic novels.

For Sainte-Beuve, if historical novels imply, by definition, the "recreation" of a past, such a past should not be temporally or spatially too remote from the author; hence, for the French critic, Walter Scott was writing about the Scottish Middle Ages from a privileged position not granted to Flaubert writing about ancient Carthage: "Walter Scott, the master and true founder of the historical novel, lived in his native Scotland, a few centuries or generations away from the events and characters he recounted with such verve and verisimilitude."[1] Whereas in Flaubert's novel "there lies between it [antiquity] and us . . . an abyss. The erudition which might bridge this gap also chills us, leaving us icy cold. . . . Antiquity can be reconstructed, but never resuscitated" (S/C, 435). *Salammbô*'s subject matter, as well as its geographical setting, are in fact so remote that Sainte-Beuve cannot understand how anybody could possibly be interested by them:

How do you expect me to take an interest in this lost war, buried among the processions and sands of Africa. . . . What do I care about the duel between Tunis and Carthage? Speak to me of the duel between Carthage and Rome, that's a different matter! There I am attentive, there I am involved. (S/C, 437)

Yet for Sainte-Beuve, if the subject matter of the novel deals with a war far too remote to be of interest to the nineteenth-century reader, the main protagonist is, on the contrary, too contemporary. In opposition to the novel's archaeological setting, the character of Salammbô is "a sentimental Elvira with one foot in the Sacré-Coeur" (S/C, 417).

Lukács's critique is close enough to Sainte-Beuve's to puzzle the reader into asking himself what might be the function, here, of a Marxist epistemology which does not displace the formulation of the problem left us by Sainte-Beuve. For Lukács too, the novel remains a "frozen, lunar landscape of archeological precision." As for Salammbô herself, she provides

a heightened image, a decorative symbol, of the hysterical longings and torments of middle-class girls in large cities. History simply provided a decorative, monumental setting for this hysteria, which in the present spends itself in petty and ugly scenes, and which thus acquired a tragic aura quite out of keeping with its real character. The effect is powerful but it shows that Flaubert, because of his embitterment with the shallow prose of his time, had become objectively untruthful and distorted the real proportions of life.[2]

The shape of both Sainte-Beuve's and Lukács's objections is easy to perceive. Both assume a purely mimetic view of narrative; both assume that the function of literature is to represent a "reality" and hence to be "true." It matters little that Sainte-Beuve expects the novel to represent what he calls "soul," "nature," "life,"[3] while the Marxist critic wants the novel to represent "the real social-historical basis."[4] What both

Sainte-Beuve and Lukács expect and demand from fiction is the represented presence of what each considers to be an "ultimate reality." The objects may be different, but not the metaphysical imperative that fiction obliterate representation by placing in front of the reader something other than itself. In the last analysis, both the Romantic Sainte-Beuve and the Marxist Lukács criticize Flaubert in the name of the same metaphysics.

That the critiques of Sainte-Beuve and Lukács are similar and stem from the same metaphysics of presence with respect to fiction is made all the more evident by the fact that Flaubert did not deny Sainte-Beuve's charges, but rather their pertinence. He admits that his novel is a mixture of old and new:

Lord knows how far I've carried scrupulousness when it comes to documents, books, information, voyages, etc. Yet I regard all that as quite secondary and unimportant. Material truth (or what is so-called) should only be a spring-board for raising oneself to greater heights. Do you think I am so stupid as to believe that in *Salammbô* I created a true reproduction of Carthage, and in *Saint Antoine* an exact depiction of Alexandrianism? Of course not! But I am sure of having expressed the *ideal* that we have of them today.[5]

Moreover, in his reply to Sainte-Beuve he states that he "wanted to transcribe a mirage by applying the methods of the modern novel to Antiquity."[6] Flaubert's insistence in his reply to Sainte-Beuve on the authenticity of *Salammbô*'s archaeological background is in the same vein as his answer to Froehner, who had questioned its exactitude. But with Flaubert, one must not confuse the fictional aspects of the novel with their antiquarian underpinnings; the "material truth" is quite distinct from the "methods of the modern novel," and their conjunction produces not the presentation of a "reality" but the transcription of a mirage. If fiction, in Flaubert's expression, is a mirage, it does represent "something," but the metaphysical status of that which is represented, both as object and as presence, is at best dubious. Flaubert also admits that the character of Salammbô does not represent an authentic Carthaginian woman, but then insists that nobody could represent one because it is impossible to know an oriental woman. On the other hand, Salammbô does not represent a contemporary woman either, but a type best exemplified by Saint Theresa:

As for my heroine, I won't defend her. According to you she resembles "a sentimental Elvira," Velleda, and Mme Bovary. Not at all! Velleda is active, intelligent, European. Mme Bovary is driven by multiple passions. Salammbô, by contrast, is riveted by her *idée fixe*. She's a maniac, a sort of Saint Theresa. No matter! I'm in no way sure of her reality—neither you nor I, nor any ancient or modern can know Oriental women, simply because it is impossible to frequent them.[7]

Salammbô, then, is either pure surface, pure representation; or, if she represents "something," that "something" is, again, neither ancient nor modern, neither oriental nor nineteenth-century French. If we accept Flaubert's characterization of his novel, we can better understand the perplexity and irritation of both the Romantic and the Marxist critics in confronting *Salammbô*. The nature of representation brought into play by the novel is not simply one of presence and identity. Its textual surface does not dissolve in front of a simple "reality"; what shimmers behind the mirage, both the archaeology and the feminine typology, escapes the possibility of simple identification of either Carthage or nineteenth-century France as epistemological objects.

For both Sainte-Beuve and Lukács, then, it is the status of representation in *Salammbô* that is problematical. The Carthaginians are too distant to be "real," the Orient too exotic to be "real," Salammbô too contemporary to be "real." The insistence of both critics on a metaphysically rooted epistemology stops them from asking a far more pertinent question, namely, why did Flaubert choose Carthage and the Orient? Instead of insisting on the question of what Carthage and the Orient represent, they might have displaced their inquiry to the question of what Carthage and the Orient could signify for the nineteenth-century author of *Salammbô*.

If it is a commonplace to state that Flaubert had a need to pursue exoticism as a reaction to what he considered the drab reality of *Madame Bovary*, more rarely have critics asked what constitutes a possible otherness to his actual environment or, more generally, what form such an escape might take. In a temporal context, for example, it is not the Carthage of the Punic Wars that is for Flaubert the ideal period, but rather imperial Rome. In a letter to Louise Colet, for example, he writes:

What wouldn't I give to see a triumph! What wouldn't I sell to enter Suburra on a night when the torches were burning at the doors to the brothels and the tambourines were echoing in the taverns! As if we didn't have enough past of our own, we ruminate on that of humanity as a whole and revel in its delightful bitterness. What difference does it make, after all, if we can only live in such a collective past, if it is the only thing we can think of with neither disdain nor pity.[8]

More specifically, in a letter to Maxime du Camp, he writes:

I have reread Michelet's *History of the Roman Republic.*—No, antiquity makes me dizzy. I lived in Rome, I am certain of it, in the time of Caesar or Nero.—Have you ever dreamt of a night of triumph when the legions were returning, with incense burning around the victor's chariot, and captive kings marching behind, followed by a venerable circus! Antiquity is where we must live, you see. Only there does one find enough poetic air to fill one's lungs, air like that on a high mountain, so much of it that it sets the heart racing. Ah, I look forward to the day when I will guzzle some down in Sicily and Greece. Will you go along with it when I say: old pal, buy yourself a rifle and have a light jacket made. Will you answer: on our way and long live the Muse! (B, 1: 266)

Before I proceed any further, a remark is in order. From the last quote it should be apparent that Flaubert's nostalgia for a given antiquity cannot be dismissed as simple exoticism. Antiquity belongs to a complex metaphorical network which has, among other functions, that of staging Flaubert's own act of writing. In the letter to Maxime du Camp, the quest for antiquity is presented as equivalent to a quest for altitude. We have already seen that altitude is a spatial metaphor for an absolute difference which would permit a textually unmediated representation. I have also tried to show how this quest for altitude and difference must fail, and how, for Flaubert, such a quest must end in spatial mediocrity, the metaphorical characteristic of the nineteenth-century prose writer, for whom representation has of necessity to be a textually mediated operation. The temporal quest for antiquity is in fact analogous to the spatial quest for altitude: "What makes ancient figures so beautiful is that they are original: to derive only from oneself is everything. Nowadays, so much study is required to free oneself from books, and so many have to be read! One has to drink in oceans and piss them back out" (C, 2: 409). In another letter he writes:

What artists we would be if we had never read, seen, nor loved anything that was not beautiful; if from the outset some guardian angel of the purity of our pens had kept us from all contamination; if we had never associated with fools or read newspapers! The Greeks were like that. As regards plastic form, they lived in conditions that will never return. But to want to wear their shoes is madness. What we in the North need are not chlamyses but fur coats. Classic form is insufficient for our needs, and our voices are not created to sing those simple tunes. Let us, if we can, be as dedicated to art as they were, but differently. Human consciousness has broadened since Homer. Sancho Panza's belly has burst the seams of Venus's girdle. (C, 3: 281)

Let us note in passing how the temporal opposition of antiquity and modernism is isomorphic to the spatial opposition of a southern Orient and a northern Europe. The nostalgia for antiquity, then, is a nostalgia for an absolutely original, unmediated form of writing.

This, of course, is not the case for either the Carthage of *Salammbô* or the Egypt of *The Temptation of Saint Anthony*. Between them and Flaubert stand the archaeological museum and the library of erudition, and it is only through the Museum and the Library that the modern writer can have access to them. The writing of *Salammbô* and *The Temptation of Saint Anthony* is for Flaubert a conscious and willed textual operation, rather than a quest for exoticism. It is, then, in relation to the metaphoric networks which they emblematize that we must try to situate the temporal and spatial characteristics of Egypt and Carthage.

Usually Polybus is quoted as the main historical source for *Salammbô*. That is no doubt exact with regard to the plot of the novel, yet Polybus is really the result of a choice on Flaubert's part, and it is in Michelet, his other source, that we stand a better chance of finding what had attracted him to Carthage in the first place.

For Michelet the confrontation between Rome and Carthage is first and foremost a war of races, and in that war one of the races will be obliterated:

It is not without reason that the recollection of the Punic Wars has remained so popular and vivid in the memory of man. That struggle was not only to decide the fate of two cities or of two empires; rather it was a matter of knowing which of the two races, Indo-Germanic or Semitic, would dominate the world. . . . On one side, heroic genius, that of art and legislation; on the other, the spirit of industry, navigation and commerce. These two hostile races encountered and attacked one another everywhere. In the early history of Persia and Chaldea, heroes ceaselessly battled their industrious and treacherous neighbors. . . . The conflict between the Phoenicians and the Greeks recurred on all of the coasts of the Mediterranean. Everywhere the latter succeeded to the trading posts and colonies of their rivals in the East, as the Romans were to do in the West. . . . Only the great Carthage and its empire which was powerful in a different way than was Phoenicia remained; Rome destroyed it. At that time something occurred never to be seen again in history: an entire civilization suddenly disappeared, at once, like a falling star.[9]

What characterizes the Carthaginians is that they are an impure race wherein sexual and genealogical differences are abolished:

This impure race, fleeing before the sword of Sesostris or the exterminating knife of the Jews, had found itself driven to the sea and had taken the coast for its country. Only the unrestrained licentiousness of the modern Malabar compares with the abominations of these Sodoms of Phoenicia. Generations of uncertain lineage overran that place, no one knowing his father's identity, giving birth, multiplying randomly, like the indigenous insects and reptiles which, after a rainstorm, swarm over their burning shores. They even spoke of themselves as born of slime.[10]

When the Carthaginians face the mercenaries, they are confronted by another racially undifferentiated group of individuals:

Carthage's first punishment, after the disgraceful peace of the Aegadian isles, was the return of its armies. Upon Carthage fell the countryless, lawless, godless throngs, the blasphemous and bloodthirsty Babel that it had once set upon other nations. Let us take this opportunity to behold the spectacle of this just recompense.[11]

It is evident, then, that what Michelet reads in the confrontation of Carthage and the mercenaries as an episode of the Punic Wars is an event *at the end* of a given history, where abolished differences *among* various peoples only lead those peoples to destroy each other, to erase the differences *between* them.

If we transpose Michelet's characterization into Flaubert's problematic, we find that, in what seemed to be an absolute temporal difference, the original term is similar to the end term. The temporal difference between Carthage and nineteenth-century France is a pseudodifference based on a primary identity. The perception that Flaubert's France is at the end of a history of which Carthage represents, if not the beginning, then at least a more primitive or even original moment, is illusory. Carthage itself is at the end of history.

It remains to show that the second term of the pseudodifference—nineteenth-century France—is not only similar to the first term by its position at the end of history, but that each of them is there, so to speak, sui generis; that nineteenth-century France is at the end of its history in the same way that Carthage was at the end of its own, and that what originally appears as temporal difference is but the mirage created by a textual interplay of identity and indifference. As described by Flaubert, being at the end of history is more than simply being at one extremity of a temporal sequence. The end of history is in fact, for Flaubert, a period characterized by nihilistic apocalypse. In that sense, nineteenth-century France is at the end of time in the same way that Carthage was for Michelet. In a letter to the Princess Mathilde, Flaubert writes: "I feel as if it were the end of a world. Whatever the result, everything I loved is lost. When the war is over we shall fall into an abominable order of things" (C, 6: 171).[12] In another letter to his niece he writes: "We are coming to the beginning of the end!" (C, 6: 196).

In a letter to Madame Regnier, this feeling for the end of history coincides, as it does for Michelet, with the end of a race: ". . . that's it! We are witnessing the end of the Latin world. Farewell to everything we love! Paganism, Christianity and boorishness are the three great developments of humanity. It is unpleasant to find oneself mired in the third" (C, 6: 201). To George Sand he writes: "Perhaps there will be a return of racial wars. Within a century we will see several million men kill one another in one go. All the East against all Europe, the old world against the new" (C, 6: 137–38).

The race, then, that will be the victim of this new war is the Latin race: "The Latin race is in its death throes. France will follow Spain and Italy; the era of loutishness is upon us. What a collapse! What a fall! What wretchedness! What abominations!" (C, 6: 184). Again, in a letter to his niece he writes: "Whatever happens, the world to which I once belonged has lived its last. The Latins are finished! Now it is the turn of the Saxons, who will then be devoured by the Slavs, and so on" (C, 6: 163). Even if there were no war to abolish races, races would disappear in any case, for they are not intrinsic essences but differential properties, and the end of time is the abolition of differential traits:

Oh how I believe in race! But there are no longer any races! The aristocratic blood has been used up; its last drops have no doubt coagulated in a few souls. If nothing changes (and that is possible), within perhaps half a century Europe will be languishing in tremendous darkness and the dark ages of history, where nothing shines, will return. (C, 3: 129)

For Flaubert, the end of history means a general collapsing of all differences—racial, social, political—into mediocrity, mediocrity understood literally as the property of being in the middle, that is to say, of not sustaining any differential space or opposition. Socially, for example, the damning thing about the bourgeois is not that he is bourgeois, but that, as the middle term between aristocratic and working classes, he is all that is left:

> . . . the only thing to be learned from the current state of things . . . is that the notion of "the people" is as worn out as that of "the king." May the worker's smock and the king's mantle both be thrown in the latrines so as to hide the blood and mud which have made them stiff. (C, 3: 211)

> There is no difference between the Socialists and the Bourgeois; or rather, there are nothing but Bourgeois.[13]

> One truth, however, seems to me to have emerged from all this: that one has no need for vulgar people, for the numerous elements of the majorities, for approval, for consecration. Seventeen eighty-nine demolished royalty and nobility, 1848 the bourgeoisie, and 1851 the "people." Nothing is left except the vulgar and stupid mob. All of us are equally mired in mediocrity. (C, 3: 349)

My purpose here is not to discuss Flaubert's political views. Suffice it to say that for him the future of history is entirely and strikingly characterized by uniformity, homogeneity and mediocrity; that is to say, by the absence of all differences:

> The world is going to become bloody stupid and from now on will be a very boring place. We're lucky to be living now. You won't believe that [Max and I] talk constantly about the future of society. For me it is almost certain that at some more or less distant time it will be regulated like a college. Schoolmasters will make the laws. Everything will be in uniform. (B, 1: 645)

It should now be apparent that Carthage, the Punic Wars, and the revolt of the mercenaries do not offer Flaubert a historical reality different from his perception of his own, but, on the contrary, one which is remarkably similar.

History for Flaubert, is periodical, and it is this periodicity which makes it possible for periods which are temporally distant to be similar to one another. Thus history is punctuated at regular intervals by periods of agony: "Perhaps we need barbarians. Humanity, the perpetual old man, requires infusions of new blood during his occasional agonies. How low we are! And what universal decrepitude!" (C, 3: 10–11).

What is important, of course, is not only the fact of similarity between Carthage and Flaubert's perception of his contemporary reality, but the fact that the categories which subtend this similarity describe equally as well the metaphorical network in terms of which he stages, for the nineteenth-century writer, the act of writing.

For Flaubert, the perception of history is itself a historical problem. It is only in periods at the ends of history that one perceives history historically, so to speak:

Poor wretches that we are, we have, I think, considerable taste because we are profoundly historical, because we accept everything and adopt the point of view of whatever we are judging. (B, 1: 645)

The sense of history dates from yesterday. And it is perhaps the best thing about the nineteenth century. (C, 4: 380)

The perception of Carthage as history belongs to the nineteenth century and, as such, partakes of the problematic of the end of history. Therefore the perception of Carthage as different is the result of the sameness which makes a sense of history possible in the first place. It is not the author of *Salammbô,* but the critics—who view that work as exotic and deny its fundamental historicity—who are the victims of a Romantic epistemology.

An identical consideration governs, for Flaubert, the question of style: "To write *the mediocre* and to do it well, in such a way that it retains its appearance, shape and even its own words, is truly diabolical" (C, 3: 338). The contemporary artist cannot escape the imperatives of a mediocre style; the problem of the modern writer is to manipulate the imperatives of a mediocre style to produce out of mediocre sameness the effect of difference as a stylistic and optical artifact.

I would like to illustrate this proposition with an example which goes beyond Flaubert. When he read Zola's *Nana,* Flaubert was terribly taken by it, especially its ending. In a letter to Zola, he wrote: "If I were to make a note of everything in it that is powerful and exceptional, I'd have to mark up every page! The personalities are marvelously true. It abounds in natural-sounding language. At the end, Nana's death is *Michelangelesque!*" (C, 8: 386). What can Flaubert mean by "Michelangelesque," since Michelangelo, along with Homer, Shakespeare, and Rabelais, is an artist who, in Flaubert's literary ideology, had access to the sort of original difference denied the modern artist?

Flaubert's central metaphor for the accomplished mediocrity of the end of history is one of rottenness and decomposition. Under the pressure of time and history, a final rotting and decomposition reduce everything to a uniform, homogeneous, repulsive medium into which individuals and civilizations are bound to be drawn. Individual existence is a continuous process of decay: "As if the corruption and infection that preceded our birth and which consumes us at death were not enough, all our lives long we are nothing but the successive decay and putrefaction invading us one upon the other" (B, 1: 418). From birth to death the process is linear and irreversible: "How nothingness invades us! No sooner are we born that putrefaction sets in, and life is nothing but a long battle it wages against us ever more triumphantly until the end—death—when its reign becomes absolute" (C, 3: 145).

But in all of our singular instances, the process of corruption is the individual emblem of the movement of history: "We are not dancing on a volcano, but on the floorboard of a latrine that seems to me quite rotten. Pretty soon society will drown itself in nineteen centuries of excrement." (B, 1: 708). The artist and the writer, who is himself submerged in the process, can only write and compose with the secondary, derived, corrupted materials handed down to him.

But finally is it not also necessary to recognize all the rooms of the heart and the social body, from the cellar to the attic, not even leaving out the latrines; above all not forgetting the latrines! In them is worked out a magical chemistry, fertilizing decompositions are made in them. Who knows to what excremental ooze we owe the perfume of roses and the taste of melons? Has anyone ever counted how many contemptible actions must be contemplated to build the greatness of a soul? How much nauseating pollution one must have swallowed, how much chagrin one must have felt, how many tortures one must have endured, to write one good page? That's what all of us are, cesspool-emptiers and gardeners. Out of its own putrefying waste, we extract things which are delightful for humanity. We grow basketfuls of flowers on a bed of misery. (C, 3: 407)

It is, then, with the belated corrupt refuse and excrement of history that the writer creates his fictions and illusions.

Let us return to the ending of *Nana*. In the striking final passage, Zola describes Nana's decomposing cadaver:

Nana was left alone, her face upturned in the light from the candle. What lay on the pillow was a charnel-house, a heap of pus and blood, a shovelful of putrid flesh. The pustules had invaded the whole face, so that one pock touched the next. Withered and sunken, they had taken on the greyish color of mud, and on that shapeless pulp, in which the features had ceased to be discernable, they already looked like mould from the grave. One eye, the left eye, had completely foundered in the bubbling purulence, and the other, which remained half open, looked like a dark decaying hole. The nose was still suppurating. A large reddish crust starting on one of the cheeks was invading the mouth, twisting it into a terrible grin. And around this grotesque and horrible mask of death, the hair, the beautiful hair, still blazed like sunlight and flowed in a stream of gold. Venus was decomposing. It was as if the poison she had picked up in the gutters, from the carcases left there by the roadside, that ferment with which she had poisoned a whole people, had now risen to her face and rotted it.

The room was empty. A great breath of despair came up from the boulevard and filled out the curtains.

"To Berlin! To Berlin! To Berlin!"[14]

This remarkable passage could not escape Flaubert's notice. Nana's cadaver emblematizes the metaphor of decomposition, undoing her body but revealing her function in the general decomposition of society. Finally, the decomposition of Nana's body coincides with the beginning of the Franco-Prussian War, which for Flaubert was the single most important event in the beginning of the end of history and the return to barbarism.[15] We begin to guess what Flaubert might have meant by characterizing the passage as "Michelangelesque." The differential element is not at the origin; on the contrary, the passage is different in the way it follows the movement of decomposition to the emblematic end of history.

What remains untouched of Nana's decomposing body is her hair, metaphorized as the sun and as gold. For Flaubert the sun is one of the metaphors of an absolute which does not fall victim to the process of corruption; it is the metaphor of an ontological state of difference which cannot be reduced to identity, of an otherness which cannot be reduced to sameness. Such a sun is, of course, *not perceptible*—"Heraclitus poked out his own eyes so as to better see the sun of which I'm speaking" (C, 3: 399)—hence it is inconceivable that it could be objectified in linguistic representation. For Flaubert, "lying above life and happiness there is something blue and incandescent, a great and unalterable and subtle sky whose radiance is sufficient to animate whole worlds. The splendor of genius is only the wan reflection of this hidden Word" (C, 3: 389). Thus the "light" by which we "see" is not that of the sun, but of some of its pale metaphors, such as candlelight or gaslight: "We have gas lighting in our brains!" (C, 3: 389). In relation to this particular metaphoric network, the passage from Zola— "And around this grotesque and horrible mask of death, the hair, the beautiful hair, still blazed like sunlight and flowed in a stream of gold"—is all the more remarkable inasmuch as by situating the metaphor of the sun as the immutable element amid an extreme decomposition, it constitutes a second-degree emblem of the nature of the literary work according to Flaubert's conception of it. Nana's corpse includes, then, the original difference—Sun, on the one hand; dark, abysmal Putrefaction, on the other—which juxtaposes Beginning and End but also opens the space in which history becomes possible and spatially emblematizes its development. It is the unfolding of this same history that will determine the evolution of the idiom of literature from a pure, transparent origin where the poetic word stood in all the glory of an adequate representation, to a contemporary corruption and decay with whose products the writer has to compose—belatedly—prosaic and representationally inadequate artifacts. Decay would be the cause and the substance of a belated literature at the end of history. Flaubert, in fact, appropriated Zola's metaphor. In a letter to Maupassant written the day after the letter to Zola congratulating him on *Nana*, he states: "Poetry, like the sun, paints gold on dung" (C, 8: 397). An ideal literature would then simply allegorize itself by representing the space which makes its deployment both possible and inevitable.

To uphold the thesis that Flaubert's "oriental" novels are dictated by a Romantic quest for the exotic, for a world temporally and spatially different from the European bourgeois world in which he lived, is to indiscriminately associate the historical element of antiquity with the geographical component of the Orient. The two are in fact neither similar nor symmetrical. The question of what the Orient meant for Flaubert is too complex, and probably too heterogeneous, to admit a simple answer. In what follows I hope to isolate briefly some of the components that go into the making of what is labeled, conveniently but inaccurately, "Flaubert's Orient."

At first it would appear that the sun resides in the orient. The sun, obscured by the Northern fogs, absent from belated European history, is in the Orient a presence: "What a sun! What a sky! . . . What *everything*" (B, 1: 663); ". . . and the sun! the sun! And an immense boredom that devours everything" (C, 3: 136). What this sun illuminates is not the bookish, costumed Orient imagined in Europe. Flaubert in fact denounces the latter: "Until now we have understood the Orient as something shimmering, screaming, passionate and full of contrasts. We have seen nothing in it but dancing-girls and curved sabers, fanaticism, sensual pleasure, etc. In a word, we haven't progressed since Byron" (C, 3: 136). What the sun in fact makes possible is the last scene of *Nana*—not as textual allegory, but as empirical reality:

On the contrary, what I like about the Orient is a certain unself-conscious grandeur and harmoniousness of disparate things. I recall having seen a bather who had on his left arm a silver bracelet and on the other a vesicatory. This is the true Orient and consequently the poetic one as well: rag-bedecked scoundrels covered in vermin. If you leave them alone, these vermin form golden arabesques in the sun. You tell me that Kuchuk Hanem's bugs degrade her in your eyes. For me, they were the most enchanting touch of all. Their noxious odor mixed with the smell of her skin which was dripping in sandalwood oil. I want there to be a bitter taste to everything, always a jeer in the midst of our triumphs, and a desolation to our enthusiasm. Which reminds me of Jaffa where, on entering the city, I smelled an odor at once of lemon trees and cadavers. In the ruined cemetery, half-rotted skeletons lay uncovered while green bushes dangled their golden fruit over our heads. Don't you feel the completeness of such poetry; that it is the great synthesis? (C, 3: 136–37)

The Orient is the simultaneous and everyday conjunction of the different, the permanent, and the original with the rotten and the corrupt. In other words, the Orient presents the monstrous as real rather than as a textual construct. The important thing, however, is that, inasmuch as difference in the Orient is given as empirical reality, it cannot be reinscribed in linguistic representation. One can see the poetry of the Orient, one can live the poetry of the Orient, but one cannot write the poetry of the Orient. In the letter just quoted, Flaubert goes on to declare: "Would I love to be a scholar! And I'd write a great book with the title: *On the Interpretation of Antiquity!* For I am sure of being in the tradition; what I add to it is the modern sentiment" (C, 3: 137).

But this brings us back to the historical problem of writing history, a history which obliterates the difference offered by the Orient. A book entitled *On the Interpretation of Antiquity* would only reveal an archaeological Orient seen through the mediation of books, and if one were to add to it "the modern sentiment," what one would have is something resembling *Salammbô* rather than a representation of what the Orient *is*. When Flaubert proposes to write a book about the Orient qua Orient, as opposed to a historical, archaeological Orient, the subject he proposes to deal with is not the Orient but the disappearance of the Orient:

If I were younger and had money, I'd go back to study the modern Orient, the Orient of the Isthmus of Suez. A big book about it has long been a dream of mine. I want to create a civilized man who becomes barbaric and a barbarian who becomes civilized, and develop this contrast of two worlds which end up blending. (C, 8: 94)

The fact is that, for Flaubert, the Orient is in its agony and will soon disappear as Orient—if it has not already done so. To Théophile Gautier, whose quest for the exotic could not have been unknown to Flaubert, he writes: "Soon the Orient will no longer exist. We are perhaps among the last to contemplate it. —You have no idea how debased it already is; the Turkish soldiers wear trouser-straps! I saw harems pass by in steamships" (B, 1: 663). And to Frédéric Baudry he writes: "It seems to me that the Orient is even sicker than the Occident" (B, 1: 654). It is thus, in the logic of Flaubert's system, that the Orient will survive only in its sun; that is to say, the Orient will no longer be perceptible as different:

Soon, the only thing that will be left of the Orient is the sun. In Constantinople, most of the men dress European-style; there's an opera there; there are reading rooms and milliners, etc. Within a hundred years the institution of the harem, after having been gradually invaded by the much-visited Frankish ladies, will succumb under the weight of the serial novel and vaudeville. . . . Soon the veil, which is already becoming thinner and thinner, will be removed from the women's faces and all Moslemism will fly off with it. Every day, the number of pilgrims to Mecca is smaller. The ulemas are as drunken as the Swiss. They talk about Voltaire! Everything is falling apart here, as it is in Europe. (C, 2: 278–79)

Even eroticism in the Orient becomes mediated by trite European Romantic representations and texts:

In another brothel we screwed some tolerable Greek and Armenian women. — The house was run by a former mistress of our dragoman. We were at home there. On the walls there were delicate engravings and scenes from the lives of Heloise and Abelard, with captions in French and Spanish. —O Orient, where are you? —Soon all that will be left of it is the sun! (B, 1: 730)

If the specter of Voltaire returns, it is because Voltaire is the metaphoric name of history: "Mohammed is also falling and without having had his Voltaire. The greatest Voltaire is time, the consumer of all things."[16] And so, in the end, the sun of the Orient will withdraw, leaving only the corruption of history.

If one were to search in the works of Flaubert for an emblematic conjunction of the corruption of space and the movement of history, one would probably find no better example than that of Jerusalem, which offers the pitiful spatial example of the temporal corruption of the center and origin of at least one history:

> Jerusalem is a charnel-house surrounded by walls. Everything there is rotting; the dead dogs in the streets, the religions in the churches: (powerful idea). There is a great deal of shit and many ruins lying about. . . . The Holy Sepulcher is the agglomeration of all possible curses. Within this tiny space there are four churches—Armenian, Greek, Latin and Coptic—all heartily insulting and cursing one another. (B, 1: 665)

And yet it is this historical ruin that, in the last analysis, offers a center from which Flaubert can write: "The pile of old religions that one finds in Syria is incredible. —I was in my center there. There is enough there for centuries of work" (B, 1: 696–97).

In conclusion, the temporal and spatial situation of the author of *Salammbô* and *The Temptation of Saint Anthony* is thus similar to that of the characters in the novels. Their temporal relationship is one of proximity and similarity rather than of distance and difference. The opposition that would sustain the accusation of exoticism leveled at Flaubert by Sainte-Beuve and Lukács is, in fact, subverted by *Salammbô*. In Flaubert's choice of Carthage, what might appear at the outset as a desire for an otherness defined as difference is dictated by the necessity of finding an otherness which would be a form of sameness. What appears as different is in fact an effect, an optical illusion, a mirage. Flaubert writes from the standpoint of the end of time, and to write at the end of time means to write from a position of mediocrity, which in turn entails writing in such a way that representation not have a direct unmediated relation to an object. *Salammbô*, like *The Temptation of Saint Anthony*, is written with an accumulation of "notes upon notes, books upon books," with an "indigestion of books." The function of art is, of course, to create the *illusion* that the language of fiction is the language of its object; that *Salammbô* is the language of

Carthage, and *The Temptation of Saint Anthony* the language of fourth-century Alexandria; and that Carthage and Alexandria exist as linguistically reachable objective entities. The quest for exoticism and for a lost object is not, then, what determines the writing of fiction. Well-constructed fiction is an optical machine that produces the exotic, the distant, and the different as illusion and mirage. Constructed illusion is the only form of metaphysical reality-sustaining representation that Flaubert subscribed to: "I only believe in the eternity of one thing: that of *illusion* which is the true truth. All the others are merely relative truths" (B, 1: 429). And the function of art is to create such illusions: "Art's first quality and goal is *illusion*" (C, 3: 344). The presumed realism of Flaubert—if there is such a thing—can only stem from an assumed identity of illusions. Art creates illusions, but these illusions are not the illusions of some presumed reality. The optical illusions of art are illusions of other optical illusions, for, "like our misfortunes, our joys are only optical illusions, effects of light and perspective" (B, 1: 419).

If there is a nostalgia in Flaubert, it is the nostalgia not for a lost object but rather, as we saw earlier, for a language and mode of representation that might achieve an original and linguistically unmediated relation to its objects. Nevertheless, Flaubert also knows such a language to be unobtainable. If it were not, one could look at the sun and name the sun.[17] Yet in the Northern fogs, at a belated time in history, one cannot look at the sun or name it by its proper name. As one might guess, Flaubert sees his destiny as temporally and spatially bound to the Northern fogs of late history:

Deep within me there is always something like the aftertaste of the medieval melancholies of my country. There is an odor of fog, of the plague brought back from the Orient, and it falls away with its carvings, its stained-glass windows and leaded joints, like the old wooden houses of Rouen. (C, 2: 348)

Bound by such constraints, the writer has no other alternative but to construct linguistic optical machines which would create the metaphorical illusion and mirage of twenty-five candles shining like the sun:

What artists those ancients were! And what language they had! Any language we may create will never equal theirs. It is there that we must live, there that we must go. —In the sunny region of the land of the Beautiful. When it rains in winter, those who understand sensual life close their shutters, light twenty-five candles, make a big fire, spike some punch and lie on tiger skins, smoking cigarettes. —They understand this in a moral sense and, as the Persian proverb puts it, "close up all five windows so that the house may see more clearly." Insect! What do I care about the world? Let it turn whichever way it wants; I live in my humble abode which I'm busy covering with diamond dust. (B, 1: 435–36)

Or, as Flaubert would remind us, "we impoverish language by comparing stars to diamonds."[18]

## Notes

1. Charles Augustin Sainte-Beuve, article on *Salammbô* dated December 22, 1862, in *Oeuvres complètes de Gustave Flaubert* (Paris: Club de l'Honnête Homme, 1971–75), 2: 435. Subsequent references to this volume will be identified in the text with the letters "S/C" and the page number.

2. Georg Lukács, "Salammbô," in *Flaubert: A Collection of Critical Essays,* ed. R. Giraud (Englewood, N.J.: Prentice-Hall, 1964), pp. 146–47.

3. A few examples: "There is what is known as the 'soul' of a work" (S/C, 429); "if everything you describe were true and copied from nature, I would take an interest in it" (S/C, 437); "Let us turn to life, to that which falls within the province and the gasp of everyone, to that which our era desires most and which can sincerely move or charm us" (S/C, 442).

4. Lukács, "Salammbô," p. 148.

5. Gustave Flaubert, *Oeuvres complètes de Gustave Flaubert: Correspondance* (Paris: Louis Conard, 1926–33), 8: 374. Subsequent references to this edition of Flaubert's correspondence will be identified in the text by the letter "C" followed by the volume and page number. In line with the argument developed in this chapter, it is interesting to note that Jean Seznec, in his *Nouvelles Etudes sur "La Tentation de Saint Antoine"* (London: Warburg Institute, 1949), quotes this same passage to argue that the *Temptation* is based on precise scholarship: "Despite its superb lack of contemporaneousness, it has deep roots in contemporary thought. It is related to a whole set of historical inquiries and poetico-philosophical speculations. It evokes and reconstructs the past, but a past which is refracted by the nineteenth century's troubled imagination" (p. 43). He adds later that in *The Temptation of Saint Anthony* "Flaubert expressed the 'ideal' of his contemporaries, their vision of the religious world in the first centuries of our era" (p. 46).

6. Gustave Flaubert, *Salammbô,* ed. Edouard Maynial (Paris: Garnier, 1961), p. 355.

7. Ibid., p. 356.

8. Gustave Flaubert, *Correspondance,* ed. Jean Bruneau (Paris: Gallimard, 1973, 1980), 1: 437. Subsequent references to this edition of Flaubert's correspondence will be identified in the text by the letter "B" followed by the volume and page number.

9. Jules Michelet, *Histoire romaine* in his *Oeuvres complètes,* ed. Paul Viallaneix (Paris: Flammarion, 1972), 2: 440–41.

10. Ibid., p. 441.

11. Ibid., p. 453.

12. I am aware of the implicit anachronism in quoting texts written by Flaubert well after *Salammbô* in order to illustrate the textual dialectics of the earlier novel. The late texts—in particular those after 1870—are consistent with a philosophy of history that Flaubert upheld throughout his life. It should be obvious that the quotes that follow are virtually interchangeable with statements by Flaubert contemporary with or preceding *Salammbô.* Again, I have chosen for simplicity's sake to do the demonstration with *Salammbô,* but the same argument could be developed with *The Temptation of Saint Anthony,* the third version of which is contemporary with or posterior to some of the quotes.

13. Gustave Flaubert, *Oeuvres complètes de Gustave Flaubert: Correspondance: Supplément* (Paris: Louis Conard, 1954), 4: 105.

14. Emile Zola, *Nana,* trans. George Holden (New York: Penguin, 1972), p. 470.

15. In some ways such a reading of Flaubert repeats that of D. H. Lawrence who, in *Phoenix II: Uncollected, Unpublished and Other Prose Works* (New York: Viking Press, 1968), p. 358, writes:

And yet humanity can only finally conquer by realizing. It is human destiny, since Man fell into consciousness and self-consciousness, that we can only go forward step by step through realization, full, bitter, conscious realization. This is true of all the great terrors and agonies and anguishes of life: sex, and war, and even crime. When Flaubert in his story—it is so long since I read it—makes his saint have to kiss the leper, and naked clasp the leprous awful body against his own, that is what we must at last do. It is the great command *Know Thyself.* We've got to *know* what sex is, let the sentimentalists wiggle as they like. We've got to know the greatest and most shattering human passions, let the puritans squeal as they like for screens. And we've got to know humanity's criminal tendency, look straight at humanity's great deeds of crime against the soul. We have to fold this horrible leper against our naked warmth: because life and the throbbing blood and the believing soul are greater even than leprosy. Knowledge, true knowledge is like vaccination. It prevents the continuing of ghastly moral disease.

And so it is with the war. Humanity in Europe fell horribly into a hatred of the living soul, in the war. There is no gainsaying it. We all fell. Let us not try to wriggle out of it. We fell into hideous depravity of hating the human soul; a purulent small-pox of the spirit we had. It was shameful, shameful, shameful, in every country and in all of us. Some tried to resist, and some didn't. But we were all drowned in shame. A purulent small-pox of the vicious spirit, vicious against the deep soul that pulses in the blood. We haven't got over it. The small-pox sores are running yet in the spirit of mankind. And we have got to take this putrid spirit to our bosom. There's nothing else for it. Take the foul rotten spirit of mankind, full of the running sores of the war, to our bosom, and cleanse it there. Cleanse it not with blind love: ah, no, that won't help. But with bitter and wincing realization. We have to take the disease into our consciousness and let it go through our soul, like some virus. We have got to realize. And then we can surpass.

And in *Phoenix: The Posthumous Papers* (New York: Viking Press, 1936), p. 312:

Thomas Mann seems to me the last sick sufferer from the complaint of Flaubert. The latter stood away from life as from a leprosy. And Thomas Mann, like Flaubert, feels vaguely that he has in him something finer than ever physical life revealed. Physical life is a disordered corruption, against which he can fight with only one weapon, his fine aesthetic sense, his feeling for beauty, for perfection, for a certain fitness which soothes him, and gives him an inner pleasure, however corrupt the stuff of life may be. There he is, after all these years, full of disgust and loathing of himself as Flaubert was, and Germany is being voiced, or partly so, by him. And so, with real suicidal intention, like Flaubert's, he sits, a last too-sick disciple, reducing himself grain by grain to the statement of his own disgust, patiently, self-destructively, so that his statement at least may be perfect in a world of corruption. But he is so late.

16. Gustave Flaubert, *Voyage en Orient* in *Oeuvres complètes de Gustave Flaubert* (Paris: Club de l'Honnête Homme, 1971–75), 10: 590–91.

17. I am referring here to the problem of proper nouns and the metaphoricity of language as developed by Jacques Derrida in "White Mythology: Metaphor in the Text of Philosophy," in his *Margins of Philosophy*, trans. Alan Bass (Chicago: University of Chicago Press, 1982).

18. Flaubert, *Voyage en Orient*, p. 522.

# 3  The Museum's Furnace: Notes Toward a Contextual Reading of *Bouvard and Pécuchet*

> *Le feu est chez vous.*  Flaubert
>
> *Nous sommes embarqués sur un microcosme volcan, prêt à s'abîmer. Pascal revu par Nietzsche pour les amateurs d'émotions cérébrales fortes.*  Michel Serres

## The Library

Flaubert's *Bouvard and Pécuchet* describes the systematic pursuit by two office clerks of a number of activities—agriculture, arboriculture, garden architecture, chemistry, anatomy, physiology, geology, archaeology, and others—which span the totality of human knowledge by systematically exhausting its various domains. Yet neither the well-meant, systematic enterprises of the two clerks nor their immense resiliency in the face of failure allows them ever to gain mastery over any of the regions of the encyclopedia. The encyclopedia, assumed to be the ultimate principle of reality, turns out to be a constantly elusive mirage. The odyssey of the two asexual bachelors stages the concept of an encyclopedic knowledge both as that which preexists and determines the various activities in which the two clerks engage, and also as the teleological end point which they indefatigably attempt to attain, without its ever being at any time present to them.

The office clerks systematically fail in each and every one of their endeavors; each field of knowledge reveals itself to be contradictory,

56

unsystematic, or simply unable to give an adequate representation of the objects it is supposed to describe. A bookish knowledge of agriculture in no way permits them to grow crops, archaeology is full of contradictions, the writing of history impossible. Having finally recognized the failure of their enterprise, they return to their original activity of copying; however, this time they simply copy anything and everything that comes to hand. Having begun with the dream and hope of a total, finite, rational domain of knowledge, they come to realize that not only is knowledge as a given totality unavailable but that also any act of totalization is by definition incomplete, infinite, and everywhere marked by accident, chance, and randomness:

They copy papers haphazardly, everything they find, tobacco pouches, old newspapers, posters, torn books, etc. (real items and their imitations. Typical of each category).

Then, they feel the need for a taxonomy. They make tables, antithetical oppositions such as "crimes of the kings and crimes of the people"—blessings of religion, crimes of religion. Beauties of history, etc.; sometimes, however, they have real problems putting each thing in its proper place and suffer great anxieties about it.

—Onward! Enough speculation! Keep on copying! The page must be filled. Everything is equal, the good and the evil. The farcical and the sublime—the beautiful and the ugly—the insignificant and the typical, they all become an exaltation of the statistical. There are nothing but facts—and phenomena. Final bliss.[1]

Most readings of *Bouvard and Pécuchet* take their point of departure from Flaubert's remarks about the composition and significance of the work. The result of the author's meanderings through the library: "I'm aghast at what I have to do for *Bouvard and Pécuchet*. I read catalogues of books that I annotate" (1324)[2]; "I am, sir, *inside a labyrinth!*" (550); "I have gotten indigestion from books. I burp in-folio" (537); "Reading is an abyss; one never gets out of it. I am becoming as dumb as a pot" (397). The novel is to portray "the story of these two men who copy a kind of farcical version of a critical encyclopedia" (1318).

Flaubert's comments could hardly have passed unnoticed by critics such as Foucault and Kenner, who—after Seznec but without acknowledging him[3]—make *Bouvard and Pécuchet* emblematic of the metaphor of the *Library-Encyclopedia*, which for them governs the modern developments of fiction's textuality, from Hegel's *Encyclopedia of*

*Philosophic Sciences* to Borges's "Library of Babel." For Kenner, "The mark of the Encyclopedia," which is its fragmentation of all knowledge into little pieces so arranged that they can be found one at a time, points only to the "burlesque . . . of fiction," to "the incompetence . . . of fiction itself which is endlessly *arranging* things."[4] For Foucault, *Bouvard and Pécuchet*, along with *The Temptation of Saint Anthony*, belongs to "a literature that exists only inside and as a result of the web of the already written: the book in which is played out the fiction of all books." Hence the *Temptation*, but also implicitly *Bouvard and Pécuchet*, "is not only a book that Flaubert had long dreamed of writing; it is the dream of other books: all those other dreaming and dreamt-of books—fragmented, taken up again, displaced, combined, distanced by the dream but also brought back by it to the imaginary and scintillating satisfaction of desire. After *The Book* Mallarmé will become possible, then Joyce, Roussel, Kafka, Pound, Borges. The library is aflame." Bouvard and Pécuchet "are tempted by books, by their indefinite multiplicity, by the rippling of works in the colorless space of the Library."[5]

Both Kenner's and Foucault's readings underscore the critical importance of the metaphor of the *Encyclopedia-Library* and its importance to the development of the Flaubertian canon. For both, *Bouvard and Pécuchet* is a book constructed out of fragments of other books; the book presupposes, then, the *Library* as its genetic memory. Such a memory, however, is neither the "constructive memory" of the interiorized world which Hegel writes about[6] and which guarantees the ontological status of representation, nor a Divine Book of Nature that the modern writer might have inherited from an earlier theological tradition. If the *Library* makes *Bouvard and Pécuchet* possible, in no way does it provide it with a privileged origin which might guarantee the mimetic or representational veracity of fiction, or the capacity of the world to fictionalize itself in an unequivocal fashion. What the *Library* imposes on the two unfortunate heroes of Flaubert's novel is the impossibility of reaching its order, its totality, or its truth. The library dooms the characters—but the author and the reader as well[7]—to an indefinite wandering in a labyrinthine space not unlike that described by the narrator of Borges's "Library of Babel." The characters' plight, as Flaubert so often indicated, is also the author's: the novel, then, stages the impossibility of its authorship and of its inscription. Flaubert, like his characters Bouvard and Pécuchet, is reduced to the role of a scribe; their failure is his failure. Through

Flaubert's signature, it is fiction which signs the dramatization of its impossible quest for privileged origins.

The final scene of the two clerks copying whatever happens to fall into their hands might then be read as an allegory of the way literature unfolds its representational texture. Flaubert's addition to the earlier scenario for the ending of the novel, quoted above and incorporated in a later, more extended version as "Give as being true, bibliographical information which is false," becomes, then, the emblem of that allegory. Literature, having shed its ontotheological illusions, shamelessly parades its fictions as "truths" to hide the staging of its hopeless quest for a privileged origin, a quest which invariably ends in fiction's dispersion into the infinite, nonnatural labyrinthine web of textuality.

Such a reading of *Bouvard and Pécuchet,* besides having the merit of accounting for the way the text inscribes its own genesis and showing how this inscription is isomorphic to the way Flaubert himself described the textual construction of the novel, permits one to read specific passages as a precise critique of linguistic representation. As I have tried to show in the previous chapter, the clerks' failure at agriculture can be derived from the failure of nominalization and rhetorical signification to sustain a stable system.[8] Their failure at writing history can be analyzed to show the generalized failure of symbolization in reaching any signified beyond the open-ended play of signifiers. In summary, it is difficult, after *Bouvard and Pécuchet,* not to arrive at the conclusion that Flaubert is a linguistic nihilist, and that in his descriptions of the two office clerks' failures, he undertook a critique of representation similar to that of Nietzsche in texts such as "Truth and Illusion in an Extra-Moral Sense."

## The Museum

The reading of *Bouvard and Pécuchet* in terms of the metaphor of the *Encyclopedia-Library,* despite its relating the novel to a crucial textual problematic and allowing for the reading of certain passages in terms of primarily linguistic or representational considerations, falls short, however, of being completely satisfactory. The reason for this is twofold. On the one hand, the *Encyclopedia-Library* is never thematized as a master term that explicitly controls the deployment of the various regions of knowledge; on the contrary Flaubert systematically stages the *Encyclopedia-Library* as one nonprivileged term in an indifferent series. On the other hand, a good number of the failures of Bouvard and Pécuchet cannot be attributed to the incapacity of linguistic or symbolic representation to account for reality. For example, when wind and rain destroy their fruit crops, or when a storm destroys their wheat crop, there is no way of accounting for the storm within any representational system. The forces at play within nature are absolutely other than those at work in the deconstruction of taxonomies, rhetoric, and semiology.

The clerks' original dream of a pastoral existence excludes the activity of writing, that is to say, of the most complex and resistant of language's representational forms: "Waking with the lark, they would follow the plough, go out with a basket to gather apples, watch the butter being made, the corn threshed, the sheep sheared, the beehives tended, and they would revel in the mooing of cows and the scent of fresh-mown hay. No more copying!" (BP, 30).[9] Carried away by their illusion, they also reject from the start any need for books. Flaubert in the *Dictionnaire des idées reçues* writes: "Library—always have one in one's home, especially when living in the country." Bouvard, on the contrary, on the verge of his new rural life decides that "we'll have no library." In their pastoral dream, Bouvard and Pécuchet dismiss the mediation of books and aspire instead to the mastery of a science which acts directly on nature. Significantly, they start their adventures equipped with an odd assortment of scientific instruments: "They purchased gardening implements and a mass of things 'which might come in useful,' such as a tool-box (every house should have one), followed by a pair of scales, a land-chain, a bath-tub in case of illness, a thermometer, and even a barometer, 'on the Gay-Lussac system,' for meteorological experiments, should the fancy take them" (BP, 30–31).

The odd assortment of books that belonged to Pécuchet before he undertook his rural adventure hardly amounts to a library. The books, in fact, are part of a group of heterogeneous objects that anticipate the "*bric-a-brac* shops" they will later visit: "and in the corners were scattered a number of volumes of the Roret Encyclopaedia, the Mesmerist's Handbook, a Fenelon, and other old tomes, as well as a pile of papers, two coconuts, various medallions, a Turkish fez, and shells brought from Le Havre by Dumouchel" (BP, 21). It can be argued, of course, that Bouvard and Pécuchet are defeated by the very thing whose importance they fail to account for in the first place. As I suggested earlier, there is no doubt that such a remark is regionally correct and that the efforts of the two clerks are sometimes undone by an unstable representational or symbolic system that they fail fully to understand or to recognize. Nevertheless, when the theme of the *Encyclopedia-Library* appears in the novel, it is thematized in such a way as to require a separate set of remarks. To return to the passage quoted above, the clerks' library—if one can call it that—is on the one hand contrasted with their scientific instruments, that is, with an otherness which is not obviously inscribed in the texture of representation; but more important, it appears in a series of heterogeneous elements. The difficulty resides, precisely, in reading a series of heterogeneous elements, since through their heterogeneity they offer what is absolutely other to the homogeneous representational space of the *Encyclopedia-Library*.

Later in the novel, when Flaubert describes the various buildings and public collections that Bouvard and Pécuchet visit, the library is again placed in a heterogeneous series:

They sauntered past the old *bric-a-brac* shops. They visited the Conservatoire des Arts et Métiers, Saint-Denis, the Gobelins, the Invalides and all the public collections. . . .

In the galleries of the Museum they viewed the stuffed quadrupeds with astonishment, the butterflies with pleasure, the metals with indifference; fossils fired their imagination, conchology bored them. They peered into hot-houses, and shuddered at the thought of so many foliages distilling poison. What struck them most about the cedar was that it had been brought over in a hat.

They worked up an enthusiasm at the Louvre for Raphael. At the Central Library they would have liked to know the exact number of volumes. (BP, 25–26)

The bric-a-brac is emblematic of the whole series. Again, it is not the bric-a-brac which is in the library; it is the latter that belongs to a series which can be characterized as bric-a-brac. Interestingly, however, the series contains one term that itself contains a heterogeneous series, namely the *Museum* (the Museum of Natural History). The term which is then representationally privileged, which allegorizes the series, is the museum and not the library, since the former contains a series of which the latter is only a term. It is then perhaps in the concept of the *Museum* that we must search for an encyclopedic totality.

If Bouvard and Pécuchet never assemble what can amount to a library, they nevertheless manage to constitute for themselves a private museum. The museum, in fact, occupies a central position in the novel; it is connected to the characters' interest in archaeology, geology, and history and it is thus through the *Museum* that questions of origin, causality, representation, and symbolization are most clearly stated. The *Museum,* as well as the questions it tries to answer, depends upon an archaeological epistemology. Its representational and historical pretensions are based upon a number of metaphysical assumptions about origins—archaeology intends, after all, to be a science of the *archēs.* Archaeological origins are important in two ways: each archaeological artifact has to be an original artifact, and these original artifacts must in turn explain the "meaning" of a subsequent larger history. Thus, in Flaubert's caricatural example, the baptismal font that Bouvard and Pécuchet discover has to be a Celtic sacrificial stone, and Celtic culture has in turn to act as an original master pattern for cultural history:

. . . whence it must be concluded that the religion of the Gauls had the same principles as that of the Jews.

Their society was very well organized. . . . Some uttered prophesies, others chanted, others taught botany, medicine, history and literature: in short, "all the arts of their epoch." Pythagoras and Plato were their pupils. They instructed the Greeks in metaphysics, the Persians in sorcery, the Etruscans in augury, and the Romans in plating copper and trading in ham.

But of this people which dominated the ancient world, there remain only a few stones. (BP, 127–28)

These stones will become the archival material displayed in the museums which are the outward manifestation of an implicit archaeological knowledge or essence.

The outstanding characteristic of the Flaubertian *Museum* is its irreducible heterogeneity. This heterogeneity becomes, in fact, caricatural in Flaubert's early scenarios for the novel. To quote from one of them:

Six months later the house looked entirely different. They possessed a collection. *Museum.*

Old junk, pottery of all sorts, shaving cups, butter plates, earthenware lamps, wardrobes, a halberd, one of a kind! Bludgeons, panoplies of primitive origins. Works of spun glass. Chest of drawers and Chippendale trunks, prison hampers. Saint-Allyre's petrified objects: a cat with a mouse in its jaws, stuffed birds. Various curios: chauffeur's cap, a madman's shoe. Objects drawn from rivers and people, etc.[10]

I have quoted this early draft because of its brevity; the lengthy description of the Museum of Bouvard and Pécuchet contains as heterogeneous a collection of objects as that of the draft, and interestingly enough contains also a library as one of the objects of the Museum. A parenthesis might be in order here. The ideology that governs the *Museum* in the nineteenth century and down to the present has often been equated with that of the *Library*, namely, to give by the ordered display of selected artifacts a total representation of human reality and history. Museums are taken to exist only inasmuch as they can erase the heterogeneity of the objects displayed in their cases, and it is only the hypothesis of the possibility of homogenizing the diversity of various artifacts which makes them possible in the first place.

As late as 1929 W. J. Holland, director of the Carnegie Institute and president of the American Association of Museums, wrote: "The ideal museum should cover the whole field of human knowledge. It should teach the truths of all the sciences, including anthropology, the science which deals with man and all his works in every age. All the sciences and all the arts are correlated." The critique of early museums is done in terms of bric-a-brac. Lord Balcarres, trustee of the National Portrait Gallery, wrote: "The modern museum of art differs essentially from its earlier prototypes. The aimless collection of curiosities and bric-a-brac, brought together without method or system, was the feature of certain famous collections in by-gone days." The success of the modern museum again depends upon the order in which the objects are displayed: "To be of teaching value, museum arrangement and classification must be carefully studied. . . . Attention must be given to the proper display and cataloguing of the exhibits. . . . Great progress has been made in the classification of objects."[11] To give one more example, in 1930 Sir Frederic Kenyon, then director and principal librarian of the British Museum, wrote:

In the galleries of these museums are gathered together examples of the art and craftsmanship of man, from the most remote stone age to the present day. The study of such objects teaches us how man has reacted to his surroundings, what products of art or industry he has achieved, how he has used or misused his opportunities. They are at once the material and the illustrations of written history, and to a generation becoming daily more dependent on the picture than on the written word their importance is increasing.

The study of history not only widens our mind by increasing our interests, but contributes to the stability of our civilisation by its record of the actions of men, and their results, in conditions more or less analogous to our own.

History is vicarious experience, and the neglect of it leads to rash ventures and disastrous experiments.[12]

These pronouncements seem to indicate as naive a faith as that of the two clerks in the capacity of giving an adequate representation of reality as it was or as it is. The ontotheological temptation to equate the *Encyclopedia-Library* with the *Museum* is as understandable as it is surprising. The *Encyclopedia-Library* is a lay version of the medieval metaphor of the *Book of Nature.* Implicit in that metaphor is the assumption that the world can be completely textualized and, vice versa, that any element of the world can be treated as a textual element. Borges, for example, significantly begins his "Library of Babel" with the words: "The Universe (which others call the Library). . . ." A linguistic critique of the ontotheological pretensions of the *Library* accentuates the open-ended boundaries of the web of language to which the *Library* tries to give a center and a limit. If the *Library* is not the mirror of a presumed World or Nature, then the *Library* is the emblem of the infinite autoreferentiality of language. Such critiques, while underscoring the open-ended play of language and its uncentered labyrinthine structure, nevertheless often maintain a nostalgia for the center—witness Mallarmé's quest for *The Book,* or Borges's search for the "Catalogue of Catalogues." This is hardly the case for the *Museum.* The set of objects the Museum displays is sustained only by the fiction that they somehow constitute a coherent representational universe. The fiction is that a repeated metonymic displacement from fragment to totality, object to label, series of objects to series of labels, can still produce a representation which is somehow adequate to a non-linguistic universe. Such a fiction is the result of an uncritical belief in the notion that ordering and classifying, that is to say, the spatial juxtaposition of fragments, can produce a representational understanding of the world. Should the fiction disappear, there is nothing left of the *Museum* but "bric-a-brac," a heap of meaningless and valueless fragments of objects which are incapable of substituting themselves either metonymically for the original objects or metaphorically for their representations.

Flaubert's critique seems radical enough to question, by means of the *Museum,* the possibility of reaching any truth, essence, or origin through a representational mode. If the *Museum* as concept has at its origin the same metaphysical ambition that the *Library* has in other contexts, namely, to give an adequate ordered rational representation of reality, nevertheless its project is doomed from the start because representation within the concept of the museum is intrinsically impossible. The museum can only display objects metonymically at least twice removed from that which they are originally supposed to represent or signify. The objects displayed as a series are of necessity only part of the totality to which they originally belonged. Spatially and temporally detached from their origin and function, they signify only by arbitrary and derived associations. The series in which the individual pieces and fragments are displayed is also arbitrary and incapable of investing the particular object with anything but irrelevant fabulations.[13] Again, the critique implied here goes beyond a critique which would limit itself to linguistic representation, even though it includes it. Linguistic representation carries within itself, in the *Library*, its own memory, its own origin, its own *archē*—displaced or hidden as it may be. The *Museum*, on the other hand, testifies to an archaeological memory that cannot be recovered except through fabulation. The chapter on Bouvard and Pécuchet's museum, in fact, repeats other statements by Flaubert to the same effect. For example, in a chapter in *Par les champs et par les grèves*, he described the ruins of Carnac, ironizing all attempts to understand them.

Thus we find this famous field of Carnac that has occasioned the writing of more stupidities than it contains rocks, and one certainly does not come across such rocky paths every day. But, in spite of our natural penchant for admiring everything, we saw in it only a hardy joke, left there by an unknown age to excite the spirit of antiquarians and stupefy travelers. In front of it one opens naive eyes and, all the while finding it quite uncommon, must admit at the same time that it is not very pretty. We understood then the irony of these granite boulders that, since the age of the Druids, have laughed in their green lichen beards at seeing all the imbeciles that came to stare at them. Scholars' lives have been spent in an attempt to determine their past usages; don't you admire this eternal preoccupation of the unfeathered biped with finding some sort of usefulness for everything? Not content with distilling the ocean to salt his stew, and assassinating elephants to make knife-handles out of them, his egotism is again provoked when he is faced with some debris or other whose utility he can't figure out.[14]

It should be obvious from such a passage that the cornerstone of Flaubert's critique is in a way remarkably similar to Nietzsche's critique of representation—namely, the anthropocentrism of meaning. If the *Museum* fails at reaching the nature and essence of the objects it displays, it is because it tries to understand them in relation to the spectator rather than in relation to the objects themselves. "Meaning," the result of metonymic or metaphoric displacements, is anthropomorphic and anthropocentric, and it is because of its anthropocentrism that it is necessarily doomed to failure. Archaeology, ultimately, is not an objective science but a fantasy of the perceiving subject.[15]

Another parenthetical remark may be in order here. Flaubert's critique is of consequence for us. Archaeology is still a discipline unlike others not only because it pretends to deal with origin and meaning, but because, today as for the nineteenth century, it offers a possible epistemological master pattern. Take, for example, Foucault's *Les Mots et les choses* and *L'Archéologie du savoir:* both books claim an epistemology based upon an archaeological master pattern. Foucault hopes, through the treatment of linguistic entities by archaeological metaphors, to avoid what he considers the implicit idealism of a problematic rooted in linguistic representation. If, however, Flaubert's critique is correct, then the whole enterprise is a fabulation unable to recognize itself as such.

Foucault describes the *épistémè*, the epistemological invariant, of the Enlightenment as being governed by a quest for a perfect representation. The taxonomies of Linnaeus and Buffon are, for the twentieth century thinker, quests for a well-constructed language that would provide an adequate representation of Nature. The isomorphism between the order of Nature and the order of Language is rooted, somehow, in their discontinuity. The relationship between the order of Words and the order of Things is presumably problematical neither for the eighteenth century nor for Foucault. Things, of course, are slightly more complicated. The botanical and zoological taxonomies did not, as the author of *Les Mots et les choses* argues, originate in or through any presumed space between the order of Nature and the order of Words which is assumed to have governed classical representation. The eighteenth century generated its botanical nomenclatures by a procedure based upon the same epistemology that would later on be applied to archaeological artifacts. The botanical and zoological taxonomies assumed that a single specimen could stand for a species, that part of a specimen could stand for a specimen, that the parts could be related and named, and finally that they could be seen to stand to each other in a contiguous ordered fashion. The possibility of a perfect representation of Nature rests, then, on a complex series of metonymies and metaphors bridging the gap between the natural object and its representation. Assuming such a *continuous* representation, the Enlightenment could then originate the idea of giving an ordered representation of Nature in various botanical gardens. It is in this idea of an ordered spectacle of Nature, supplemented by an ordered language that would describe the spectacle, that the idea of the *Museum* was born.

At the beginning of the nineteenth century the development of an archaeological method, and an archaeological idea of the *Museum*, was simply the displacement onto human history of what was until then considered "natural history." This displacement guaranteed archaeology a metaphysical basis by providing it with a "natural" master pattern. Such a metaphysical basis was all the more necessary in that the passage from the fragments of archaeology to the discourse of history is much more problematical than the passage from Nature to the language of botanical and zoological taxonomies. At any rate, Foucault's epistemology is rooted in the epistemology of the Enlightenment he describes so well and, like it, is vulnerable to a critique that takes as its point of departure the questioning, through representation, of the continuity between Word and Thing, Taxonomy and Nature, and Language and Stone.

To return to *Bouvard and Pécuchet,* if the *Museum* as both theme and concept is important, then it ought to account for more than the central chapters related to archaeology and history.

In *Bouvard and Pécuchet,* and in the nineteenth century generally, the archaeological metaphor is closely linked with geology and its specific epistemology. It is, in fact, the scientific nature of geology which guarantees the displacement of its metaphors toward archaeology. The central name in geology is that of Cuvier, whom the two clerks, of course, had read: "Cuvier . . . had appeared to them in the brilliance of an aureole, on the peak of a science beyond dispute" (BP, 108). This is not surprising, since Cuvier's *Discours sur les révolutions de la surface du globe* was a very widely read text whose influence in the earlier part of the century was comparable to that of Claude Bernard's *Introduction à la médecine expérimentale* in the latter part. Cuvier described his enterprise as that of an archaeological antiquarian:

Antiquarian of a new type, I found it necessary to learn at the same time to restore these monuments of past revolutions and to decode their sense; it was my task to collect and to put together in their original order the fragments which composed them, to reconstruct the antique creatures to which these fragments belonged; to reproduce them conserving their proportions and their characteristics; to compare them finally to those which live today at the earth's surface. . . . I was sustained in this double work by the fact that it promised to be of equal import both to the general science of anatomy, the essential basis of all those sciences which deal with organized bodies, and to the physical history of the earth, the foundation of mineralogy, of geography, and even, one could say, of the history of men, and of everything that it is most important for them to know concerning themselves.

If it is of interest to us to track down in the childhood of our species the nearly eradicated traces of so many extinct nations, would it not be of greater interest to search in the darkness of the childhood of the earth for the traces of revolutions that took place prior to the existence of all nations? . . . Would there not be some glory for man in knowing how to overstep the limits of time, and in rediscovering, by means of a few observations, the history of this world and a series of events which preceded the birth of the human race?[16]

Cuvier's text is exemplary; for him, geology is a form of archaeology. The function of the geologist is to reconstruct a continuous temporal history out of the fragments handed down to him. His task, like that of the archaeologist, is twofold: to reconstruct the entities to which the fragments belonged and then to arrange those same entities in a series so as to discover the history of the globe—a history which, incidentally, is of necessity as anthropocentric as that proposed by archaeology: "All of these ages have been separated from each other by cataclysms, of which our deluge was the last. It was like a fairy-tale in several acts, having man for the finale" (BP, 98). To the geologist, the earth in its entirety is a museum.

When Bouvard and Pécuchet, their fancy having been caught by geology, attempt such a reconstruction in imitation of Cuvier, they fail, but their failure is the failure of the epistemology of the *Museum* to offer an adequate continuous representation between Words and Things. That is to say, attempting to understand the history of the globe through geological fragments is as futile as trying to understand human history through archaeology. Disordered fragments lead only to a multitude of contradictory fabulations, something that even the two clerks seem to understand, since to Bouvard's "Geology is too restricted!" Pécuchet replies, "Creation takes place in an up-and-down and haphazard manner. We should do better to start on something else" (BP, 112). Their only blindness is in not seeing that what they will pursue next through archaeology is the same thing they attempted to find in geology, namely, a continual temporal order where there are actually only disconnected fragments.

The figure of the *Museum* is so pervasive that Bouvard and Pécuchet's failure at the various branches of agriculture can also be read as a failure of the *Museum*, or, more exactly, their failure at agriculture should signal to the reader from the start the failure of the *Museum*. Mouchard had already put forth the argument that the two clerks' concern with agriculture, being aesthetic, deals primarily with the question of selecting and ordering, that is to say with precisely the activities upon which the *Museum* is based.[17] I believe the argument can be generalized, and that perhaps the fact is that we still have a theological nostalgia for the *Museum* that has in part prevented us from seeing the obvious. If the Museum of Natural History is singled out, it is because, as I stated earlier, the ideology of the *Museum* was first applied to Nature. The Museum of Natural History was, strictly speaking, the first French museum.[18] Its function was to give an ordered representation, a spectacle of Nature. By displaying plants, metonymically selected and metonymically ordered, it meant to produce a *tableau* of Nature. The botanical failure of Bouvard and Pécuchet points directly to the failure of understanding Nature. In spite of our hopes and wishes, nature will always escape any attempt on our part to comprehend it through the representation we give of it to ourselves, in our cultured, cultivated, tame fields and gardens.

Soon after their failure in the various branches of botany, Bouvard and Pécuchet undertake a study of anatomy. The order of succession seems random only if one does not take the *Museum* into account. Edward Said has already perceptively pointed out how anatomy in the eighteenth century epistemologically belongs to the realm of the laboratory and the museum:

Both linguists and anatomists purport to be speaking about matters not directly obtainable or observable in nature. . . . The text of a linguistic or an anatomical work bears the same general relation to nature (or actuality) that a museum case exhibiting a specimen mammal or organ does. What is given on the page and in the museum case is a truncated exaggeration . . . whose purpose is to exhibit a relationship between the science (or scientist) and the object, not one between the object and nature.[19]

This is also true, in a caricatural way, of the anatomical episode in *Bouvard and Pécuchet*. In the first place, the two clerks do not study the anatomy of a "natural specimen" but of a mannequin, that is to say, a representation: "It was brick-coloured, airless, skinless, striped with numerous blue, red and white filaments. This was not so much a corpse as a kind of toy, horrible-looking, very spick-and-span, and smelling of varnish" (BP, 76–77). The function of each part of the mannequin, instead of having any relation to a presumed nature, is the cause of imaginary fabulations; for example, "the brain inspired them with philosophical reflections" (BP, 78). More important, however, throughout the eighteenth and beginning of the nineteenth centuries anatomy was, along with botany, very much a part of the *Museum*. Anatomy stands in the same relation to animals and humans that botany does to plants. Significantly, the Museum of Natural History had from its very beginnings a chair of anatomy attached to it.[20] By taking up anatomy after the various branches of botany, Bouvard and Pécuchet in fact exhaust what were the domains of knowledge associated with the Museum of Natural History and its major epistemological ideology from approximately the time of Buffon to that of Cuvier.

In summary, then, *Bouvard and Pécuchet* retraces the changes, the evolution and the archaeological metaphor on which the *Museum* is based. Representation of Nature, representation of the globe, representation of history, the *Museum* believed it possible to make visible the implicit order of Nature and of History. It failed. It failed not only at its pretense of displaying the order of Nature and History, but in comprehending them as well. Behind our gardens and our fields hides a Nature to which we cannot have access. As for the past of our globe or of human societies, it is given to us only in the form of senseless fragments without a memory, and any attempt of ours to reconstruct a history is nothing but vain fabulation. We are irrevocably cut off spatially from Nature and temporally from our past. There is no continuity between Nature and us, any more than between our past and us. And in this sense, beyond language, Flaubert is an epistemological nihilist.

## The Furnace

Bouvard and Pécuchet fail systematically: they fail in their dealings with Nature, with the world, with society, and, up to a point, in their private lives. Some of the failures seem to be intrinsic to their pursuits;

if they fail at history, geology, or archaeology, it is because these enterprises are epistemologically doomed from the start. Their botanical failures seem to be of a different kind. If our cultured nature has no epistemological privilege, it nevertheless need not fail as long as our concerns, like those of the count of Faverges or of the peasants who surround Bouvard and Pécuchet, are pragmatic rather than theoretical. However, as we mentioned earlier, their botanical enterprises fail in part because of storms, wind, and rain. Storms, wind, and rain belong to Nature proper, and not to the spectacle of Nature that the cultured botanical museum and garden offer. Storms, in fact, are there to remind us that the two are discontinuous. Once, when Flaubert's own garden at Croisset was badly damaged by a storm, he wrote in a letter to Louise Colet:

Not without some pleasure, I beheld my destroyed espalier trees, all my flowers cut to pieces, and the vegetable garden in total disarray. In beholding all these little artificial arrangements created by man which five minutes of Nature sufficed to overturn, I admired true order reestablishing itself within false order. These things tormented by us—sculptured trees, flowers growing where they have no desire to, vegetables from other lands, got a type of revenge in this atmospheric rebuff. All this has a *farcical side* to it which overcomes us. Is there anything more ridiculous than bell-glass covers for melons? So, these poor bell-glass covers have had quite a time of it! Ah! Ah! To what fantasies of little useful purpose this Nature whom we exploit pitilessly, whom we make ugly with so much impudence, whom we disdain with such fine speeches, abandons herself when the temptation seizes her! This is right. It is widely believed that the sun has no other useful purpose on earth except to make cabbages grow. (407)

An essential form of our contact with Nature is through the forces it brings into play which cannot be understood as such, but which wreak havoc with our ordinary representations of Nature.

If we were to search for other instances of the unaccountable manifestations of such a force in the novel, we should easily find them in the way the two clerks encounter, time and again, fire and heat and all of their literary and historical metaphors without ever realizing exactly what it is they face, nor ever knowing how to come to terms with it.

Their first encounter with fire occurs when the hay spontaneously ignites. As in the case of the storm, they no more have a way of understanding this event's origin than of coping with its results. Their second encounter, this time in the form of an explosion, is far more significant. During their experiment at distillation, the container explodes:

> Suddenly, with the detonation of a shell, the still burst into a score of pieces which leapt to the ceiling, cracking the pots, knocking over the ladles, shivering the glasses; the coals were scattered, the stove demolished. . . .
> The pressure of the steam had broken the apparatus—naturally so, as the cucurbit turned out to be blocked at the mouth. . . .
> When they recovered their speech, they asked themselves what could be the cause of so much ill-luck, especially the last? And they could make nothing of it, except that they had escaped death. Finally, Pécuchet said: "Perhaps it is because we never studied chemistry!" (BP, 72–73)

What is particularly relevant, of course, is Pécuchet's inability to determine the cause of the explosion. Steam is a concern not of chemistry but of thermodynamics. Thermodynamics, on the other hand, is the one science they are not capable of recognizing, because it constitutes the new science which will sweep away the old Newtonian physics as well as all the epistemologies based upon the temporality it predicates. The tools that Bouvard and Pécuchet take with them to the country are in themselves significant. They are tools that belong to the old physics of mechanical devices and not to the new physics of heat and fire.

The point, of course, is not to make Flaubert the proponent of one system as opposed to the other. The case for Flaubert's knowledge of the new physics and what it entailed could easily be stated and is rather uninteresting—the hasty extrapolation of the second law of thermodynamics, according to which the solar system will cool down and our universe will die a frozen death, an idea that the nineteenth-century imagination found striking, is even mentioned in *Bouvard and Pécuchet*. What is at stake is something different. The new physics brought with it a new concept of time and history, differing from and subverting the one postulated by archaeology and the *Museum*. What is significant is the fact that Flaubert subscribes to a view of history which assumes a temporality similar to that predicated by the new physics.

Before we turn to that subject, however, a remark is in order. Heat, as the object of thermodynamics, possesses in the literary imagination of the nineteenth century a number of metaphorical equivalents, in particular, revolutions, gold, and sexuality. It is interesting to note that Bouvard and Pécuchet encounter all three of these metaphors without understanding them. They live through the revolution of 1848 without realizing its historical implications. They disperse, through their financial failures, a fortune in gold without realizing it. Finally, their attempts at integrating sexuality into their lives are resounding failures. Let us return to the problem of history. The Newtonian model of time displays its object as forever identical to itself, based upon an eternal, circular, and recurring movement. Time, the clock as an emblem, moves from point to point, each point considered identical to the others. In this sense, the Newtonian model moves from point of presence to point of presence and does not have, intrinsically, a temporality that describes systems as changing. As Laplace would have it, given Newtonian mechanics:

An intelligence that at a given instance was acquainted with all the forces by which Nature is animated and with the state of the bodies of which it is composed would—if it were vast enough to submit these data to analysis—embrace in the same formula the movements of the largest bodies in the Universe and those of the lightest atoms: nothing would be uncertain for such an intelligence, and the future like the past would be present to its eyes.[21]

It is easy to see how the model of Newtonian physics and the *Museum* depend epistemologically on the same temporal scheme, for the *Museum* also makes of time a spatial continuum in which each point is equivalent to each other point.

The revolution introduced by thermodynamics is a revolution at the very heart of history. The second principle, so striking to the Romantic imagination, states that energy goes from a differentiated to an undifferentiated state. The consequences are enormous; henceforth, systems will move inexorably in a given direction. The process of a history patterned after the new science will be an abolition of differences. Finally, the system has no memory. From the state of the system at a given moment, it is impossible to deduce what conditions were at its origin. In Michel Serres's characterization:

The final equilibrium à la Fourier or Boltzmann implies an ignorance of initial conditions and of duration. Whatever the origin of history may be, its end is unequivocal, determined, everywhere identical and necessary, no matter what the length of the process is. Universal equilibrium, monotonous distribution, maximum entropy. . . . Inevitable, the boltzmanian world is without individualizing memory, it wipes out progressively both memory banks and differences. It has its discrete events, without causal preconditions; it is subject to this single linear law which gives a distribution over an orderless space as the end point of history. And no matter how long the time necessary, one only need wait; and whatever one may do . . . [22]

What thermodynamics makes impossible is a history conceived as archaeology. In the long run, the metaphors of thermodynamics will rob Cuvier's geology, as well as the museums of natural or human artifacts, of any epistemological privilege, reducing them to the status of a bric-a-brac collection of disparate objects, which they always were and had remained for the author of *Bouvard and Pécuchet*, despite the illusions of an archaeological history.

In contrast to Newtonian history, based upon points of presence, thermodynamics will substitute a notion of history based upon the metaphors of decay, decadence, corruption; in a word, a notion of history based upon any metaphor that can be read as abolishing differences.

Bouvard at one point is overtaken by a "frenzy for manure," and furiously begins to produce fertilizer out of manure, excrement, and anything else he can find that is in an advanced state of decomposition.

In the compost-trench were flung together boughs, blood, entrails, feathers— everything that could be found. He employed Belgian dressing, Swiss fertilizer, lye, pickled herrings, seaweed, rags; he sent for guano, and tried to manufacture it; then, pushing his tenets to the extreme, would not let any urine be wasted. He suppressed the privies. Dead animals were brought into the yard with which he treated the soil. Their carcasses were scattered over the country in fragments. Bouvard smiled in the midst of the stench. (BP, 50)

Bouvard, who was unable to recognize the forces which ushered in the new science, is unable to recognize his emblematic fabrication of the metaphor of the very history in which he is caught and which determines his failures. What escapes the characters does not escape the author, who recognizes in the products of Bouvard the very metaphors of the history in which his work is inscribed: "We are not dancing on a volcano, but on the floorboard of a latrine that seems to me quite rotten. Pretty soon society will go drown itself in nineteen centuries of excrement and they'll scream themselves hoarse."[23] It is then precisely at the level of the metaphors of decomposition that we must localize the lucid irony that constitutes the distance between the characters and the author, who can but write from where he stands and compose with what history has handed down to him. A passage quoted in the previous chapter bears repeating here:

But finally is it not also necessary to recognize all the rooms of the heart and the social body, from the cellar to the attic, not even leaving out the latrines; above all not forgetting the latrines! In them is worked out a magical chemistry, fertilizing decompositions are made in them. Who knows to what excremental ooze we owe the perfume of roses and the taste of melons? Has anyone ever counted how many contemptible actions must be contemplated to build the greatness of a soul? How much nauseating pollution one must have swallowed, how much chagrin one must have felt, how many tortures one must have endured, to write one good page? (446)

It is with the rotting by-products of history that one grows tasty melons, not with the botanical taxonomies cherished by Bouvard, who "had grown different species next to one another, the sweet variety got mixed with the bitter, the big Portuguese with the great Mongolian, and the presence of tomatoes completing the anarchy, there resulted abominable hybrids of a pumpkin flavour" (BP, 48).[24] In the same way that it takes excrement to grow proper melons, it takes the rotting by-products of history and the ruins of the Museum to construct a book such as *Bouvard and Pécuchet.*

In conclusion, then, *Bouvard and Pécuchet* stages within itself the conflict of two epistemologies, one characterized by the *Museum,* the other by a *Force* that escapes the domain of representation, and the undoing of one by the other.

*Bouvard and Pécuchet* does not so much argue for one system as opposed to the other; rather it denounces the optimism of the first system in the name of the implicit nihilism of the latter. In part an epistemological nihilism that denounces the possibility of ever attaining an essential knowledge of the world, it manifests itself more explicitly as a historical nihilism. The *Museum* displayed history as an eternally present spectacle with transparent origins and anthropocentric ends. The history ushered in by thermodynamics is a different one. Origins are forever erased, differences disappear, and the end foreseen is an indifferent universe governed by the laws of chance and statistics. More important, in this perspective, nihilism becomes an event at the end of time, and as such, *Bouvard and Pécuchet* is a book at the end of time about the end of time.

This permits us, perhaps, to read the ending of the novel, from which we began, as the final state of indifferent events governed purely by chance: "Everything is equal . . . exaltation of the statistical. There are nothing but facts—and phenomena." In this sense the ending of *Bouvard and Pécuchet* and the creation of *The Copy,*[25] "the orderless space" of the text, rather than being emblematic of a literature yet to come, intends, instead, to be damningly prophetic.

## Notes

1. *Oeuvres complètes de Gustave Flaubert* (Paris: Club de l'Honnête Homme, 1971), 6: 607. Flaubert died before finishing *Bouvard and Pécuchet* but left a number of scenarios for the ending of the novel. I have slightly modified the text and have not taken into account words or expressions erased by Flaubert nor reproduced the diacritical marks the editors have used to indicate words and expressions added by Flaubert at a later date.

2. All quotes followed by a number refer to the Conard edition of Flaubert's *Correspondance* in *Oeuvres complètes de Gustave Flaubert* (Paris: Conard, 1923–33).

3. See in particular his *Nouvelles Etudes sur "La Tentation de Saint Antoine"* (London: Warburg Institute, 1949), in which he writes, for example, "To understand the worker Flaubert . . . it is necessary to lose one's way with him in the labyrinth of libraries" (p. 11).

4. Kenner, *The Stoic Comedians: Flaubert, Joyce and Beckett* (Boston: Beacon, 1962), pp. 12–13.

5. Michel Foucault, "La Bibliothèque fantastique," introduction to Flaubert, *La Tentation de Saint Antoine*, ed. Henri Ronse (Paris: Gallimard, 1967), p. 11.

6. On this question of the relationship of memory to representation, see Derrida's "The Pit and the Pyramid: Introduction to Hegel's Semiology," in *Margins of Philosophy*, trans. Alan Bass (Chicago: University of Chicago Press, 1982). In the example of the Abbé Faria in *Le Comte de Monte-Cristo*, the nineteenth century has provided us also with the literary example of an internalized "constructive memory" which is not only the internalization of the outside world, but the internalization of the outside world through the internalization of a library: "In Rome, I had approximately five thousand volumes in my library. By dint of reading and rereading them, I discovered that with one hundred fifty well-chosen works, one has, if not a complete summary of human knowledge, at least all that is useful for a man to know. I devoted three years of my life to reading and rereading these one hundred fifty volumes, with the result that I knew them almost by heart when I was arrested. In prison, with a slight effort of memory I was able to recall them in their entirety."

7. Claude Mouchard, in a recent article entitled "Terre, technologie, roman: A propos du deuxième chapitre de *Bouvard et Pécuchet*," in *Littérature* 15 (1974): 67, has again, after Seznec, further expanded the problem of the dilemma of the reader: "The reader who really wants to 'comprehend' what

the text of the novel deals with should refer to the manuals mentioned by Flaubert. But this would involve the risk of entering into an unending game of cross-references, which is one of the temptations of technological discourse despite its claims to immediate and effective clarity. . . . And this movement toward a knowledge that must always be clarified further would make reading the novel even more problematic than the immediate obscurity of the quotations."

8. Charles Bernheimer's "Linguistic Realism in Flaubert's *Bouvard et Pécuchet*," in *Novel* 7 (Winter 1974), provides an interesting discussion, in spite of the different conclusions at which he arrives, of the problems of linguistic representation and symbolization in *Bouvard and Pécuchet*.

9. All quotes from *Bouvard and Pécuchet* are from the translation of T. W. Earp and G. W. Stonier (New York: New Directions, 1954), indicated by "BP" and the page number in parentheses.

10. *Oeuvres complètes* (1971) 6: 662.

11. In "Museums of Science" and "Museums of Art," *Encyclopedia Britannica*, 11th ed. (1911), 19: 64–65, 60.

12. *Libraries and Museums* (London: E. Benn, 1930), pp. 69–70.

13. To the best of my knowledge, the first to underscore the epistemological importance of archaeology and of museums is Raymond Schwab in *La Renaissance orientale* (Paris: Payot, 1950). In particular, he writes: "the scriptural document . . . ceases to have sole and absolute reign. The advent of the archaeological method forcefully heightens the authority and efficiency of history. . . . The museum is no longer so much a conservatory of models as a storehouse of information; the masterpiece, formerly a source only of pleasure and a standard of taste, now must share the same room with household artifacts; it is placed side by side with the commercial object on an exhibit table; it is removed from the class of aeroliths in order to become a number in these series. . . . The object is contrasted to the text, the inscription to the chronical, the statue or the vase to the narrative, the king's deeds to his legend" (p. 410).

14. *Oeuvres complètes* (1971) 10: 99.

15. The metonymic displacement of the archaeological objects of the museum which makes them unsuitable for an objective science makes them, on the contrary, very suggestive to the literary imagination. The archaeologist's loss is the novelist's gain; witness *Salammbô*.

In 1851 Flaubert went to England with his mother to visit the "Great Exhibition of the Works of Industry of All Nations." There is no particular rationale to the objects that caught Flaubert's fancy. Seznec notes, for example, that in the Indian section Flaubert "pauses for a long time in front of a harnessed elephant; then examines a chariot, then instruments of music, a cannon on a camel's saddle, a coat of mail, a divan, a vest, some fans, three Indian dancing girl dresses, and some turbans." Even taking into account the "unusual nature of the Exposition," the question remains as to why Flaubert chose to describe one object rather than another. I believe Seznec's answer to be very convincing. The function of the objects chosen by the novelist is to permit him to reconstruct a *fictional image* of a particular culture: "I am inclined to believe that an object is chosen on account of its special power of evocation. This knick-knack, that accessory, is the fragment of a civilization which, by itself, it is capable of suggesting. 'Is not *all of China* contained in a Chinese woman's slipper decorated with damask roses and having embroidered cats on its vamp' (421). In basing itself on objects, the imagination reconstructs that universe whose quintessence they express" (Jean Seznec, *Flaubert à l'Exposition de 1851*, Oxford: Clarendon Press, 1951, pp. 16–17).

16. In Georges Cuvier, *Recherches sur les ossemens fossiles . . .* (Paris: E. d'Ocagne, 1834–36) 1: 93–95.

17. Specifically Mouchard writes: " 'Pécuchet spent . . . delightful hours there unpodding the seeds, writing tickets, arranging his little pots. He used to rest on a box at the door and mediate improvements' [BP, 46]. From Rousseau to Goethe or Jünger, we note the contemplative meticulousness of botany and the charms of manipulating the plant kingdom. The concerns of classifying and conserving plants are very close, in the nineteenth century, to those which regard the library. In this way, these few lines enter into a game of mirrors with many other passages of *Bouvard and Pécuchet,* and even with the entire book in its ever-present tendency to classify" ("Terre, Techonologie," p. 68).

18. For a history of the Museum of Natural History, see Joseph Philippe François Deleuze, *Histoire et description du Muséum royal d'histoire naturelle* (Paris: A. Royer, 1823). Michelet in a curious passage gives a good illustration of how for his generation the first museum with a pedagogical function that comes to mind is the Museum of Natural History: "The young people from the provinces, who arrived trembling with excitement, found the immense creation of the museums and of the libraries ready to welcome them. . . . These museums, these gardens, were our education for us, the children of Paris. When from dreary neighborhoods, from dark streets, we went there to dream before so many beautiful enigmas, what things did we not feel instinctively, from our hearts! Did we understand? Not everything. . . . It was there and nowhere else that history first made a deep impression on me" (quoted by Schwab, *La Renaissance orientale,* pp. 412–13).

19. Edward Said, *Orientalism* (New York: Pantheon, 1978), p. 142.

20. A nineteenth-century description of the gallery of anatomy attached to the Museum of Natural History gives a clear illustration of its similarity to collections of bric-a-brac: "the gallery of comparative anatomy, established by Cuvier, . . . is made up of several rooms; the first of them presents bones and skeletons of gigantic fossils, skeletons of cetaceans and of whales; then come skeletons of all the human races, of heads of birds, of reptiles, of fish, of mammals, etc., etc. Other rooms are devoted to ovology, to phrenology, to

teratology. The anatomy gallery contains approximately twenty-five thousand specimens, six thousand of which are stuffed, five thousand preserved in alcohol, the rest in wax or in plaster." In Pierre Larousse, "Jardin des plantes de Paris," *Grand Dictionnaire universel du XIXᵉ siècle* (Paris, 1865–90) 9: 906–7.

21. Quoted in David Layzer, "The Arrow of Time," in *Scientific American,* December 1975, p. 69. The opposition between a geological history and a thermodynamic history runs throughout the nineteenth century. The opposition is made even more evident by curious attempts, such as Renan's, at synthesizing the two. For Renan there are three histories: the history of the universe before the creation of the earth (Laplace's history), the history of the world before the advent of man (geological history—the history of Cuvier), and finally the history of man (the history of the sun—thermodynamic history): "The history of our planet before the advent of man and of life is in some respects beyond our reach for it hinges on a less delicate order of things. It is the geologist who in this context becomes a historian. With the help of general physics, he narrates the transformations that the earth has undergone since the first day it existed as an independent globe. . . . One can truthfully say that the geologist holds the secrets of history. . . .

"The *System of the World* of Laplace is the history of a preterrestrial era, the history of the world before the formation of the planet Earth, or if one prefers, of the Earth in its unity with the Sun. In fact, we have reached a point in our reasoning where the history of the world is the history of the sun." Letter to Marcellin Berthelot in Ernest Renan, *Oeuvres complètes* (Paris: Calmann-Lévy, 1947) 1: 638–39.

22. *Hermes III: La Traduction* (Paris: Minuit, 1974), p. 62. Serres has most convincingly argued for the importance of understanding thermodynamics in order to understand the nineteenth century. My argument is derived entirely from his analysis. On this same subject, see also his *Jouvences sur Jules Verne* (Paris: Minuit, 1974). For a less analytic but more descriptive treatment of the influence of thermodynamics on the Romantic imagination, see S. Brush, "Thermodynamics and History," in *The Graduate Journal* 7 (1967): 477–566.

23. From a letter to Louis Bouilhet in Flaubert's *Correspondance,* ed. Jean Bruneau (Paris: Gallimard, 1973), 1: 708.

24. For a reading of this passage in terms of linguistic taxonomies, see chapter 1.

25. Flaubert had projected a second volume for *Bouvard and Pécuchet* which was to be made up of a collage of quotations and was to constitute the "Book" composed by Bouvard and Pécuchet.

# 4 Gnostic Fictions: A Reading of the Episode of the Heretics in *The Temptation of Saint Anthony*

> *Egypt is the country of symbols.* Hegel

> *Quoique les mots en soient d'une langue perdue et que la bouche humaine ne puisse les dire, tu les liras tout courant comme les lettres de ton nom.* Flaubert

> *Supposing that Truth is a woman—what then?* Nietzsche

> *So that all deified Nature absolutely paints like a harlot whose allurements cover nothing but the charnel-house within.* Melville

The section concerning the heresies constitutes one of the major episodes of *The Temptation of Saint Anthony*. Yet, except for Seznec's magisterial essay which shows how Flaubert composed it through an extraordinary use of his sources, little has been said about it.[1] Critically we are left, for example, with the vague statements of a Thibaudet or a Foucault that damn or praise the *Temptation* in very general terms for its "textual" quality. Flaubert does not "invent" his text, but reinscribes what is already, to use Foucault's expression, in the general domain of the "déjà dit" of the *Encyclopedia-Library*. Nevertheless, as with *Bouvard and Pécuchet,* granting that the text constitutes itself by a mechanism of genetic repetition does not help us much with its elucidation.

Regarding the specific episode where Flaubert stages the assault upon Anthony by various heresies and heretics, the critic is forced to take his point of departure from Seznec's analysis and ask why Flaubert chose to privilege the Gnostics. Of all the heresies available to Flaubert, any number were colorful enough in their rites or metaphysically complex enough to lend themselves readily to an imaginative fictional treatment. Nevertheless, as Seznec put it: "The majority of the heresies with which the *Temptation* abounds are Gnostic heresies. In fact, if Renan is to be believed, certain critics claimed that Flaubert 'wanted to write a history of Gnosticism.' "[2] Why the Gnostics then?

We might, perhaps, begin to answer this question by noting that for Flaubert the Gnostics were part of a privileged history and a privileged geography. Gnostic heresies are primarily *oriental* heresies. If one were to set up an oversimplified opposition between Rome and the Orient, the Gnostic heresies are typically oriental and characteristically belong to a land which, from a fictional standpoint, is strategically privileged for the nineteenth-century writer. In the same way that the war between Carthage and the mercenaries is an oriental war peripheral to the dominant antiquity of Rome, the Gnostic heresies belong to a specific context: they are Alexandrian heresies.

Flaubert himself described his project as one of "sketching out a dramatic exposition of the fourth-century Alexandrine world."[3] Fourth-century Alexandria is the emblem of a belated syncretism of old, displaced, subverted beliefs. As Jacques Matter, one of Flaubert's principal sources on Gnosticism, put it:

Alexandria became the theater of every teaching, of every revolution, and of all the combinations to which they gave rise. In its beginnings, Platonism predominated; soon afterward, Pythagorianism and Aristotelianism were introduced. But none of these systems retained its primitive purity, and none managed to conserve whatever purity remained to it. The ancient doctrines of Egypt and Greece, the mysterious teachings of Thrace and Samothrace, of Elysis and of Sais all penetrated the three principal Greek systems. Doctrines which up to that time had had neither contact nor affinity with these systems came to combine with their principles, or at least draw from them. In the person of Aristobulus, Judaism took hold of Aristotle; in that of Philon, Judaism adopted Platonism; the Essenes and the Therapeutes brought together all that was most sublime in the teachings of Pythagoras and Plato, and the priests of Egypt and Persia. The kabbalists went even further, incorporating into their teachings nearly the entirety of Zoroastrianism.[4]

In the same way that the mercenaries of *Salammbô* emblematize through a mixture of races another belated agonizing civilization, fourth-century Alexandria represents, at the level of ideologies, a crepuscular moment in the history of ideas in antiquity.[5] At the religious level, Gnosticism likewise represents a belated, decayed, and heterogeneous form of what were once original, singular religious beliefs. As Matter would have it:

Ever since the general upheaval which was the result of Alexander's wars in the three parts of the world, the doctrines of Greece, Egypt, Persia, and India encountered one another and became intermingled everywhere. All of the barriers which had hitherto separated nations from one another disintegrated and the peoples of the Occident, who had always traced their beliefs to those of the Orient, hastened to do so again . . . their [the Greeks'] Platonists . . . hurriedly embraced the strongest beliefs that Palestine, Egypt, Chaldea, Persia, and India had to offer.[6]

Gnostic ideologies plainly, therefore, belong to a particularly *late* moment in the history of ideas and are of a *secondary* and *composite* nature. For Flaubert, who viewed the nineteenth-century writer as being at the end of another history and obliged to compose with its textual by-products, the historical and ideological context of Gnosticism, rather than being spatially and temporally removed in a distant and bygone past, was remarkably similar to his own. The exoticism of Gnostic beliefs comes not from their absolute difference but is based instead on an apparent difference hiding a more fundamental identity.[7]

We might also point out that the problem of heresy in general, and of Gnosticism in particular, is above all one of identity and undifferentiation. Gnostic ideologies were too similar to and undifferentiated from the religions from which they drew their various elements. Of the Gnostic divinities it was impossible for Christians to say categorically that they were false gods, as they might have of the Greek and Roman pantheon. The Christian dilemma was, in fact, that of trying to reestablish differences in a situation where differences tended to disappear.

It must be emphasized, however, that these syncretic, constructed ideologies that the Gnostics produced out of past fragments did in fact generate something distinctly original. Again, in Matter's words:

"So then," it will be said, "gnosticism was only a *copy*, a kind of mosaic made up of the most remarkable portions of each of these systems?" Just as it is to badly misjudge the human spirit to compare its works with those of a crude mechanism, to consider *gnosis* from this point of view is to misunderstand it, as has been done for too long now. Gnosticism is perhaps the most original of the systems produced by the ancient world; at the very least it is the richest of them.[8]

If Gnosticism is a syncretic, secondary construct from the ideological remains of an earlier history, then the constitution of Gnostic ideologies is isomorphic to the text in which Flaubert refers to them. Both Gnostic ideology and Flaubert's text are produced from repeated, "copied" fragments handed over by past history; both are "mosaics" which stand as original syntheses.

Gnostic ideologies are primarily "textual" ideologies based on sacred writings, a multiplicity of gospels, secret books, occult names. The third version of the *Temptation* lists some of them: "*the Gospel of the Hebrews, the Gospel of the Lord, the Gospel of Eve, the Gospel of Thomas, the Gospel of Judas, the treatise of the arisen soul, the prophecy of Barcouf*" (OC, 540). This proliferation of texts is underscored by all Flaubert's sources, including one from the earliest Epiphanius: "They possess many books. For they publish certain 'Questions of Mary,' and others issue a number of books on the aforesaid Ialdabaoth or in the name of Seth. There are others which they call Revelations of Adam and they have dared to compose others in the name of the disciples."[9]

The original, unique, sacred writing is multiplied into a plurality of contradictory texts. In Flaubert this multiplication and degradation of texts is itself emblematized in the way they are presented: "Then they all held aloft rolls of papyrus, wooden tablets, pieces of leather, and swatches of fabric" (OC, 540). The Gnostic *Library*, in short, relates to a unique, original text in the same way that *Bouvard and Pécuchet's Encyclopedia* is reinscribed in the multiplicity of texts the two scribes use at the end of that novel to compose *La Copie*.

One particularity of Gnostic texts is their pretension to a direct, unmediated, nongraphic origin. Regarding their origin and authority they postulate what, for lack of a better expression, we might call a "transcendental pastoralism." They systematically assume the possibility of a direct, unmediated access to what Flaubert, in another context, calls the Idea. A good example of this "visionary textuality" can be seen in the first version of the *Temptation* where, after Epiphanius, Flaubert refers to the book of Noria:

We have the prophecy of Bahuba, who cried on the mountains with the Gospel of Philip that neither fire nor water can destroy. Do you wish to know the life of Christ before his apparition on Earth, his exact stature, the name of the star on which he has his throne? Here is the book of Noria, wife of Noah. She wrote it aboard the ark for nights on end while seated on the back of an elephant, illuminated by the flashes of lightning. Adrift among the huge waves churning the yellow slime of the primordial creation, looking through the fissures which the thunder had torn in the sky, she saw God, the luminous spirits turning on their spheres, and the traveling angels moving through space on wings of flame. (OC, 393)

The irony, of course, is that all these texts fail to give access to a transcendental signification. The problem is succinctly summarized by the expression, "The word *Abraxas* signifies . . ." (OC, 394). The word *Abraxas* will never signify, but will remain a pure signifier, an irreducible linguistic entity without signification, translation, or referent. *Abraxas* is to language what the stones of Carnac are to Celtic archaeology. The third version of the *Temptation* expands the list of occult names and finally reduces them to a pure graphic mark on stone:

The Supreme Being with all the infinite emanations is called Abraxas; and the Savior with all his virtues, Kaulakau—otherwise line-upon-line, rectitude-upon-rectitude. One obtains the strength of Kaulakau with the help of certain words, inscribed on this chalcedony to facilitate memory. *And he points to a little stone engraved with bizarre lines hanging from his neck.* (OC, 537)

In the same way that the stones of Carnac permit the wildest archaeological speculations, the "texts" of the Gnostics allow for the most uncontrolled allegorical translations. There is no continuity between stone and word but, once a relation is assumed, one has only to coin a metaphor and mistake the metaphor for a name. Then, through an open system of metaphoric and metonymic displacements, one can, from the first trope, elaborate the most complex linguistic constructs which, while continuing to function as pure signifiers without "real" signification, accumulate a "false" referentiality.

Epiphanius, again, gives example after example of such "improper" translations, which are at the heart of Gnostic ideological constructs. To quote just two: "These men who are in alliance with Nicolas . . . produce for us certain names without meaning and forge books one of which they call Noria. . . ." The example he gives of improper allegorical translation is even more striking:

And the text, "When ye see the Son of Man going up where he was before" (John 6:62) means the emission which is taken up to the place from which it came, and the saying "Unless ye eat my flesh and drink my blood" (John 6:53), unless the disciples were perplexed and said, "Who can hear this?" (John 6:60)—they quote this as if the saying referred to indecency, this being the reason why they were overcome and "went backward" (John 6:66); for he says, they were not yet established in the Pleroma. And when David says, "He shall be as a tree that is planted by the springs of the waters, which shall give forth its fruit in due season" (Ps. 1:3), he refers, he says, to the male member.[10]

The most extravagant example of language caught in a vertiginous delirium of metonymic displacements can be seen in a passage from one of the sacred books of the Gnostics which Flaubert consulted called *Pistis Sophia.* In it we find the following paragraph:

> This is the name of the *immortal one:* ααα ωωω; and this is the name of the voice for the sake of which the *perfect man* is moved: ιιι. But these are the *interpretations* of the names of these *mysteries:* the first name which is ααα, its *interpretation* is φφφ; the second, which is μμμ, its *interpretation* is ωωω; the third, which is ψψψ, its *interpretation* is ooo, the fourth which is φφφ, its *interpretation* is ννν, the fifth which is δδδ, its *interpretation* is ααα. That which is on the throne is ααα; this is the *interpretation* of the second: αααα αααα αααα; this is the *interpretation* of the whole name.[11]

We reach here a level of allegorical delirium in comparison to which the mad elucubrations of Bouvard and Pécuchet concerning their Museum, Archaeology, and History are models of lucidity and sanity. In his description of Gnostic heresies, Flaubert has given us the equivalent of a *linguistic museum.* In this particular museum, made of linguistic quotes and linguistic interpretations, what we have is the ultimate recourse to a mute stone, wall, or object which, if it never reveals its essence or meaning, nevertheless acts as a transcendental signifier ensuring the illusion that one might block the mad merry-go-round of a language with its own intrinsic tropological devices.

Not the least interesting aspect of Gnostic texts is the way the problematic of textual allegorization is related to a complex sexual metaphorics. Indeed, the maze constituted by the conjunction of textuality and sexuality constitutes one of the most difficult thematic networks in the entire Flaubertian canon. Our reading of it will force us to situate it within a broader context than the single episode of the Gnostics and to treat that episode as an emblem for a more general problem in Flaubert's text.

The importance of women in Gnosticism has been underscored by Seznec, who quotes Matter on the subject: "The role of women in the history of Gnosticism is as considerable as in the history of Christianity itself. Women occupy an important place among the ranks of the dissidents."[12] Interestingly it is in the episode of the Gnostics that, with the exception of the Queen of Sheba, we encounter most of the major female figures in the *Temptation*.

The relation between textual and theological questions on the one hand, and sexual thematics on the other, is important as regards Flaubert's choice of sources, his use of them, and finally, his influence on other historians of Gnosticism such as Renan.

Matter is particularly discreet on the subject. His discussion of sexual matters, couched in the most decorous prose, hints at sexual matters, dismisses them, and then tries to discredit Epiphanius as the most explicit and graphic source on this subject.[13] The texts in question, relatively unknown, are worth quoting in some detail to illustrate the problems Flaubert faced in translating into his own work the textual/sexual nexus of Gnostic ideologies.

Speaking of the Barbelognostics, for example, Matter writes:

The *Borbonians* or the *Borborians,* who were also given the name of *Barbelonites,* were doubly unfortunate in their relations with other sects: first, they fell into bizarre errors, and second, they were accused of deviations which were even more serious than those they really professed. Theodoret couldn't imagine that a man could be sufficiently wretched to want to describe what went on in their secret ceremonies: the most depraved conceptions cannot do justice to the extent of their deviance. Such exaggeration is but one token of the injustice and hatred which have prevented even the written name of this sect from reaching us.[14]

Turning his attention to the Philibonites, he adds:

This society was founded not by the Greeks of Alexandria, who were equally well versed in the mysteries of Platonism, Kabbalah, Zenda-Vesta, and the New Testament and more at home in the world of ideas than in the sensuous one. Rather, it was established by a few obscure Egyptians or sensual Cyrenacians who had been reduced to recruiting among the lowest ranks of the populace. Here what is revealed is no longer the human soul in its sublime ecstasies. Rather, what dares to rear its head is man's second nature: his most trivial inclinations.[15]

Finally, in a footnote he adds: "It is not possible that Saint Epiphanius was not the victim of the credulity of his century in providing us with the details he does."[16] Epiphanius, of course, lacks the delicacy, the verbal reticence, and the apologetic intentions of matter. In his *Panarion* he writes:

First they have their women in common. . . . After this recognition of each other they proceed at once to a feast and they serve up lavish helpings of meat and wine, even if they are poor. Then, when they have had their drinking-party and so to speak filled their veins to satiety, they give themselves over to passion. For the husband withdraws from his wife, and says these words to his own wife: "Rise up, make the love (feast) with the brother." When they have had intercourse out of the passion of fornication, then, holding up their own blasphemy before heaven, the woman and the man take the man's emission in their own hands, and stand there looking up towards heaven. . . . And so they eat it, partaking of their own shame and saying, "This is the body of Christ." Similarly with the woman's emission at her period; they collect the menstrual blood which is unclean, take it and eat it, together, and say "This is the blood of Christ." For this reason when they read in the apocryphal writings: "I saw a tree which bears twelve fruits each year, and he said to me, 'This is the tree of life,' " they allegorize this to refer to the woman's monthly emission. And while they have intercourse with each other they forbid the bearing of children. For this shameful conduct is pursued by them not for the bearing of children but for the sake of pleasure. . . . But if one of them mistakenly implants the natural emission and the woman becomes pregnant, attend to the further outrage that these men perform. They extract the embryo when they can lay hands on it and take this aborted infant and smash it with a pestle in a mortar, and when they have mixed in honey and pepper and other condiments and spices to prevent them from vomiting, then they all assemble, every member of this troop of swine and dogs, and each one with his fingers takes a piece of the mangled child. And so when they have finished their feast of human flesh, they pray to God and say, "We have not been deceived by the Archon of lust, but we have retrieved our brother's transgression." And this they consider the perfect Passover.[17]

Flaubert will, of course, turn for his sources more toward the colorful Epiphanius than the discreet Matter and, among the Church fathers, more toward Epiphanius than the more restrained Irenaeus or Clement of Alexandria.

Flaubert gives us a literary, dramatic version of his patristic sources regarding the libertine practices of some of the Gnostic sects. The question as to whether in doing so he gives a reasonably accurate account of Gnosticism is a false question. Flaubert's argument, in his answer to Sainte-Beuve's objections to *Salammbô* regarding the impossibility of a "real" rendering of Carthage, could be equally well applied to the Alexandria of the fourth century and its heterogeneous collection of ideologies. The argument that Flaubert chose his sources because of their dramatic and gory details does not explain much either. Flaubert's rendition of his sources in the first version of the *Temptation* is, in comparison with the original texts, very sober. This is even more accentuated in the third version, where Flaubert alludes to the libertine practices of some Gnostic sects in a far more indirect, allusive, and euphemistic fashion. Finally, the argument that Flaubert's toning down of his sources was dictated by fear of censorship is not very convincing either. This might have been true of the earlier versions, had he published them, but by the time he wrote the third version not only had Flaubert less to fear from censorship, but there is little doubt that he wrote the last version thinking that he would never publish it.

Before attempting to understand the function of Flaubert's transcription of Gnostic sexual practices, let us look at another example of a nineteenth-century reaction to them, namely Renan's. Flaubert had of course read, between the first and third versions of the *Temptation*, part of Renan's *Histoire des origines du Christianisme*—specifically the *Vie de Jésus* (1863), *Les Apôtres* (1866), and *Saint-Paul* (1869). What Flaubert had not consulted was *Marc-Aurèle et le fils du monde antique* (1882), which deals with the same historical period as the *Temptation*. The long developments on the Montanists in the first version are condensed in the third to let Montanus himself express the highlights of his dualistic theology and his rituals of mortification. Priscilla and Maximilla, on the other hand, narrate in both versions how they first met Montanus and how they left their husbands, children, and households to follow him. Priscilla, being also a prophetess, announces the forthcoming end of time: "I am the last of the prophetesses; and after me, the end of the world will come" (OC, 538). Renan, on the other hand, reduces Montanus to a vile seducer and tries to discredit him on sexual grounds:

The Church of Markos was more than a den of iniquity. It was also a school for debauchery and secret infamies. . . . Such a man was particularly dangerous in Lyons. The mystical and passionate character of the women of that city, their slightly material pity, their taste for the bizarre and for tangible emotion, exposed them to all manner of degradations. . . . The Christians who were thus abased did not take long to become disenchanted. Their consciences tormented them and a pall was cast over their lives.[18]

Renan, of course, does try to give an account of Montanus's theology and its importance. Nevertheless, the passage quoted above is revealing because it shows that Renan reacted to the sexual aspects of Gnosticism in the same way as did Matter. Both dismiss them: one in the name of a presumed human propensity to debauchery and licentiousness; the other in the name of the inherent weakness that the women of Lyons are supposed to have had regarding matters of the flesh![19] We can thus better understand Flaubert's affinity for Epiphanius. Both refuse to separate Gnostic beliefs from Gnostic practices, theology from ritual, textuality from sexuality. The passage from Epiphanius on the sexual practices of the Gnostics is thus of a piece with the earlier quoted passage on the Gnostics' multiplicity of apocryphal books and their propensity to allegorize.

This inseparability of a textual and sexual problematic is even more accentuated in Flaubert's text. The section of the *Temptation* on the Gnostics is so homogeneous as to make any separation of the two a critical artifact. In fact, given the metaphorical equivalence of textuality and sexuality, any attempt to read the text through an allegorical movement describing its genetic constitution will of necessity encounter a nexus of sexual and textual metaphors. When Valentinus at one point exclaims that "the world is the work of a delirious God," this statement is less a mere point of Valentinian theology than a perfect reading of the whole passage to which it belongs. The episode of the Gnostics is first and foremost a textual construct displaying the unredeemable nature of any textual/sexual performance.

Let us briefly review the sexual practices of the Gnostic sects as they appear in the more explicit 1849 version of the *Temptation*. The Gnostics masturbated and consumed their sperm: "We who sift God out from nature, who both purify and extract him from it, let us stave off the captivity in which he languishes, let us destroy at its source the cause which enslaves him, let us absorb it: let us thus swallow the sperm of men!" (OC, 393). They tried not to consummate intercourse: "Beware of the terrible moment when the harmony of evil, combining parallel projections, tends to melt them together in a fertile stagnation; extract yourselves from the arms which embrace you" (OC, 393). They practiced sodomy: "Glory unto Cain" (OC, 396). They preached an indiscriminate form of sexuality: "The eyes are made to behold light, the teeth to grind up meat, the skin of the hands to handle fabrics, and the sex organ for enjoying oneself over a woman" (OC, 396). Finally, after Epiphanius, Flaubert has his Gnostic destroying embryos: "Let us kill the man who perpetuates the curse, slaughter the woman who reproduces it, and crush the child who suckles at the breast" (OC, 401).

The preceding passages form a coherent unit. On the one hand, the Gnostics seem to overvalue sexuality; on the other, they systematically refuse paternity and generation. But then Flaubert will use a parallel set of sexual metaphors to describe the act of literary writing. For Flaubert, treating a new literary subject is not unlike approaching a woman for the first time: "A subject to write about is for me like a woman one is in love with: when she is about to give in, one trembles and is afraid. It's a voluptuous terror. One dares not attain one's desire."[20] To write is a sexual activity:

Oh to go back to my youth, when I would lay out [*où je foutais*] a five-act play in 3 days. With our scruples we resemble nothing so much as those poor believers who never manage to live, for fear of hell, and who wake their confessor early in the morning to unburden their consciences of having had a miscarriage in a dream. Let's worry less about results. The thing is to keep fucking, keep fucking [*foutons, foutons*]: who cares about the child the muse will give birth to? (B, 1: 677)

This sexual relationship is, however, never consumed. The muse will always remain a virgin: "The Muse is a virgin with a bronze-hard chastity" (B, 1: 471); "O Muse, how tough your virginity is to crack!" (B, 1: 511). The unsuccessful modern writer, incapable of consuming his affair with the muse, will find his writing reduced to an unproductive solitary activity: "perhaps by masturbating my meager spirit I will manage to squeeze a spark out of it";[21] "let's masturbate the old art right down to its deepest joints" (C, 4: 284).

"At every line, every word, language fails me, and the insufficiency of vocabulary is such that I am very often forced to change details. It will kill me, my friend, it will kill me. No matter: it begins to be tremendous fun. I've finally achieved the erection, Monsieur, by dint of self-flagellation and masturbation." (C, 4: 287)

The writer's activity is solitary and futile inasmuch as it is incapable of engendering, authoring, fathering a literary work. For Flaubert this situation is not his alone but the lot of the modern writer:

Ah, blessed peaceful times, blessed times of powdered wigs! You lived with complete assurance, poised on your high heels, twirling your cane! But beneath *us* the earth is trembling. Where can we place our fulcrum, even assuming that we possess the lever? The thing we all lack is not style, nor the dexterity of finger and bow known as talent. We have a large orchestra, a rich palette, a variety of resources. We know many more tricks and dodges, probably, than were ever known before. No, what we lack is the intrinsic principle, the soul of the thing, the very idea of the subject. We take notes, we make journeys: emptiness! emptiness! We become scholars, archaeologists, historians, doctors, cobblers, people of taste. What is the good of all that? Where is the heart, the verve, the sap? Where to start out from? Where to go? We're good at sucking, we play a lot of tongue games, we pet for hours: but—the real thing! To ejaculate, beget the child! (B, 1: 627–28).

The failure to generate a *work* is a modern incapacity. To father a work with all the authorial authority it implies is a modern dilemma, that is to say, *the* historical dilemma of the nineteenth-century writer writing at what he takes to be the end of history. And it is perhaps in this impotence, this inability to generate at the end of history, that Flaubert's affinity for the Gnostics, with all their presumedly bizarre sexual practices, lies.

The *Temptation* contains a long passage devoted to the Queen of Sheba. A distant mythical figure, she is at the same time desire's ultimate *object*—"all the shapes half seen or imagined by your desire, ask for them every one! I am not a woman, but a world"—and she possesses the totality of *fiction:* "Simorg-anka . . . circles the world in his flight. At eve he returns; he perches at the foot of my bed and tells me all he has seen—the seas which passed far beneath him with all their fishes and ships, the great void deserts he has contemplated from the heights of the sky, the harvests bowing in the valleys, and the plants that were growing on the walls of cities abandoned" (OC, 532). We are perhaps in a better position now to understand why the Queen of Sheba must remain inaccessible to Anthony. Anthony, a character in a belated history, cannot have access to her as the emblem of a supreme sexuality any more than the modern writer can have access to the supreme fiction she represents.

In the episode concerning the Gnostics, Flaubert introduces another character, Helen-Ennoia, who in many ways parallels the Queen of Sheba. She represents a synthetic and supreme sexuality:

She was the Helen whose memory Stesichore cursed and who became blind to punish him for his blasphemy; she was Lucretia who was raped by the kings and who killed herself out of pride; she was the infamous Delilah who cut the hair of Sampson; she was that daughter of the Jews who strayed from camp, surrendered herself to goats, and was stoned to death by the twelve tribes; she was a lover of corruption, fornication, lying, idolatry, and stupidity.[22]

Where the Queen of Sheba stood for a supreme fiction containing all fictions, Helen-Ennoia is a primal *Idea* containing all possible ideas: "She is the one called Charis, Sigé, Ennoia, Barbelo; she was the thought of the Father, the We which created the universe and the worlds" (OC, 395).

In spite of their similarities, the Queen of Sheba and Helen-Ennoia differ in important ways. The Queen of Sheba has a center, a kingdom, an original homeland where she invites the hermit to join her; Helen-Ennoia has lost her original birthplace: "I have a memory of a faraway country, a forgotten country; a huge, fanned-out peacock's tail defines its horizon and, through the feathers, one can see a sky as green as emerald" (OC, 394). The Queen of Sheba is a mythical, atemporal, synthetic character. She is all that she is at the same time and outside of time. Helen-Ennoia is a sequential character; she has been all her incarnations one after another. Her being is, so to speak, serial. She is a historical character or, more exactly, she is the product of a certain history: a history with an order, an order of decadence. Expelled from her celestial abode, she has undergone incarnations that are the history of a constant degradation. Beginning as Helen, she has gone through a process of constant and inevitable decadence: "she has demeaned herself with all manner of corruptions, debased herself through all sorts of wretchedness, and has prostituted herself for all nations; she has sung at every crossing and has kissed every face" (OC, 395).

If, for Flaubert, textuality and sexuality are inseparable, it is Helen-Ennoia and not the Queen of Sheba who emblematically represents the writer's plight.[23] She also nostalgically yearns after a lost homeland, the sun, height, purity, and unmediated transparency; yet she is also, like the modern writer, obliged to live among the degraded products of an irrevocably decadent history.

It has been argued that the common characteristic of Gnostic ideologies is a view of history which considers man as the result of an original fall precipitated by an evil deity, and which entailed the degradation of his spirit into a history and temporality governed by matter and from which he must escape.[24] Such a view is similar to Flaubert's perspective on the tyranny of history in the act of writing. And Helen-Ennoia is the perfect incarnation of such a history.

Helen-Ennoia's final degradation brings her to prostitution. Flaubert's interest in prostitution is often mentioned but rarely analyzed. In his correspondence we have two important references to prostitutes and prostitution. The more extensive appears in a letter to Louise Colet; in spite of its length, the passage deserves to be quoted in its entirety:

I like prostitution—and for its own sake, independently of what lies underneath. My heart has never failed to pound at the sight of one of those provocatively dressed women walking in the rain under the gas lamps, just as the sight of monks in their robes and knotted girdles touches some ascetic, hidden corner of my soul. Prostitution is a meeting point of so many elements—lechery, frustration, total lack of any human relation, physical frenzy, the clink of gold—that a glance into its depths makes one giddy and teaches one all manner of things. It fills you with such sadness! And makes you dream so of love! Ah, elegy makers, it is not on ruins that you should lean, but on the breasts of these light women.

Yes, that man has missed something who has never awakened in an anonymous bed beside a face he will never see again, and who has never left a brothel at sunrise feeling like throwing himself into the river out of pure disgust for life. And just their shameless way of dressing—the temptation of the chimera—the aura of the unknown, of the *maudit*—the old poetry of corruption and venality! During my first years in Paris, I used to sit in front of Tortoni's on hot summer evenings and watch the streetwalkers stroll by in the last rays of the sun. At such moments I used to gorge myself with biblical poetry. I thought of Isaiah, of "fornication in high places," and I walked back along the rue de la Harpe saying to myself: "And her throat is smoother than oil." I swear I was never more chaste. My only complaint about prostitution is that it is a myth. The kept woman has invaded the field of debauchery, just as the journalist has invaded poetry; everything is becoming mongrelized. The courtesan does not exist any more than the saint does; there are only "soupeuses" and "lorettes"—even more sordid than grisettes. (C, 3: 216–17)

Prostitution as a phenomenon of the end of history at the end of history has a temporality similar to that of the literary text. Prostitution has its own poetry, the poetry of decadence. Yet the poetry of prostitution is to be contemplated in its own abyssal structure rather than possessed. As such the poetry of prostitution does not have a present, at least not a textual present; it either brings back the memory of a poetry of the past or it permits the imagination to project dreams, pure representations which do not coincide with the reality of the present. Prostitution, like Helen-Ennoia, is a textual myth. Even as a phenomenon of decadence, it does not coincide with the decadent historical moment of the author's present; as such, the myth of prostitution is the myth of decadence. Prostitution is the essence of decadence in its inaccessibility to decadence except as floating image, wishful projection, or ungrounded text. Thus its privileged moment is always a liminal, crepuscular one.[25]

In "Novembre," the story of an encounter between a young virgin and a prostitute, the crepuscular quality of prostitution is so pronounced that we can hardly doubt its significance. The narrator, looking back on his memories, writes: "I lived in a perpetual twilight."[26] Both he and the prostitute yearn for a bright sun: "I used to love the sun; on sunny days my soul would partake of the serenity of the radiant horizon and the loftiness of the sky"; "our lives would be beautiful if only it were so, if we went to live in a country where the sun makes the flowers grow" (OC, 258, 270). Nevertheless, the bright sun will remain an object of temporal and spatial nostalgia. The lighting of the narrative is different; the tale is told at a time when "everything seemed like it was becoming more pale and frozen; on the horizon, the sun's form was beginning to become indistinguishable from the white color of the sky which it permeated with some of its waning life" (OC, 248). Modernity is bathed in a pale, shadowy light: "Oh the pale winter sun! It is as sad as a happy memory. We are surrounded by shadow. Watch our hearth burn, the exposed coals are covered with a great network of black lines which seem to beat like the animated veins of another life; let us wait for night to come" (OC, 253).

Seznec sees in Marie, the prostitute of "Novembre," a prefiguration of Helen-Ennoia. She is, in fact, more than just a prefiguration; she is a parallel character. Marie, like Helen-Ennoia, has gone through all the steps of degradation. Once a queen—" 'Be a queen,' I said to myself, 'and make the crowd fall in love with you.' Well, I've been a queen, in the only way that one can nowadays" (OC, 267)—she has gone through all forms of sexuality, from the most exalted to the most vile. Willingly, for her whole history is determined by a quest, which she knows to be impossible, for "the man who has always escaped me, whom I have pursued in the beds of sophisticates, in the balconies of theaters; a dream which is only in my heart and that I want to hold in my hands; one fine day, I hope, someone will doubtless come, . . . someone greater and more noble" (OC, 267). Her quest is hopeless because the gods and divine men all belong to an irrevocable past: "So there is no longer any of the heavenly youth of ancient times!

No Bacchuses or Apollos, and no more of those heroes who would promenade naked, crowned with laurel wreaths!" (OC, 267). Her quest, then, is a search through a hopeless future for an event doomed to an irrevocable past by a decadent present—a temporality which we can now recognize as typical to Flaubert's quest for an absolute fiction: "The future torments us and the past holds us back. No wonder the present is slipping from our grasp" (B, 1: 730).

That such a temporality is inherent to prostitution, that the temporal dialectic of recovering a past memory only through a never-present future implies a form of chastity or impotence is, amusingly, illustrated by an episode from Flaubert's trip to Egypt. Solicited by some prostitutes, he refused to give in for fear of spoiling the scene: "We return to the street where the dancers are; I intentionally start strolling; the women call out to me: '*Cawadja, cawadja, batchis! batchis, cawadja!*' I give piastres to each of them; several try to lead me off, holding me around the waist. I forbid myself to screw them, so that I may preserve the melancholy flavor of the memory, and I leave."[27]

That the temporal modes determining Flaubert's fictional enterprise should eventually lead to a problematic of memory was perhaps predictable. The whole of "Novembre" is predicated upon the act of writing as a failed means to recapture a lost memory. The main part of the story is told by a dead narrator who writes in the hope of recapturing a lost memory, a representation which has lost its original referent, a representation without any possible form of presence. The narrator, having lost Marie, searches for her everywhere without success, commenting: "What all men seek is perhaps only the memory of a love conceived in heaven or in the very first days of life; we are in pursuit of anything connected to it" (OC, 270). Marie, then, is the image of that lost origin but, as such, she is only a representation. Marie *is* no more than Helen-Ennoia *is*. Their reality is a pure textual representation in the impossible present of the text: "I wrote what precedes as a way of remembering her, hoping that the words would bring her back to life for me. I failed" (OC, 271).

The failure of the narrator is the failure of the text. All the text can represent is a forgotten memory—that is, something which by definition is not, but which is the transcription of a lost memory whose only reality is textual. The knowledge beyond the illusory representations of this text, which we might have gained had the manuscript continued, is also illusory. The text can only reveal its own nature as a complex machine of tropes and figures. The second editor/narrator ironically writes that "the manuscript stops here, but I knew its author. If someone has come to this point after having passed through all of the metaphors, hyperboles, and other figures with which the preceding pages are filled, and wants to know their end, let him continue reading. We are about to provide him with it" (OC, 272). The reader who continues through the second narrator's text discovers only that the first narrator led a futile life and died. The logic of the text is rigorous: at the end of writing as an interminable and futile enterprise to recapture a lost memory, there is only death. The story again allegorizes Flaubert's entire literary enterprise— "the page must be filled"—until death punctuates his discourse by placing the final period that he himself could not place.

And perhaps it is in writing considered as a doomed act, a hopeless quest to recapture the memory of a lost *Sun*, a lost *homeland*, a lost *origin*, that one finds the closest affinity between Flaubert's literary enterprise and the Gnostics' search for salvation.

## Notes

1. Jean Seznec, *Nouvelles Etudes sur "La Tentation de Saint Antoine"* (London: Warburg Institute, 1949). In particular, see chapter 2, "Les Hérésies."

2. Ibid., p. 19.

3. In a letter to Mlle Leroyer de Chantepie dated July 8, 1870; quoted by Seznec in *Nouvelles Etudes*, p. 34.

4. Jacques Matter, *Histoire critique du Gnosticisme* (Paris, 1838), pp. 120–21.

5. Curiously, even though the Gnostic heretics are oriental, when they first appear in the *Temptation*, Flaubert describes them as of mixed races, not unlike the army of mercenaries in *Salammbô:* "There are men from the land of the Germans, from Thrace and from Gaul, from Scythia and from the Indies— snow on their beards, feathers in their hair, thorns in the fringes of their garments, sandals black with dust, skins burnt by the sun." In Gustave Flaubert, *Oeuvres complètes* (Paris: Editions du Seuil, 1964), p. 535. All references to the first or third version of *The Temptation of Saint Anthony* will be to this edition, and will be indicated in the text by the letters "OC" followed by the page number.

6. Matter, *Histoire critique*, pp. 10–11.

7. Closer to Flaubert, Renan offers us another example of an ideological

rapprochement between fourth-century Alexandria and nineteenth-century France, the latter viewed as the locus of conflicting mystical ideologies. In his description of the Gnostics, he writes:

The tremendous confusion of ideas which reigned in the Orient brought with it the strangest sort of syncretism. Small mystical sects in Egypt, Syria, Phrygia, and Babylonia took advantage of apparent resemblances with Church teaching and were able to claim to be part of it and were even sometimes welcomed. All the ancient religions seemed to spring back to life in order to anticipate Jesus and claim him as one of their adepts. The cosmogonies of Assyria, Phoenicia, and Egypt, the doctrines regarding the mysteries of Adonis, of Osiris, of Isis, and of the great goddess of Phrygia, all came to invade the Church as the continuation of what one might call the—scarcely Christian—oriental branch of Gnosticism. Sometimes Jehovah, the god of the Jews, was identified with the Assyrio-Phoenician demiurge *Ialdabaoth,* "the son of chaos." At other times, the ancient Assyrian IAΩ, which shows unusual signs of an affinity with Jehovah, was brought into vogue and related to his quasi-homonym in such a way that it is difficult to distinguish the mirage from the reality. . . . Wavering between genius and madness, Gnosticism defies all absolute judgments. In it one finds Hegel and Swedenborg, Schelling and Cagliostro rubbing shoulders. We must not be repelled by the apparent frivolity of some of its theories. Any law which is not the pure expression of positive science is subject to the vagaries of fashion. Hegelian formulae which were in their time considered the supreme perspective from which to view the world are now objects of derision. Any phrase by which we would presume to sum up the universe will someday seem hollow and faded. One must thus show indulgence toward those who sink in the sea of infinity. (In Ernest Renan, *Oeuvres complètes,* Paris: Calmann-Lévy, 1952, 5: 283–84, 832.)

Another way of viewing the nineteenth-century interest in Gnosticism is to note the similarities between its theology and the vague, general aspirations of Romanticism. Seznec has developed this thesis at some length (*Nouvelles Etudes,* pp. 40–46). As I shall try to show, such a view is fundamentally correct, but Seznec does not develop it in terms which are specific enough to make the comparison significant.

    8. Matter, *Histoire critique,* pp. 16–17.

    9. For convenience I shall quote Epiphanius from the selections published by Werner Foerster in *Gnosis: A Selection of Gnostic Texts* (Oxford: Oxford University Press, 1972), 1: 320.

    10. Ibid., pp. 317, 321.

    11. *Pistis Sophia,* trans. Violet Macdermot, ed. Carl Schmidt (Leiden: E. J. Brill, 1978), p. 126. On the importance of the figure of Pistis Sophia for the Romantics, see Seznec, *Nouvelles Etudes,* pp. 41–43, where he discusses a poem by André de Guerne entitled "La Passion de Pistis Sophia" and draws a parallel between de Guerne's treatment of Pistis Sophia and Flaubert's treatment of Helen-Ennoia in the *Temptation.*

    12. Seznec, *Nouvelles Etudes,* p. 21.

13. Seznec noticed the discrepancy between Flaubert's text and some of his sources, but limits his reading of the discrepancy by attributing it to Flaubert's personal obsessions. See *Nouvelles Etudes,* pp. 35–36.

14. Matter, *Histoire critique,* p. 280.

15. Ibid, p. 281.

16. Ibid., p. 282.

17. Foerster, *Gnosis,* pp. 319–20.

18. Renan, *Oeuvres complètes,* 5: 821.

19. An incidental remark: From our contemporary point of view one might think that Matter and Renan were in the right, since an enormous amount of scholarship has shown us the originality and the importance of Gnostic theology and epistemology. Nevertheless, most contemporary scholars who write on the question—Hans Jonas, Robert Haardt, Werner Foerster, Henri-Charles Puech, and others—fall into the same trap as do Matter and Renan, but in a more systematic way: namely, they divorce the theological, cosmological, and epistemological speculations from the rituals, as if the latter were not an integral part of Gnosticism. What Epiphanius and Flaubert refuse to do, each in his own way, is to separate theology from ritual.

20. Gustave Flaubert, *Correspondance,* ed. Jean Bruneau (Paris: Gallimard, 1973), 1: 390. Subsequent references to this edition of Flaubert's correspondence will be identified in the text by the letter "B" followed by the volume and page number.

21. Gustave Flaubert, *Oeuvres complètes de Gustave Flaubert: Correspondance* (Paris: Louis Conard, 1926–33), 4: 175. Subsequent references to this edition of Flaubert's correspondence will be identified in the text by the letter "C" followed by the volume and page number.

22. OC, 395. For my discussion of Helen-Ennoia, I shall quote from the more explicit 1849 version of the *Temptation.*

23. That Helen-Ennoia can be taken as a textual allegory is confirmed by one of Flaubert's major sources for the Gnostic episode, namely Isaac de Beausobre who, in his *Histoire critique de Manichée et du Manichéisme* (1739; rpt. Leipzig: Zentral-antiquariat der Deutschen Demokratischen Republik, 1970), 2: 327, writes:

One must admit that Saint Epiphanius and his peers provide us with strange tales of the Heretics and their sentiments. Audaciously, he tells us "that Simon assured that his Helen was the same Helen over whom the Greeks and Trojans engaged in such a long and bloody war." The Moderns have not yet managed to avoid repeating this view. It seems that the greater the absurdity, the more care they take to report it. However, Saint Epiphanius fools them, and I want no other witness to it than him. Simon never uttered so great an impertinence. Even cursory attention would have demonstrated to everyone what I noticed immediately. Here is what the Heresiarch said. He had the idea, which today still captivates several scholars, that the fictions of Homer contain Philosophical Truths. Based on this principle, he claimed that Homer and the Poets had spoken in an allegorical way of his Ennoia, that therefore the Helen of Homer was at root none other than this celestial Virtue, that the Trojan war referred to the war waged by the Princes of this world to carry her off and possess her. . . . In short, Simon allegorized the Fable of Helen in order to confirm his own.

24. See for example Henri-Charles Puech, "Gnosis and Time," in *Man and Time: Papers from the Eranos Yearbook* (New York: Pantheon, 1957).

25. In another letter Flaubert again associates prostitutes with a crepuscular moment and the capacity to evoke memories which console us for the present:

The weather has been quite nice since yesterday and there should be a good many scantily-clad prostitutes on the boulevard this evening. Especially between the rue de Grammont and the rue de Richelieu; that's where it's best. The supreme moment in Paris at 8 o'clock in the evening reminds me of antiquity. It's a sight which can console great sorrow. And isn't it sensible to be able to delight in something which afflicts the moralists and philosophers? (B, 1: 100)

26. Gustave Flaubert, "Novembre," in *Oeuvres complètes* (1964), p. 255. All subsequent references will be indicated in the text by the letters "OC" followed by the page number.

27. Gustave Flaubert, *Voyage en Orient* in *Oeuvres complètes* (Paris: Club de l'Honnête Homme, 1971–75), 10: 485. This same scene is described in much greater detail in a letter to Bouilhet (B, 1: 605).

# 5 Who Signs "Flaubert"?

*In telling a story I pretend to speak the dead.* Louis L. Marin

*The Self: a cemetary guard.* Jacques Derrida

In a letter written on June 26, 1852, addressed to Maxime Du Camp, who had just moved to Paris and invited his friend to come there in order to make "a name" for himself, he whom we choose to call Flaubert protests:

It seems to me that with regard to my situation you suffer from a *tic* or a redhibitory vice. It *does not bother me*, have no fear of that. I have long since made up my mind on the matters you mention.

I will merely tell you that all the words you use—*hurry, this is the moment, it is now time, your place will be taken, establish yourself*, and *outside the law*— are for me a vocabulary empty of meaning. It is as if you were speaking to an Algonquin—I don't understand.

*To get somewhere*—what for? . . .

*To be known* is not my main concern.[1]

The site of literary fame is not the theater wherein the writer would like to inscribe his name; that others occupy center stage does not trouble him at all: "I don't give a damn about whether or not Augier is successful and I won't become frantic if Vacqueir and Ponsard so broaden their shoulders that they take my place, and I have no intention of troubling them to give it back to me."

The letter is not signed with a proper name but simply "Your

Quarafon," the nickname that Maxime Du Camp had given to Flaubert and which for Flaubert remained associated with the mimetic talents of his friend—mimetic talents which were part of a certain literary activity, precisely that which permits one to "make a name for oneself": "Maxime has developed a great mimetic talent . . . I call him father Etienne; he calls me Quarafon."[2] It is thus the addressee, in the process of making himself a name among other names, who determines what Flaubert chooses to sign. . . .

Flaubert's refusal to make a literary name for himself is linked to his refusal to move to Paris and to his choice to remain in Croisset, the privileged place of his writing. If Flaubert chooses to live in the country, it is not in order to do what one usually does when living in the country but because Croisset is the place of another literature, a literature different from that which is written in the capital: "If I really led a provincial or rural existence, devoting myself to the playing of dominoes or the growing of melons, I could understand the reproach. But if I am becoming stupefied it is Lucian, Shakespeare, and writing a novel which are to blame."[3] We sense the error of Bouvard and Pécuchet who, within this same Normandy, cultivated melons before understanding that "happiness" in the country consists of setting oneself at a double writing desk in order to produce there, through a pure act of writing, La Copie. Already in 1852 Flaubert qualifies his literary activity as "neutralizing"—"As for so bitterly deploring my 'neutralizing' life, it is as though you were to reproach a shoemaker for making shoes."[4]

But if Croisset in particular and Normandy in general are privileged places for the consummation and production of a certain literature, it is because that same literature participates in a scene of writing which implicates Flaubert the individual. Normandy is the place of Flaubert's dead and it is these dead who, by being associated with the literary act, put into play a series of texts which produce, in their turn, the space in which a form of writing which engenders the series of texts signed Flaubert becomes possible. In a letter written barely a week before the one addressed to Maxime Du Camp, Flaubert explains to Louise Colet:

We carry away . . . the fatherland on the soles of our heels and we carry in our heart, without knowing it, the dust of our dead ancestors—As for me, I personally rely on a demonstration by A + B—It is the same in literature. I recover all of my origins in the book which I knew before I knew how to read,

*Don Quixote,* and there is still, over and above this, the agitated froth of the Norman seas, the English malady, the stinking fog.[5]

This phantasmatic Normandy will therefore be the place where, for Flaubert the individual, a certain number of the dead come to be intimately associated with a certain literature which has always carried within it the imaginary space wherein he chooses to live. For Flaubert, the possibility of being able to produce a certain number of texts signed "Flaubert" will depend upon this precise choice.

And yet the necessary condition for Flaubert to be able to produce the texts signed "Flaubert" would exclude the possibility that Croisset's recluse could ever come to know his own name. In that same letter of June 26, 1852, to Maxime Du Camp, Flaubert writes this extraordinary sentence: "one almost always dies in the incertitude of one's own proper name."[6]

But then what might be proper to that signature which we—we who?—read as being that of "Flaubert"? The textual production which subtends the engenderment of a proper name—whose proper meaning would consist precisely in the production of an oeuvre signed by a name—would consequently have to constitute the representation of a subject always distinct from that of the psychological ego of the writer and from all the identifications and significations which the writer or the reader would come to invest in it. By the signing of a text, the proper name produces itself, presents itself, gives itself to be seen and to be read, simply by producing the conditions of its illegibility. In the end, then, a signature can only engender the mark of a necessary nonadequation or nonattribution of a representation, or more exactly, of what represents itself in a name to the writer insofar as he is an individual. At least, of course, insofar as we try to determine the margin of possible exception permitted by the "almost"—"one almost always dies in the incertitude of one's own proper name"—or insofar as we believe it possible to say what is proper to imbecility—"unless one is an imbecile."

Without pretending to offer a response to the conditions of a proper name's legibility and without believing myself able to say what is proper to the imbecile, I would like to weave around the proper name "Flaubert" a phantasmatic scenario which might at least permit us to displace the proper name "Flaubert" onto other proper names. These other proper names would not be any more legible than that of Flaubert; nonetheless, if to try to read a proper name can only end by displacing it onto another proper name, then this transfer, this translation, this metaphorization would at least be one of the determining conditions of its illegibility. My hypothesis is the following: if the proper name "Flaubert" remains illegible, it is partly because it is engendered by another proper name which could almost be said to be that of "Loulou—Le Poittevin"; however, "Loulou—Le Poittevin," being a name of a dead person, itself remains illegible except through the proper name "Flaubert," which it renders possible by its own encryptment (*mise en crypte*).

If the signature of a certain number of titles problematizes the proper name "Flaubert," it does not do so in a unified way over a uniform corpus. On the contrary, the signature "Flaubert" divides the Flaubertian corpus in two and gives it a particular morphology. Flaubert the writer does not sign his works—or only expresses his intention to sign his works beginning with the first *Temptation of Saint Anthony*, that is, beginning in 1849. If his refusal to publish the works of his youth remains comprehensible, we understand less his lack of interest in publishing the first *Sentimental Education* or "Novembre," which he nevertheless allowed to circulate among his friends.

The *Temptation of Saint Anthony*, in any case, plays a privileged role for Flaubert. It is the first of his works that he assumes without reserve; through its three versions it therefore frames his career as a writer and, by his own admission, constitutes the work of his entire life. For Flaubert, it is *The Temptation of Saint Anthony* and *Bouvard and Pécuchet* which occupy a privileged position among his works, and not *Madame Bovary* or *Sentimental Education,* which are ultimately valorized by the naturalist myth of a so-called realist Flaubert.

It is precisely here, within the register of proper names, and beginning with *The Temptation of Saint Anthony,* that a series of metaphorizations of the writer's ego takes place in Flaubert's writing, by way of a series of proper names based on imaginary identifications which determine, in their fashion, not only the possibility of being for Flaubert's works, but also the condition of their signature. If the phrase "Madame Bovary is I" is known and cited at every turn, it is important not to forget that Flaubert the writer will identify himself on several occasions with St. Anthony and that he will end by identifying himself with Bouvard and Pécuchet—"Bouvard and Pécuchet overwhelm me to such an extent that I have become them! Their stupidity is mine, I die from it."[7] Nor should one forget that this mechanism of identification is finally based upon a more general process: "Everything that is there within St. Theresa, within Hoffman and Edgar Poe, I have *seen*." Or again: "My imaginary characters haunt me, or rather, it is I who am in them."[8] If these imaginary identifications are essential to the production of the text, it is because they procure for the writer an enjoyment essential to the libidinal economy which governs his writing: "good or bad, it is a delicious thing to write, to no longer be *oneself*, but to circulate within every creation of which one speaks."[9]

"Flaubert" is thus not the proper name of the writer; the latter calls himself, by turns, St. Anthony, Madame Bovary, Bouvard, Pécuchet, and so on. These names permit the engenderment of a text which, itself, will be signed "Flaubert." "Flaubert" would only be at the limit one of the names of that heterogeneous assemblage of names. The writer only lives for, and only *enjoys* himself through, a series of names which never properly return to him but which permit him to make himself a single name, the knowledge of which will always remain enigmatic for him.

A first indication of this strange dialectic between the writer Flaubert and the name of that which signs "Flaubert": sentences such as "the writer does not write in order to be published. . . . I do not in any way dream of this, thank God. . . . It is necessary more than ever to make Art for itself, for itself only"[10] recur constantly in his correspondence and express a resolution that the writer repeats in practically each one of his novels. On the other hand, the other name, the proper name "Flaubert," only exists because of publication and only as the signature of a published text.[11] A second indication: the names of the imaginary characters with which the writer identifies himself engender, in their turn, by association, other names which the writer does not hesitate to assume; this is what permits him, for example, to sign letters with "St. Polycarpe" or "the last of the Church Fathers."

Among all the proper names which circulate in Flaubert's novels, I single out two of them, Alfred Le Poittevin and Loulou, which seem to me to be of particular interest because of their particular relationship with the name "Flaubert." The first appears only on the occasion of a dedication, the second is the name of Félicité's parrot in *A Simple Heart*.

In 1874 Flaubert finally publishes the third version of the *Temptation* and dedicates it to Alfred Le Poittevin, whose name comes to be associated with the name "Flaubert" in a privileged fashion. The text of the dedication is not content simply to mention the name of his childhood friend but also indicates the date and place of his friend's death— "To the memory of my friend, Alfred Le Poittevin, who died in Neuville-Chant-D'Oisel on the third of April, 1848." Flaubert himself recognizes the importance of Alfred Le Poittevin's name to the *Temptation*. On October 30, 1872, he writes to Laure de Maupassant: "In my mind *The Temptation of Saint Anthony* has always been dedicated to Alfred Le Poittevin. I had spoken to him about this book six months before his death. I have finally finished it, this book which has occupied me off and on for 25 years!"[12] Four months later, in another letter to Laure, Flaubert speaks again of Alfred Le Poittevin and generalizes his point: "He remains in my memory beyond all comparison. Not a day passes that I do not think of him. Besides, the past, the dead (my dead) obsess me."[13]

The writer thus carries within himself, among his dead, the memory of his friend. If it remains true that Flaubert had spoken to the latter about his project of writing a *Temptation of Saint Anthony*, and if it is to Alfred Le Poittevin that he announced, before his project, his discovery of the Bruegel tableau,[14] it remains no less true that the bond of the *Temptation* to the memory of his friend is more fundamental. Even on an anecdotal level, if Flaubert thinks of the project of writing a *Temptation*, it is only in May 1848, after Alfred Le Poittevin's unexpected death on April 3 of the same year, that he begins to compose the first version.

That the possibility of beginning "the work of all his life" and of inaugurating the signed part of his work are intimately linked, for Flaubert, to the work of the mourning of his friend, is suggested to us by a letter to Maxime Du Camp in which he describes in detail the wake and burial of Alfred Le Poittevin. I cite here some extracts from it:

Alfred died on Monday night at midnight. I buried him yesterday and I am now back. . . . I buried him in his shroud, I gave him the kiss of farewell and I saw his coffin being sealed. I spent two very full days there. While watching over him, I read Creuzer's *Religions of Antiquity*. The window was open, the night was superb, one could hear the cock crow and a moth was fluttering around the torches. I shall never forget all that, neither the aspect of his figure, nor the first night at midnight, the distant sound of a hunting horn that came to me through the woods.

The last night I read *Les Feuilles d'automne*. I kept coming across pieces that he liked best or that for me had some relation to the present situation. From time to time I got up and went to lift the veil that they had placed on his face, and looked at him. I was myself bundled up in a coat that belonged to my father and that he had worn only once, the day of Caroline's wedding. . . . There, my dear friend, you have what I have lived through since Tuesday night. I have had unheard-of perceptions and flashes of untranslatable ideas. Many things have been coming back to me with choirs of music and whiffs of perfume. . . . I feel the need to say incomprehensible things.[15]

In telling of the vigil and burial of Alfred Le Poittevin, Flaubert effectively ends up creating nothing less than a phantasmatic scenario of the origin of a certain type of literary representation. At first the presence of his friend's corpse drives the writer to read. The choice of texts is doubly marked. Flaubert begins with the French Translation of Creuzer's *Symbolik und Mythologie*. Of all the readings that Flaubert will go through for the *Temptation,* the *Religions of Antiquity* is not only one of his most important sources, but it is also the very book that will provide him with indispensable iconographic material. In other words, Alfred Le Poittevin's corpse will at first permit Flaubert to read one of the important sources for the work that will inaugurate his career and to allegorize the birth of a type of literature whose most extreme form will be *Bouvard and Pécuchet.* The *Temptation* in effect belongs to a literature whose pre-text is no longer a "reality" or "imagination" conceived of as outside the text, but rather a pre-text which is itself textual and which affirms itself as such. In order to be able to write the *Temptation* or *Bouvard and Pécuchet,* Flaubert will have to be able to say: "I have gotten indigestion from books; I burp in-folio."[16]

Flaubert then read the *Feuilles d'automne:* if in this case the question is not that of a text which will be part of the literary genesis of one of Flaubert's works, the choice of texts is nevertheless dictated to him by the preferences of the dead man. What the corpse gives him to understand and to feel—"choirs of music," "whiffs of perfume"—does not belong to a system of textual representation. The only possible translation of the intuitions produced by the presence of the dead man will be a series of contradictory metaphors—"unheard-of perceptions," "flashes of untranslatable ideas." Flaubert's ultimate desire to say "incomprehensible things"—what he will elsewhere call the Idea—will end by opening an unbreachable gap between what is written and the intended meaning, which will be the very space of Flaubertian prose— a prose which "is never finished" and which condemns him "no longer to expect anything from life but a series of sheets of paper to scribble upon in black."[17] In order to pass from the wish to say "incomprehensible things" to writing, "one must undertake a kind of permanent translation, and what an abyss that creates between the absolute and the work."[18] In other words, if the corpse of Alfred Le Poittevin determines the literary practice which will produce the texts signed "Flaubert," it will engender as well the aesthetic which subtends such a practice.

We might be tempted, because of the way in which Flaubert represents his literature to us as a thanatography, to conclude that what is proper to the Flaubertian signature belongs to Alfred Le Poittevin. Such a conclusion is more incomplete than false. On the one hand, it neglects the fact that there are other names apart from that of Alfred Le Poittevin which belong to that phantasmatic scenario of the origin of Flaubertian writing; yet on the other hand, it forces us to ask what is theoretically at stake when we declare that, in the last analysis, the signature of Flaubert belongs to one or several corpses.

The conditions under which Flaubert composes the end of *A Simple Heart* are well known. He borrows a stuffed parrot from the Museum of Natural History at Rouen which he places in front of him on his work table: Félicité's parrot is a textual transposition of the representation of the dead parrot that the writer has in front of him. Félicité's parrot is named Loulou, an unusual name for a parrot: "Many are surprised when it does not answer to the name of Jacquot, since all parrots are named Jacquot."[19] Félicité's parrot will die and in turn become a stuffed bird. Yet this is not the essential point.

For the author of *A Simple Heart* thus summarizes his tale: "She [Félicité] successively loves a man, the children of her mistress, a nephew, an old man whom she cares for, then her parrot; when the parrot dies, she has it stuffed and when she in turn is dying she confuses the parrot with the Holy Spirit."[20] Flaubert's tale is based upon the series of Félicité's libidinal objects, a good part of which disappear in her dying. The series is itself engendered by the double death of Félicité's parents and Mme Aubain's husband. The parrot, the last object of the servant's affection, suspends the play of substitutions among which it is the privileged term, since it is the only one which, in being dead, continues to "live" stuffed in the form of a simulacrum, and the only one which will eventually be transformed into the Holy Spirit by Félicité's death.

Now Loulou has a very particular relationship to language. Alive, the parrot utters only pure signifiers that are indefinitely repeated by a voice that the deaf Félicité hears and understands; dead, it will be transformed into the symbol of the only name that we can say is truly proper, the transcendental signifier of all signification, the proper name of what is proper to the name, namely, the Holy Spirit. But it is within this last transformation that the role of the parrot becomes paradoxical for, if *in principium erat Verbum*, at the origin the parrot is also the endless babble of language, the indefinite repetition of a signifier without signification. If the Holy Spirit calls itself Loulou, then the only properly proper name is itself only composed from the repetition of the insignificant signifier "lou." In other words, through Félicité's death the dead parrot divides language in two; on the one side, an indefinite babble of "sonorous inanities"; on the other side, an always inaccessible transcendental signified.

We have often approached the description of Virginie's corpse in *A Simple Heart* through the description that Flaubert gives us of his dead sister, Caroline. We must not forget, however, that the daughter of Mme Aubain is named Virginie (and her son, Paul) and that her name is only a reference to a literary antecedent. Moreover, Loulou is also one of the names that Flaubert gives to his niece Caroline, the daughter of his sister Caroline. It is also important to note, as Philippe Bonnefis has emphasized,[21] that during the entire period of the writing of *A Simple Heart,* in all of his letters addressed to his niece, he calls her only by the name of Loulou. If *A Simple Heart* returns us to the death of Caroline Flaubert, it does so through a series of transpositions which puts into play Félicité's parrot and the name of Loulou. If, for Félicité, the parrot replaces the lost object, Virginie, the name of the parrot remains associated, for Flaubert, with that of his niece which, in turn, repeats and replaces the name of his dead sister.[22] *A Simple Heart* evokes the corpse of Caroline Flaubert by transposing it into that of a parrot, that is to say, by inscribing it into a textual problematic of the proper name.

The description of the corpse of Caroline Flaubert, dead in 1846, two years before the death of Alfred Le Poittevin, is itself significant, insofar as it also proposes to us a phantasmatic scenario of the genesis of Flaubert's literary production.[23] In a letter to Louise Colet in 1847 Flaubert describes the vigil of his sister in the following manner:

When my sister died, I stood vigil over her at night; I was on the edge of her bed; I was looking at her lying on her back in her wedding dress with a white bouquet.—I was reading Montaigne and my eyes were going from the book to her corpse; her husband was sleeping and breathing heavily; the priest was snoring; and I was saying to myself, in contemplating all this, that forms pass and that only the idea remains, and I had shivers of enthusiasm from the way in which the author worded some of his sentences.—Then I thought that he too would pass; it was freezing, the window was open because of the odor, and from time to time I got up to see the stars, calm, caressing, sparkling, eternal; and I told myself that when, in turn, they should become pale, when they should send, like the eyes of those in agony, lights full of anguish, all will be said and everything will be even more beautiful.[24]

Again we have a scene of reading created by the displacement of a libidinal investment in a dead object into the literature that Flaubert proposes to us. In front of his sister's corpse the writer, who will in the future sign "Flaubert," reads Montaigne. But it is precisely this transposition of a dead body into a written representation, this *translatio*, this metaphorization of the corpse into a text, which positions language between the already-said of a literature to be read and the text to be written, between plural forms and effects of style, between the source of the writer's enjoyment and the Idea—the transcendental signified. As in *A Simple Heart,* this play of oppositions works only to announce an eschatology within the indefinite future of an eventual end of time. It is only when the speakable (*le dicible*) has used up the time engendered by the anteriority of the corpse and the aftermath of the text, when "everything has been said," and when the corpse has finally recuperated the textual representations that belong to it, that a final epiphany will be possible.[25]

A few sentences before the description of the dead Caroline, Flaubert had written: "Perhaps I am only a violin."[26] What he will not say, or more exactly what he will not name, is the name of whoever holds the bow or the name of the melody which is being played. We might be tempted to say that what holds the bow is nothing other than the corpse, to name the corpse Caroline Flaubert, Loulou, or Alfred Le Poittevin, and to recognize, within the melody, the work signed "Flaubert." However, we must leave to the corpse the capacity to remove the limits of our discourse and to determine the theoretical stakes of attributing the name "Flaubert" to "Loulou Le Poittevin."

To try to explain the relation of the corpse to the subject, we have no theoretical vocabulary other than that proposed by psychoanalysis, and no model other than that which psychoanalysis offers us, in order to think the work of mourning. It is thus a question of understanding the relation of the lost object to the representations that it might engender in terms of the notions of incorporation and introjection. I shall discuss in the concluding chapter of this study the psychoanalytic implications of the notions of incorporation and introjection, and their relationship to the genesis of literature. What I simply want to emphasize here is that, if we accept the possibility of their being two distinct concepts, they differ precisely in their conditions of reading: if the incorporated object is always readable, the introjected object never is.

It is Derrida who deserves credit for having radicalized, in "Fors," the notion of crypt and marked the problems of reading that this notion poses. A crypt would be a phantasmatic, hermetically sealed space which surrounds and hides a corpse introjected by the ego. The status of the corpse is a peculiar one, for we cannot say whether it is dead or alive. But the phantasmatic space of the crypt is also a linguistic space. As such, it encloses an occulted name through the elaboration of a cryptic code whose function is to displace and to translate, by *misreading it,* every sign which tries to penetrate it or to read the name that it hides.

In other words, to propose a concept in order to read the proper name of an encrypted corpse, a corpse which is properly attended by a certain literary representation, would be equivalent to re-creating a phantasmatic scenario of the genesis of literature, as Flaubert has already left us to understand. Thus, to try to read "Loulou Le Poittevin" as the proper name of "Flaubert," to say that what is proper to his name belongs to one or several names or introjected corpses, is a necessary but ultimately derisory critical enterprise. For if such is the case—and we have every reason in the world to believe that this is in fact the case—it is neither readable nor sayable.

Flaubert, "stuffed by funerals," vomits the names which in turn permit him to retell their stories. However, the texts thus engendered always hide from us their ultimate signatories. We can always read the signature "Flaubert" as being that of "Loulou Le Poittevin." But this deciphering, this decrypting, this archaeological restoration is itself only the trace left by the impossibility of a translation without remainder of that which a proper name gives us to read of what properly belongs to a proper name.

The attempt to read a proper name always ends by problematizing the proper name which serves us within our own signatures. I have chosen the name "Flaubert," but what if in its place I had substituted mine or yours? Can we ever know who signs our sayings or our writ-

ings? It is he who writes, in the third person, his impossible autobiography: an autobiography which, as Louis Marin has admirably
shown, is always a thanatography.

## Notes

This chapter was translated by Eduardo Cadava.
1. Gustave Flaubert, *Correspondance*, ed. Jean Bruneau (Paris: Gallimard,
1973, 1980), 2: 113–15. I will indicate this edition by the letter "B" followed
by the volume and page number. I will indicate the *Correspondance* collected
within the Conard edition of Flaubert's *Oeuvres complètes* (Paris: Louis Conard, 1926–37) by the letter "C" followed by the volume and page number.
2. B, 1: 641.
3. B, 2: 115.
4. Ibid.
5. B, 2: 111.
6. B, 2: 114.
7. C, 7: 237.
8. C, 4: 169; C, 5: 350.
9. C, 3: 405.
10. C, 6: 250.
11. It is interesting to note that, aside from a few exceptions demanded by
protocol, Flaubert almost never signs his letters in his own name.
12. *Oeuvres complètes* (Paris: Club de l'Honnête Homme, 1971–75), 15:
178.
13. Ibid., 205–6.
14. B, 1: 230: "I have seen a tableau by Breughel representing *The Temptation of Saint Anthony* which has made me think of composing a *Temptation of
Saint Anthony* for the theater. But that would require a merry fellow other than
me."
15. B, 1: 493–94.
16. C, 4: 189.
17. C, 3: 252; C, 7: 235.
18. C, 4: 239.
19. Flaubert, *Trois contes* (Paris: Garnier/Flammarion, 1965), p. 66.
20. C, 7: 307.
21. For an analysis of the theme and function of the parrot in Flaubert, see
Philippe Bonnefis's brilliant essay, "Exposition d'un perroquet," *Revue des
Sciences Humaines* 181 (1981): 59–78. Bonnefis has been the first to emphasize the connection between the name of Loulou and that of Caroline.
22. We have often wanted to see in Julie, the servant of Flaubert's who
entered into his service in 1825 and stayed with the writer for three years, a

model for Félicité. In line with certain historical research into Flaubert's models, the identification is not a false one. Yet on a phantasmatic level we might propose another kind of identification between Félicité and Flaubert himself. If Félicité is a martyr to her work, Flaubert is one to his. Flaubert says of himself that he is a "hysterical woman." Félicité occupies herself by taking care of other people's children and particularly Virginie; Flaubert takes care of his niece Caroline. When Virginie dies, Félicité keeps a lock of her hair; Flaubert does the same at the death of his sister. Before taking care of Virginie, Félicité had cared for her nephew Victor, whose father "never appeared." Flaubert will have paternal sentiments for Guy de Maupassant, the son of Alfred Le Poittevin's sister.

If we accept this phantasmatic identification between Flaubert and Félicité, we may be able to read the end of *A Simple Heart* as a wish on the writer's part to finally reconcile, by way of Félicité's death, the interminable prose to which he is condemned with the Idea to which he aspires but can never reach. The end of *A Simple Heart* would then be the linguistic equivalent of the third version of *The Temptation of Saint Anthony*, when Anthony finally discovers "happiness" through an identification with substance.

23. We must also note that Caroline died in 1846, and thus within the period which separates the first version of *Sentimental Education* from the first version of *The Temptation of Saint Anthony*. It is this period which separates Flaubert's youthful works from the first work that he has the intention of signing. The only work of Flaubert's between Caroline's death and that of Alfred Le Poittevin is a set of chapters from *Par les champs et par les grèves*, a text of which we can neither say it is a part of the "works of his youth" nor a part of the works that were signed.

24. B, 1: 431. This letter is to be completed by Flaubert's earlier description of his sister's wake in a letter written on March 25, 1846, to Maxime Du Camp:

It was yesterday at eleven o'clock that we buried her, poor girl. We put on her wedding gown, with bouquets of roses, immortelles, and violets. I spent the whole night watching over her. She was stretched out on her bed in that room where you have heard her play music. She seemed taller than when she was alive, with the long white veil that went down to her feet. In the morning, when everything was done, I gave her a long and last farewell kiss in her coffin. I leaned over her, I put my head into the coffin and I felt the lead crumple under my hands. (B, 1: 258)

This description should be put in relation with Saint Anthony's recollection, in the first *Temptation of Saint Anthony*, of his having had a necrophiliac desire for a dead young girl dressed in her wedding gown:

By dint of letting your eyes wander from above, it seemed to you at times that the pall was trembling from one end of its length to the other, and you took three steps to see the figure; with a hand slower than that of a mother opening a cradle, you raised the veil and you uncovered her head:

A funeral wreath with closely tied knots surrounded her ivory forehead, her blue pupils paled in the milky tint of her sunken eyes, she seemed to be sleeping with her mouth open, for her tongue passed over the edge of her teeth. . . . Then you imagined yourself her husband, you thought that you might have been able to be him, that you had been him; you felt her girdle tremble under your fingers and her mouth moved upward toward your lips.

You looked at her: on her neck, on the left side, you saw a rose-colored blemish; desire, like a thunderbolt, ran through your vertebrae, you extended your hand a second time. (*Oeuvres complètes,* Paris: Garnier/Flammarion, 1957, 1: 379–80)

In order to put the letters describing Caroline Flaubert's vigil and burial in relation to the letter which describes those of Alfred le Poittevin, it would be necessary to consider Flaubert's "mourning" when Alfred le Poittevin decided to get married in 1846. In a letter to his friend written on May 31, 1846, two months after Caroline's death, Flaubert writes:

In all my artistic hopes, I was united with you. It is this aspect which makes me suffer. It is too late! Let be whatever will be! You will always find me here for you. It remains to know if you will be there for me. Do not protest! Time and things are stronger than we are. (B, 1: 268)

25. In this regard it is perhaps useful to emphasize that if, for example, *Madame Bovary* and *Salammbô* end with a series of deaths, and if *The Temptation of Saint Anthony* and *A Simple Heart* finish with phantasmatic epiphanies, it is only in *Bouvard and Pécuchet* that Flaubert refuses to "conclude" and that the already-said repeats itself in the insignificance of *La Copie*. Whence the absolutely unique character of this work even within the context of Flaubert's corpus.

26. B, 1: 431.

# 6  Lancelot Brown, Rousseau, and the Enlightenment's Rhetoric of Nature

I have argued in preceding chapters that the epistemology implicitly subtending the production of any "natural representation" is identical with the epistemology responsible for creating botanical gardens in the eighteenth century, and that the transposition of this same epistemology to cultural artifacts was responsible for the archaeological museums. Now I wish to examine the epistemology of botanical gardens in relation to that of the so-called English garden in general and of landscape gardens in particular, especially Lancelot Brown's, in order to argue that botanical gardens are only the appropriate development of an epistemology of nature which is, in fact, a rhetoric of nature.

Before proceeding, though, we should pause to give ourselves a working definition of "garden." And, following Flaubert, we might as well begin with the trite remark that gardens are not natural entities, nor do they simply exist in nature. To be sure, certain aesthetic ideologies identified nature and garden, but such an identification is problematic. When, for example, Horace Walpole praised Kent in his oft-quoted remark, "he leaped the fence, and saw that all nature was a garden,"[1] he bequeathed us a problem in interpretation. If all nature is a garden, then what is the difference between gardens and nature? What does the fence, wall, boundary separate? Where does nature stop being simply nature and become also a garden? Those who read Walpole's statement as praising the naturalness of Kent's gardens are insufficiently attentive to Walpole's careful yet ambiguous formula. Walpole does not say that Kent attempted to make his gardens in the image of nature but that Kent—presumably having built a fence, that is to say, a garden—was *then* capable of seeing that nature is a garden. The question is one of logical priority. It is not the perception of nature which provides a model for the garden; instead it is the garden—albeit a certain type of garden—which serves as an epistemological tool to help us perceive nature in such a way as to postulate the identity of the two.

Gardens, we should remember, are always constructed, even when they aspire to be as "natural" as, say, the Elysée of *La Nouvelle Héloïse* (if we may suppose, that is, an Elysée actually, and not just textually, created). And the construction of a garden requires a certain number of natural botanical species selected for their properties—color, size, shape—and arranged in a certain order. The botanical species are not, strictly speaking, natural specimens, because they are inseparable from the rhetorical system that governs their selection as well as their display. In this sense, gardens are what I have called "natural representations."

A distinction is necessary here. A garden may be a "natural representation," but what a garden represents may not necessarily be "natural." In other words, one may use the representational properties of gardens to make them represent something different from what is perceived as "nature." In this sense the eighteenth-century gardens that tried to be "natural" did not attempt an impossible return to what might have been considered "nature." Instead, they provided a representation of what they took nature—more exactly, the order of nature—to be. It is in this supposed identity of a secondary representation and a primary object, a rhetorically constructed order and a presumed original order, that one must situate the Enlightenment's "return" to nature in its gardens.

French formal gardens in the style of Le Nôtre or the Dutch topiary gardens, against which English landscape architects reacted so vehemently, are not meant to be representationally "natural." The Le Nôtre garden is not a garden in the same sense that, say, a Lancelot Brown garden is a garden. The Le Nôtre garden did not attempt the representational reconstruction of "nature," unless one understands "nature" in terms of geometry and assumes that geometry—that is, "nature"— is better represented by architecture than by parks. A Le Nôtre garden is, first and foremost, an architectural construct, and its ideological rationale can be found in the buildings of Le Brun and Mansard.

Derek Clifford cites Thomas Burnet to illustrate the earlier belief that the order of nature was geometric. He implies that this same belief gave rise to the architectural gardens of Le Nôtre:

Thomas Burnet, theologian and cosmogonist, in his *Theory of Earth,* asserted that the universe would have been a great deal better if the land had been made level, the seas in regular shapes, and the stars arranged in geometrical patterns. That we had been cheated of this desirable state of affairs was, in the nature of things, a prime fault which man slowly and laboriously must set himself to amend. This was the garden of Louis XIV on a vaster scale even than Versailles. Others, less theoretically inclined than Burnet, had begun to find even fifty acres staged in such a fashion tedious.[2]

But even closer to our concern is Addison, who criticized the geometric nature of trimmed plants in topiaries: "I do not know whether I am singular in my opinions, but for my own part I would rather look upon a tree in all its luxuriancy and diffusion of boughs and branches than when it is thus cut and trimmed into a *mathematical figure.*"[3]

If we turn to an influential treatise of gardening like Dézallier D'Argenville's *La Théorie et la pratique du jardinage,* which takes the Le Nôtre garden as a model, we find it explicitly stated that gardens are primarily meant to be architectural artifacts:

'Tis, therefore, the great Business of an Architect, or Designer of Gardens, when he contrives a handsome Plan, with his utmost Art and œconomy, to improve the natural Advantages, and to redress the Imperfections, Shelvings, and the Inequalities of the Ground. With these Precautions he should guide and restrain the Impetuosity of his Genius, never swerving from Reason, but constantly submitting, and conforming himself to that which best suits with the natural Situation of the Place.

This is no such easy Task, as some imagine, a fine Garden being no less difficult to contrive and order well, than a good Building, and that which makes a great many Architects, and such as take upon them to give Designs of Gardening, often miscarry, is, that most of them form Designs in the Air, no way proper for the Situation of the Place and at best but stolen, and pick'd here and there from others.[4]

But if a garden is primarily conceived in architectural terms, it is because "nature" is understood in geometric terms. The landscape garden's "return to nature" was, then, not so much an escape from the formality of French gardens or the artificiality of topiary gardens as it was a substitution of one representational order for another, a substitution which was effected by an understanding of "nature" in pictorial rather than geometric terms.

Studies of eighteenth-century landscape gardens make up a bibliography so elaborate and erudite that it might seem there is little more to say about either them or the more modest French version known as the English or Anglo-Chinese garden. But most such studies have concerned themselves with a very small number of gardens, and have celebrated the gardens of Bridgeman and Kent at the expense of Brown's, which are far more significant both culturally and quantitatively. The reasons are easy to understand. Without oversimplifying, we can say that studies of eighteenth-century gardens have accepted the premise that they came about from a desire to imitate the landscapes of Poussin and Claude on the one hand and, on the other, to make gardens serve a poetics of allusion and association. This premise finds some basis in an important literature concerned with gardens: Pope's *Epistle to Burlington,* Walpole's *History of the Modern Taste in Gardening,* Shenstone's *Unconnected Thoughts on Gardening,* and Rousseau's *La Nouvelle Héloïse.* As a consequence, most historians have thought it proper to treat landscape gardens within a literary context, and such an approach has its merits, of course. Yet the results are finally more helpful for our understanding of the literature concerning gardens than for the gardens themselves. It would be foolish to read Pope's epistle without taking into account his garden at Twickenham, his friendship with Kent, or his admiration for Stowe. Yet it may be equally foolish to think that Pope's epistle or Shenstone's *Unconnected Thoughts* are particularly relevant to our understanding of the gardens of Blenheim or Kew.

The thesis that eighteenth-century landscape gardens are characterized by an attempt to imitate the landscapes of Claude and Poussin and belong to a poetics of allusion and association owes its acceptance to the works of Christopher Hussey and H. F. Clark. In particular, Clark's influential article entitled "Eighteenth-Century Elysiums" has encouraged the widespread assumption that the most characteristic eighteenth-century gardens were those designed by Kent, especially the garden at Stowe. But Clark's thesis leads to three problems.

First, Clark is obliged to overestimate the importance of Pope's garden at Twickenham and Shenstone's *ferme ornée,* the Leasowes. As Clark puts it, in words reminiscent of Flaubert's description of Bouvard and Pécuchet's garden:

In . . . [Pope's] garden are either suggested or actually constructed most of the elements of those landscapes which were to be the greatest achievements of the movement. And Pope brings to the scene associations and emotions which later were to be consciously invoked; murmuring waters for pleasant melancholy; the ivy-clad ruins, a stimulus for romantic fanciers; urns which were to be inscribed with nostalgic lines to departed friends; the "awful and solemn" effects, so necessary to invoke the "sublime"; the venerable broken walls; and lastly, the paths which, leading from seat to seat, were to be employed to show "the diversity, taste and what the natural genius of the place had to give.[5]

As for Shenstone, Clark categorically declares that "the last and greatest of the landscape gardens was The Leasowes."[6] Yet even though Pope's and Shenstone's gardens were important for the problems of literary allusion or the general history of eighteenth-century aesthetics, they can hardly be said to exemplify or to have affected the forms of parks designed by Bridgeman, Kent, Brown, or Repton. Shenstone may have advocated the imitation of pictorial landscapes, but one would be hard-pressed to see the connection between the landscapes of Claude, Poussin, or Rosa on the one hand, and the gardens at Stowe, Blenheim, Chiswick, or Kew on the other. Besides, Clark fails to realize that Twickenham, The Leasowes, and Stowe are effectively three different kinds of garden, and that, if Stowe can be considered an example of the dominant genre, then Twickenham and The Leasowes must be considered idiosyncratic exceptions.

Second—as I said earlier—Clark's thesis forces him to disregard the gardens of Brown, the single most important landscape designer of the eighteenth century. Clark's list of important landscape architects does not include Brown: "Writers in the eighteenth century declared it was a sudden change in fashion and taste, chiefly as a result of the personal expression of genius, and named such gardeners as London and Wise, Bridgeman and Kent, as responsible."[7] In fact, the continuity between Bridgeman, Kent, and Brown was evident to the eighteenth century: witness, for example, Walpole.[8] The trouble is that Brown cannot be easily assimilated to Clark's thesis, which stresses a poetics of allusion and association, and as a result Clark postulates a discontinuity which is historically highly problematic.[9] Because of the controversies that surrounded Brown, Clark is of course obliged to mention him, but does so only to dismiss him without discussing his achievements. In Clark's words, Brown "did not, like Kent, 'use the pencil of his imagination.' By this is meant that a very vital element in landscape has been discarded, that of the principle of association."[10] That Brown had a "theory," Clark is obliged to admit; the trouble is that Brown's "theory" does not seem to fit into the scheme of Clark's "theory." In a later work Clark again denigrates Brown without attempting to understand him:

Brown's style is easily recognizable. His fault lay in endless repetition of a formula, the most obvious features of which were circular clumps of trees, the boundary ride or belt, serpentine rivers and his undulating lawns brought up to the very walls of the house. He was, as Mr. Hussey calls him, "that most dangerous phenomenon, a practical man inspired by a theory. But a theory, moreover, that although derived from visual qualities, had become intellectual and standardised."[11]

Third, Clark's insistence upon finding a purely literary or aesthetic problem in the development of the landscape garden obscures for us the connection between that development and the equally important development of the botanical garden. His insistence also distracts our attention from the general problems of the representation of nature posed by the great botanical taxonomies of Bouffon and Linnaeus, which, it should be said, provide the epistemological background for such grandiose projects as the Jardin des Plantes in Paris or the Botanical Gardens at Kew.

The only scholar who has resisted the temptation to find a purely literary problem in the history of landscape gardens is Derek Clifford, who, to the best of my knowledge, is the first to have treated that history descriptively instead of normatively. Clifford has not only shown that Brown was important, but also, and curiously enough, that the problem of the eighteenth-century landscape garden is in its own way a textual problem.[12] I shall return to this question later. On the other hand, Clifford's desire to separate gardens from purely literary problems leads him to denigrate Rousseau's contribution to the debate. In spite of the extraordinarily rich critical literature concerned with the importance of the Elysée in *La Nouvelle Héloïse*, Clifford curtly dismisses it as a text that can in no way shed light on the nature of eighteenth-century landscape gardens.

But Chambers was not the sole, most important, nor earliest publicist in Europe of what was still misleadingly known as "nature." The natural garden on the continent was very much more the creation of Jean-Jacques Rousseau than of the English or the Chinese, though this was not because Rousseau had any original contribution to make but solely because of the manner in which his thoroughly unsatisfactory life and half-baked doctrines succeeded in capturing the imagination of his contemporaries. In *Julie, or La nouvelle Héloise*, published in 1760, he described a garden in which there is to be discerned no trace of man's hand. Flowers spangle the fields; rivulets meander through the pasture or purl among the rocks; birds fly freely and are no longer confined in aviaries. This is in the tradition of Bacon's wilderness and of Addison's untrimmed trees. The Marquis de Girardin, the patron upon whom this eighteenth-century version of an angry and ill-adjusted adolescent battened for the last years of his life, formed at his Château of Ermenonville a park on this model. But whereas Rousseau's ideal garden contained no buildings, no tombs, nothing bearing the mark of man's hand, the park at Ermenonville collected a variety of poetic adjuncts; a windmill; a hamlet; a temple of philosophy; an obelisk; a rustic temple; an altar of "reverie"; a brewhouse; two curious pieces of historical reconstruction—the "Tomb of Laura," and the "Tower of Gabrielle d'Estrées"; and finally, on an island of poplars in the lake in the fullness of time was built the tomb of Jean-Jacques Rousseau himself, the Mecca of the sentimentalists.[13]

Of course Clifford is right in a sense: the Elysée of Clarens in no way resembles an English landscape garden. But Rousseau's text does not offer us a treatise on gardening. When lecturing Saint-Preux in *La Nouvelle Héloïse*, Monsieur de Wolmar attacks formal gardens in the style of Le Nôtre, with their straight alleys, their *pattes d'oie*, their trimmed trees and sculptural decorations. Rousseau, then, attacks the Le Nôtre garden for its architectural features, which he found unnatural. Through Saint-Preux, Rousseau also criticizes Chinese gardens, presumably aiming his remarks at Attiret's *An Account of the Emperor of China's Gardens at Peking* and Chambers's *Designs of Chinese Buildings, Furniture, Dresses, Machines, and Utensils* (1757), a work containing ideas on Chinese gardens which Chambers was later to develop in his influential *Dissertation on Oriental Gardening* (1772).

Chambers's praise for Chinese gardens is based on arguments similar to those used by Rousseau in justifying the Elysée:

NATURE is their pattern, and their aim is to imitate her in all her beautiful irregularities. Their first consideration is the form of the ground, whether it be flat, sloping, hilly, or mountainous, extensive, or of small compass, of a dry or marshy nature, abounding with rivers and springs, or liable to a scarcity of water; to all which circumstances they attend with great care, choosing such dispositions as humor the ground, can be executed with the least expense, hide its defects, and set its advantages in the most conspicuous light. . . . The perfection of their gardens consists in the number, beauty, and diversity of these scenes. The Chinese gardeners, like the European painters, collect from nature the most pleasing objects, which they endeavor to combine in such a manner, as not only to appear to the best advantage separately, but likewise to unite in forming an elegant and striking whole.[14]

Rousseau agrees that such gardens have some concern for nature, but nonetheless criticizes them for being too expensive and, more important, for constituting an unnatural whole. The argument is a curious one for Rousseau to be making, for he concedes that these gardens successfully, so to speak, erase the rhetorical traces of the gardener, but he denies that they successfully identify the representational copy with its original:

I have seen in China gardens such as the ones you asked for and built with so much art that art was not apparent, but at such expense and maintained at such cost that the very idea took away any pleasure that I might have had in seeing them. There were rocks, grottos, artificial cascades in flat and sandy places where only well-water is available. There were flowers and rare plants from all the regions of China and Mongolia assembled and cultivated in a single soil. In truth one saw neither beautiful alleys nor regular divisions, but one saw piled one upon another a profusion of marvels that one only finds dispersed and separated from each other. Nature presented itself in a thousand manners but the whole itself was not natural.[15]

After unfavorably comparing Chinese gardens with the Elysée at Clarens, Rousseau turns to Stowe, which he also compares unfavorably with the Elysée; in doing so, he significantly identifies the aesthetics of Chinese gardens with those of Stowe:

I feel that this place could be more agreeable but please me infinitely less, as does, for example, the famous park of Milord Cobham at Stowe. It is composed of very beautiful and very picturesque places, their aspects having been chosen in different countries, and all the parts seem natural except the way in which they are assembled, like the gardens of China about which I just spoke to you.[16]

Rousseau, of course, knew Stowe only indirectly through a number of engravings.[17] But for more than one reason Stowe was and remains historically one of the most important landscape gardens. Even though it is not the best example of the genre developed by Lancelot Brown, it became famous in the Enlightenment and was often cited as a model.

This was, no doubt, because it offered a striking and well-documented example of a formal garden gradually changed into a landscape garden and because the changes were made successively by Bridgeman, Kent, and Brown, the three men chiefly responsible for the transformation of the English landscape garden in the eighteenth century.

Curiously enough, Rousseau's intent in creating the Elysée was not very different from that ascribed to Lancelot Brown. Rousseau asked for a representation of nature so close to the original that the work of the gardener—the rhetorical transformations that nature must undergo in order to yield a perfectly identical representation of itself—would have to remain invisible. The human agency that generates the representations has to erase its traces completely:

There is here, however, one thing that I cannot understand. A place so different from what it was could only become what it is through culture and care; however, I do not see anywhere the slightest trace of cultivation. All is green, fresh, and vigorous and the hand of the gardener cannot be seen; nothing dispels the idea of a desert island I had on entering and I do not see any traces of human steps. "Ah!" said Monsieur de Wolmar, "that is because we have gone to a great deal of trouble to erase them." I have often been a witness to this mischief.[18]

Here Rousseau simply repeats a commonplace. Pope had already written that "half the skill is decently to hide,"[19] and Walpole would add: "having routed *professed* art . . . the modern gardener exerts his talents to conceal his art."[20] The commonplace is nevertheless important since it both signals an awareness that art, and therefore representational schemes, are inevitable, and notes the necessity of hiding, concealing, erasing that same art if one is to produce an *effect* which gives the illusion of being natural.

One eighteenth-century interpretation of Lancelot Brown's aesthetics characterizes them as identical to Rousseau's. We learn the following from *A Guide to Burghley House* (1797):

It was the genius of the late Launcelot Brown, which brooding over the shapeless mass, educed out of a seeming wilderness, all the order and delicious harmony which now prevail. Like the great Captain of the Israelites, he led forth his troop of sturdy plants into a seemingly barren land; where he displayed strange magic, and surprised them with miracle after miracle. Though the beauties with which we are here stuck are more peculiarly the rural beauties of Mr. Brown than those of Dame Nature, she seems to wear them with so simple and unaffected a grace, that it is not even the man of taste who can, at a superficial glance, discover the difference.[21]

Repton, sometimes considered a follower of Brown, is even closer to Rousseau in his definition of the ideal design for a landscape garden: "Art . . . can only perform its office by means of deception, effecting its purpose well in proportion as that deception remains undiscovered."[22] Repton's four rules for "the perfection of Landscape Gardening" are even more explicit:

First, it must display the natural beauties and hide the natural defects of every situation; Secondly, it should give the appearance of extent and freedom, by carefully disguising or hiding the boundary; Thirdly, it must studiously conceal every interference of art, however expensive, by which the scenery is improved; making the whole appear the production of nature only; and, Fourthly, all objects of mere convenience or comfort, if incapable of being made ornamental, or of becoming proper parts of the general scenery, must be removed or cancelled.[23]

Even Chambers, who differed from Brown, indirectly confirmed Brown's success in giving a natural representation of "nature" indistinguishable from the original:

Our gardens differ little from common fields so closely is vulgar nature copied in most of them. . . . These compositions rather appear the offspring of chance than design, and a stranger is often at a loss to know whether he be walking in a common meadow or in a pleasure ground, made and kept at a considerable expense.[24]

Chambers, of course, reverses Brown's logic—or Rousseau's, for that matter—by describing Brown's gardens as mimetic copies of nature, when in fact the perception of nature is mediated by the artifact of the garden. Yet, given the similarity between Brown's and Rousseau's presumed aesthetics, one cannot avoid asking two questions: why is Clifford so dismissive of Rousseau while laudatory of Brown and, more important, if the art of the landscape gardener is to produce exact replicas of nature, why create these representations in the first place?

Brown has left us no treatise explaining his intentions, motives, or aesthetic principles. But there exists an important and oft-quoted passage in Hannah More's *Memoirs* recording a conversation she had with him about his procedures when designing landscapes:

He illustrated everything he said about gardening with some literary or grammatical allusion. He told me he compared his art to literary composition. Now there, said he, pointing with his finger, I make a comma, and there, pointing to another part (where an interruption is desirable to break the view) a parenthesis—now a full stop and then I begin another subject.[25]

If we are to take this statement seriously, Brown reverses the normal aesthetic terms of eighteenth-century landscape gardens. Brown, it seems, did not create a representation of nature in order to erase the rhetoric that sustains it. Instead, he saw the representation of nature as a mere pretext for the display of a textual rhetoric. Nature, for Brown, presumably exists only to permit the conversion of landscape into text.

Clifford is therefore right to see in Brown a limit-case. All that remained to do after Brown was to turn gardens into pure textual entities by denaturing their natural component. As Clifford puts it:

In England, indeed in Europe, the abstractionist approach to garden designing could, at that time, go no farther. Conditions were not ripe for the next stage, which would have transmuted the park landscapes of Brown into the stone gardens of the Japanese architect/priest Soami. Capability Brown was as much at the end of his road as Le Nôtre had been at the end of his.[26]

The oriental garden represents for Clifford the most extreme form of a textual garden: "just as Chinese painting with its economy of line and its nervous relationship to calligraphy becomes at times almost a form of written language, so at its most extreme did the Far Eastern garden become a brief note sketched on the surface of the ground."[27]

We may now turn to our second question and simply say that Brown answers it: the repetition of nature in nature has as its main function the constitution and display of a textual rhetoric. But we must still ask why Brown's and Rousseau's positions are not identical, and why Brown is not just an unashamed version of Rousseau, emphasizing an artifact that Rousseau wishes to cancel or hide. In fact the original "nature," which Chambers calls "vulgar nature" and which the author of *A Guide to Burghley House* calls a "shapeless mass" or a "seeming wilderness," is not perceivable without its rhetorical reduplication, and even then it can only be perceived as an orderless and formless mass. The order and form of nature are a consequence of the rhetoric that constitutes the representation of nature: they do not precede it.

Curiously enough, Rousseau himself is not far from this position. The creation of the Elysée is necessary because nature in its original form is not immediately perceivable by man:

Nature seems to wish to hide from the eyes of man its true beauties, to which they are not very sensitive and which they disfigure when they have them at hand's reach. It is at the top of the mountains, deep within forests, on desert islands that she spreads her most charming touches. Those that love her and cannot go that far in search of her, are reduced to doing violence to her, to force her in some way to come and cohabit with them, and all this cannot be achieved without some illusion.[28]

Nature, then, is not simply present to the willing beholder. It is the artifact of a "natural representation" which constitutes nature and makes it available as a presence. Rhetoric is, in fact, the necessary condition for nature's return to its original plenitude. Rousseau certainly knew that this reconstituted nature was only an illusion, that nature is itself only on mountain tops, in forests, or on desert islands. He knew, in short, that nature is not perceivable as original presence. But it is his desire to maintain the illusion that makes him hide the artifact that created it. The difference between Rousseau and Brown resides, perhaps, in the fact that Brown, oblivious to the illusory nature of his creations, was willing to proclaim the gardener's rhetoric his tool, and his landscapes the result of an essentially textual practice.

The development of botanical taxonomies in the eighteenth century is normally treated as a separate subject from that of the development of the landscape garden. But the question of whether the two are in some way related is nonetheless worth asking.

Foucault has argued that the development of botanical and zoological taxonomies was made possible by an assumed continuity between language as a representational system and the "Order of Things" to which "Nature" belongs, taxonomies being an attempt to give a perfect, isomorphic representation of the order that governs nature:

The Classical age gives history a quite different meaning: that of undertaking a meticulous examination of things themselves for the first time, and then of transcribing what it has gathered in smooth, neutralized, and faithful words. It is understandable that the first form of history constituted in this period of "purification" should have been the history of nature. For its construction requires only words applied, without intermediary, to things themselves. The documents of this new history are not other words, texts or records, but unencumbered spaces in which things are juxtaposed: herbariums, collections, gardens; the locus of this history is a non-temporal rectangle in which, stripped of all commentary, of all enveloping language, creatures present themselves one beside another, their surfaces visible, grouped according to their common features, and thus already virtually analysed, and bearers of nothing but their own individual names. It is often said that the establishment of botanical gardens and zoological collections expressed a new curiosity about exotic plants and animals. In fact, these had already claimed men's interest for a long while. What had changed was the space in which it was possible to see them and from which it was possible to describe them.[29]

Foucault identifies gardens, botanical gardens, and zoological collections with nature in an unproblematic way, then postulates another unproblematic passage between such a nature and a discontinuous order of language. But we have already seen that the passage from nature to garden and its relationship to language are considerably more complex than Foucault makes them out to be. I should like to suggest that the constitution of botanical taxonomies is problematic in a way similar to the construction of a garden, and that landscape gardens, botanical taxonomies, and botanical gardens belong to the same representational configuration.

A botanical taxonomy is a representation of nature, and the constitution of a taxonomy pretends to give an adequate representation of "Nature"; its purpose is to display an order presumed in nature which is not visible to the naked eye. In a botanical taxonomy, as in a garden, the assumption is that nature does not give its reality in an unmediated fashion to the beholder, that it is necessary to re-present nature in order to see what, in the original, remains hidden. To constitute a representation of nature in a botanical taxonomy, one again needs a specific rhetoric that is finally inseparable from the "natural representation" it generates. Minimally, a botanical taxonomy employs a series of synecdoches: species for genus, individual for species, part of an individual plant for a whole plant; the plant as object is then reconstructed by a set of metonymies which find the name implied in the properties and re-create a totality out of leaf, flower, stem. Finally, the plant is named by a metaphor. The linguistically or pictorially reconstructed object is not meant to exist in a space distinct or discontinuous from that of nature. On the contrary, it pretends to remain in a continuous relationship with its original object. The continuity is important, since on it depends the possibility of postulating an identity of object and representation which would, so to speak, erase the tropology that subtends the representation.

Like gardens, botanical representations function as a means of possibly recovering the original order of "Nature." Thus, at the beginning of the nineteenth century, Alexander von Humboldt summarized in *Cosmos* the Enlightenment's view of nature in order to justify his own botanical and zoological journeys:

> The most important result of all thoughtful exploration . . . is to recognize in the apparent confusion and opulence of nature a quintessential unity—to study each detail thoroughly, yet never to be defeated by the contradictions of a mass of fact, to remember the elevated destiny of homo sapiens and thereby to grasp the spirit of nature, its essential meaning which lies concealed under a blanket of multifarious manifestations.[30]

The "essential meaning," the "quintessential unity" of nature, remains hidden: what nature gives in so unmediated a way is only "confusion" and "contradictions." The hidden order of nature can become apparent only through a complex rhetoric that the eighteenth century had to postulate as neutral, and in order to guarantee neutrality, the eighteenth century also had to assume the identity of original and representation.

The actual relationship between botanical taxonomies and landscape gardens would have been more evident, if historians of gardens had paid more attention to the development of botanical gardens, which are usually put in a separate class from landscape gardens and then summarily dismissed.[31] In fact, botanical gardens tried to offer a more systematic version of what landscape gardens had attempted in an aesthetic key. The botanical garden of the Enlightenment tried, that is, to offer a total representation of one of nature's realms, the function of the representation being none other than to present a visual tableau of an order which is otherwise unperceivable. Inasmuch as this "natural representation" was the textual product of a specific rhetoric, the natural history represented in botanical gardens could—by uncritically identifying object and identification—be considered the "Script of Nature." Planting botanical gardens helped nature tell the tale of its hidden order. As Voltaire so aptly put it: "I too cultivate natural history, but I do it by planting trees."[32]

Among the English landscape gardens of the eighteenth century most often cited by historians, Kew is relatively neglected. Stowe and Claremont are mentioned as important instances of the way the landscape garden developed; Blenheim is mentioned as an excellent example of Brown's art; but Kew, more often than not, is cited only for the buildings and ruins with which Chambers decorated it. Kew nevertheless deserves special mention, since it contains on one side a landscape garden designed by Brown and, on the other, the botanical garden that was to acquire considerable importance under the directorship of Sir Joseph Banks. This juxtaposition of landscape garden and botanical garden constitutes what we might, after Flaubert, characterize as an exemplary emblem of the Enlightenment's Rhetoric of Nature.

## Notes

1. Horace Walpole, "The History of the Modern Taste in Gardening," in Isabel W. Chase, *Horace Walpole: Gardenist* (Princeton: Princeton University Press, 1943), p. 25.

2. Derek Clifford, *A History of Garden Design*, 2nd ed. (New York: Praeger, 1966), p. 123.

3. Quoted by H. F. Clark, "Eighteenth-Century Elysiums," in *England and the Mediterranean Tradition*, ed. Warburg and Courtauld Institutes (Oxford: Oxford University Press, 1945), p. 155; my italics.

4. A. J. Dézallier D'Argenville, excerpt from *The Theory and Practice of Gardening*, trans. John James (1712), in *The Genius of the Place*, ed. John Dixon Hunt and Peter Willis (New York: Harper and Row, 1975), pp. 125–26.

5. Clark, "Elysiums," p. 156.

6. Ibid., p. 164.

7. Ibid., p. 154.

8. Chase, *Walpole*, pp. 24–25, 37.

9. This denigration of Brown's achievements is continued by Nikolaus Pevsner, who declares that "the landscape garden was conceived in England between 1710 and 1730. It was conceived by philosophers, writers and virtuosi—not by architects and gardeners" (*Studies in Art, Architecture and Design*, New York: Walker, 1968, 1:100). Pevsner thus eliminates not only Brown's contributions but those of Bridgeman and Kent as well.

10. Clark, "Elysiums," pp. 167–68.

11. H. F. Clark, *The English Landscape Garden* (London: Pleiades Books, 1948), p. 27.

12. Thus, for Clifford, "[Brown's] scenery has been compared with that of Claude and Poussin, but there is only a superficial similarity. It would show more penetrating discernment of his achievement to measure his grounds against an arabesque or the pattern upon a Chinese silk or a woodcut by Haronobu" (Clifford, *Garden Design*, p. 159).

13. Ibid., p. 151.

14. William Chambers, excerpt from *Designs of Chinese Buildings, Furniture, Dresses, Machines, and Utensils*, in *The Genius of the Place*, pp. 283–84.

15. Jean-Jacques Rousseau, *Collection complète des oeuvres de J. J. Rousseau* (Geneva: n.p., 1782–89), 3: 127–28. My translation here and in subsequent quotations from this work.

16. Ibid., p. 128.

17. For Rousseau's knowledge of Stowe, see Peter Willis, "Rousseau, Stowe and *Le jardin anglais:* Speculations on Visual Sources for *La nouvelle Héloïse*," *Studies on Voltaire and the Eighteenth Century* 90 (1972): 1791–98. This identification of Stowe with the gardens of China is puzzling. Could Rousseau have had in mind the work that Chambers was supervising at Kew? Chambers had complained that a garden could only be built there at great expense, because the soil was unsuitable. Kew contained a number of chinoiseries, including the famous pagoda designed by Chambers. Moreover, the buildings there do indeed give the impression that they were "chosen in different countries and all the parts seem natural except the way in which they are assembled." The buildings at Kew include a Temple of the Sun, a Temple of Pan, a House of Confucius, an Alhambra, a Pagoda, a Mosque, a Gothic cathedral, Ruins, and so forth.

18. Rousseau, *Collection complète*, p. 120.

19. Alexander Pope, *Epistle to Burlington*, in *The Works of Alexander Pope* (New York: Gordian Press, 1967), 3: 176, l. 54.

20. Chase, *Walpole*, p. 30.

21. Quoted in William George Hoskins, *The Making of the English Landscape* (London: Hodder and Stoughton, 1955), p. 176.

22. Humphry Repton, excerpt from "The 'Red Book' for Blaise Castle" (1795–96), in *The Genius of the Place*, pp. 359–60.

23. Quoted in Clifford, *Garden Design*, p. 169.

24. Quoted in Clark, *The English Landscape Garden*, pp. 16–17.

25. Quoted in Clifford, *Garden Design*, p. 159.

26. Ibid., p. 159.

27. Ibid., p. 115.

28. Rousseau, *Collection complète*, p. 121.

29. Michel Foucault, *The Order of Things*, (New York: Pantheon, 1970), p. 131.

30. Quoted in Desmond Wilcox, *The Explorers* (London: British Broadcasting Corp., 1975), pp. 161–62.

31. See, for example, Clifford, *Garden Design*, pp. 165–66.

32. Quoted by Geoffrey Murray, "Voltaire's *Candide:* the Protean Gardener, 1755–1762," *Studies on Voltaire and the Eighteenth Century* 69 (1970): 33; my translation.

# 7 Divine Agonies: Of Representation and Narrative in Romantic Poetics

> *But for you it would perhaps be a duty since you could occupy yourself with awakening the dead of Tübingen. The undertakers will, certainly, try to harm you as much as possible. If your efforts should be in vain I think, of course, that it would be a self-betrayal to bother yourself with that species. But are you going to find a more favorable field of action among your Swiss than among our Swabians? That is the question.* Hölderlin to Hegel, letter of November 25, 1795, from Stuttgart

> *One has only to say the words "College of Tübingen" to grasp what German philosophy is at bottom—a cunning theology. . . . The Swabians are the best liars in Germany, they lie innocently.* Nietzsche

Nietzsche's resounding proclamation that "God is dead," by the lucid forcefulness of its statement, may easily lead us to neglect the fact that Nietzsche's harrowing of that event is only one episode—even if we should eventually discover that it is the most decisive episode—in the history of a topos that is central to the Romantic imagination. Within the corpus of Nietzsche's writings it appears more than once. If Section 125 of the *Joyful Wisdom*, entitled "The Madman," is the most important version of the theme, the theme reappears again in various places, particularly in *Zarathustra* and the *Posthumous Fragments*. It is not certain in fact that, as we shall see later, we should treat all the occurrences as equivalent.

At any rate, if the theme that "God is dead" has important but unrelated historical antecedents, the topos does not become obsessive, but more importantly does not acquire significant variations, until the Romantics. The young Hegel, for example, will remind his readers that Pascal had already anticipated that theme. Nevertheless, for Hegel, the theme belongs to modernity:

Formerly, the infinite grief only existed historically in the formative process of culture. It existed historically as the feeling that "God Himself is dead" upon which the religion of more recent times rests; the same feeling that Pascal expressed in, so to speak, sheerly empirical form: *"la nature est telle qu'elle* marque *partout un Dieu* perdu." By marking this feeling as a moment of the supreme Idea, the pure concept must give philosophical existence to what used to be either the moral precept that we must sacrifice the empirical being or the concept of formal abstraction. Thereby, it must re-establish for philosophy the Idea of absolute freedom and along with it the absolute Passion, the speculative Good Friday in place of the historic Good Friday. Good Friday must be speculatively re-established in the whole truth and harshness of its Godforsakenness.[1]

Anticipating for a moment, we may already note the characteristically Christian form that the theme takes in Hegel, who metaphorically connects the topos of God's death with the Christian Passion. The theme of "God is dead," in fact, grounds the birth of a certain philosophy—Hegel's—but this grounding has to follow the particular pattern set by the Gospels for Christ's death: that, in fact, God's death announces the death of religion and of a number of philosophies—specifically, Kant's and Fichte's—to be resurrected at the end of a unique process in the glorified luminous, timeless, body of Hegel's own philosophical discourse.

The double function of speculation is that of bringing back to a privileged incorruptible form of life an older philosophical discourse that died from its incapacity to overcome a corruptible materiality, and to contemplate the final luminous spatial manifestation of the new philosophy. It is worth noting, however, that the basic narrative pattern that will ground the advent of the new philosophy is the Christian model of the narrative of the Passion, namely death/entombment/resurrection. It is the existence of the Christian model that permits the transubstantiation of religion into philosophy and the rebirth of the old philosophy into the new.

Since the variations that the theme may take are important and significant, one must be careful not to disregard the specific aspects that the topos may take in individual poets or thinkers. Schiller, who was among the earliest of the Romantics to use the theme, in opposition to Hegel, places it in a strictly Greek context. Part of his poem "The Gods of Greece," neglected today but popular in the nineteenth century, in an awkward Victorian translation reads thus:

Beauteous World, where art thou gone? Oh, thou,
Nature's blooming youth, return once more!
Ah, but in Song's fairy region now
Lives thy fabled trace so dear of yore!
Cold and perish'd, sorrow now the plains,
Not one Godhead greets my longing sight;
Ah, the Shadow only now remains
Of yon living Image bright! . . .
                    . . .
All that's bright and fair they've taken too,
Ev'ry colour, ev'ry living tone,—
And a soulless world is all we view.
Borne off by the Time-flood's current strong,
                    . . .
All that is to live in endless song,
Must in Life-time first be drown'd![2]

The contrast with Hegel is striking. Even though the disappearance of the Greek gods constitutes the genesis of Schiller's text—since the poem is the nostalgic evocation, the "song that mourns," inscribed by the trace (*Spur*) left by their absence—Schiller's world does not have the possibility of a resurrection; the past lost forever dooms the modern poet to a belatedness that divides history into two distinct moments: one of Gods and "golden years of nature," and one of elegiac poets and presumably art. Nature for Schiller does not belong to the same temporal category as art. We can begin to see how the choice of the versions of the theme of the Death of God organizes different narrative structures that in turn will produce different "Histories." Thus if, for Schiller, belatedness conditions the idiom of the artist, for Hegel belatedness is necessarily philosophical according to a scheme that localizes art and religion in an equivalent temporal moment. At any rate, Hegel and Schiller are useful because they provide us with early examples of the two fundamental centers—Greek and Christian—around which the topos will organize itself throughout the nineteenth century before taking a more generic form with Nietzsche. The two centers are not always clearly distinguishable. If Keats, in the "Hyperion" and "The Fall of Hyperion" fragments, resorts to a Greek model, in as complex a poet as Hölderlin the theme of the withdrawal of the Divine often uses the Greek model, but at times, as Szondi has shown, the Greek and Christian models are indistinguishable.[3] The best known version—and certainly the most popular version in the nineteenth century—of the theme before Nietzsche is Jean-Paul's, which was translated into French by Mme de Stael and influenced Vigny's and Nerval's treatment of the topos.[4] Jean-Paul's text was also translated more than once into English, the most famous English version probably being Carlyle's.

Jean-Paul's Christian version of the topos is particularly interesting because, in contrast to Hegel, he uses in a paradoxical fashion the Christian model to propose a nonredemptive, noneschatological form of history. Jean-Paul's text is worth quoting at some length. In Carlyle's version it reads:

I passed through unknown Shadows, on whom ancient centuries were impressed.—All the Shadows were standing round the empty Altar; and in all, not the heart, but the breast quivered and pulsed. One dead man only, who had just been buried there, still lay on his coffin without quivering breast; and on his smiling countenance stood a happy dream. But at the entrance of one Living, he awoke, and smiled no longer; he lifted his heavy eyelids, but within was no eye; and in his beating breast there lay, instead of a heart, a wound. He held up his hands and folded them to pray; but the arms lengthened out and dissolved; and the hands, still folded together, fell away. Above, on the Church-dome, stood the dialplate of *Eternity*, whereon no number appeared, and which was its own index: but a black finger pointed thereon, and the Dead sought to see the time by it.

Now sank from aloft a noble, high Form, with a look of uneffaceable sorrow, down to the Altar, and all the Dead cried out, "Christ! is there no God?" He answered, "There is none!" The whole Shadow of each then shuddered, not the breast alone; and one after the other, all, in this shuddering, shook into pieces.

Christ continued: "I went through the Worlds, I mounted into the Suns, and flew with the Galaxies through the wastes of Heaven; but there is no God! I descended as far as Being casts its shadow, and looked down into the Abyss and cried, Father where art thou? But I heard only the everlasting storm which no one guides, and the gleaming Rainbow of Creation hung without a Sun that made it, over the Abyss, and trickled down. And when I looked up to the immeasurable world for the Divine *Eye*, it glared on me with an empty, black, bottomless *Eye-socket;* and Eternity lay upon Chaos, eating it and ruminating it. Cry on, ye Dissonances; cry away the Shadows, for He is not!"[5]

We can now observe how the topos of the Death of God is, in fact, governed in either the Greek or Christian version by a more fundamental opposition. The topos can be used to allegorize a redemptive eschatological history grounded in a privileged narrative, as in Hegel, or on the contrary used, as in Keats or Jean-Paul, to deny the very possibility of an eschatological end, a privileged *Telos* to history, and hence to problematize the very nature of narrative.

That the theme of the Death of God, whatever else it may signify in any one particular author, allegorizes the specific temporal mode that governs narrative and hence history is made explicit by one of the more interesting and neglected versions of the topos, namely Flaubert's in *The Temptation of Saint Anthony.*

Flaubert's variant offers a number of unique characteristics. Flaubert, instead of writing of the Death of God, transforms the theme into the death of the gods. This change allows him to portray as a history, as a narrative history, a topos that deals with the temporal modes of history. Like Hegel's, Flaubert's history moves from East to West. First he describes the death of the gods of India, then the death of those of Persia followed by those of Egypt and Greece. Unlike Hegel's, the movement of history is not a redemptive one. Instead of placing at the end of his series the triumphant appearance of a "true" philosophical or theological discourse, he situates his literary description in the belated moments of a decaying history.

The different moments of Flaubert's history are interesting in themselves. The Buddha dies within the context of a cyclic history: "And having in this last existence, preached the law, nothing now remains for me to do. The great period is accomplished! Men, animals, the gods, the bamboos, the oceans, the mountains, the sand-grains of the Ganges, together with the myriad myriad of the stars,—all shall die;—and until the time of the new births, a flame shall dance upon the wrecks of worlds destroyed!"[6] The death of the Egyptian gods ending with the death of Isis is, on the other hand, inscribed in a linear history that leaves in its wake only archaeological ruins: "The breath of Typhon devours the pyramids. . . . Egypt! Egypt! Thy great motionless gods have their shoulders already whitened by the dung of birds; and the wind that passes over the desert rolls with it and the ashes of thy dead!"[7]

If, in the Egyptian context, nature becomes the antithetical enemy of history, it is this same nature that decrees the necessary nonredemptive nature of history. The death of the Greek gods is preceded by a voice which "rises, indistinct and awful like the far roar of waves, like the voice of forests in time of tempests, like the mighty moaning of the wind among the precipices" and states: "We knew these things!—We knew them! There must come an end even for the Gods! Uranus was mutilated by Saturn,—Saturn by Jupiter. And Jupiter himself shall be annihilated. Each in his turn;—it is Destiny!"[8]

The Flaubertian Greek gods, in a gesture not unrelated to the withdrawal of the Divine in Hölderlin's poetry, do not die but withdraw to leave behind the last remnants of a history whose law is one of decay and corruption. Jupiter withdraws, saying: "I no longer desire to receive those [the souls] of men. Let the Earth keep them; and let them move upon the level of its baseness. Their hearts are now the hearts of slaves;—they forget injuries, forget their ancestors, forget their oaths,—and everywhere the folly of crowds, the mediocrity of individuals, the hideousness of races, hold sway!"[9]

The withdrawal of Apollo into what Flaubert calls "pure thought"—"No! enough of forms! Further, higher!—to the very summit!—to the realm of pure thought"[10]—will make it impossible for the belated history to succeed as an artistic undertaking. The final moment in the episode of the history of the death of the gods coincides with Hegel's and describes the death of the Christian God, but his death places a nihilistic void at the place of, and an answer to, Hegel's triumphant philosophy: "Woe! Woe! the Holy of Holies is open, the veil is rent, the perfumes of the holocaust are dissipated by all the winds of heaven! The jackal whines in the sepulchres; my temple is destroyed; my people dispersed! . . . An enormous silence follows—the deepest night."[11] Flaubert's narrative of the death/withdrawal/disappearance of the gods is a historical narrative that, by sequentially stratifying a number of possible temporal models for history, constitutes a historical allegory with an absolute nihilistic end associated with the impossibility of a Christian redemptive history. If such a historical allegory emblematizes the belated situation of the modern artist, the latter's temporal position does not coincide with the nihilistic moment of the disappearance of the Christian God but instead with that of the withdrawal of Apollo that renders the Idea—Flaubert's expression for absolute form—hopelessly beyond the reach of the modern artist. As we shall see later, the emblematization of the belatedness of the modern associated with the nostalgic valorization of an impossible art form, through the figure of Apollo, is not unique to Flaubert—it is, in fact, Keats who offers us the most complex version of the problem, which is significant in relationship to the Hegelian model of the topos.

Hegel's Christian redemptive scheme in the last analysis is the basis for the final dialectical sublation of history and of art as well into the domain of philosophical discourse. As the ending of the *Phenomenology* makes clear, philosophical discourse is to climax a history in which art represents a single moment. Flaubert's narrative, then, on the face of it, is a parody of the Hegelian project. Like Hegel, Flaubert writes a "history" that appears to have the same orientation as Hegel's. Flaubert's "history," however, is constituted by a series of disconnected and different histories that are grounded in an artistic—and not philosophical—text. It is the Apollonian moment and not the Christian moment that makes the narrative possible. Yet the possibility opened by the Apollonian moment, by allegorizing the nonredemptive nature of the history by which it is constituted, states the future impossibility—or the impossible future—of dialectically sublating philosophical discourse.

An appreciation of the radicality of the Flaubertian gesture could be aided by a parenthetical digression. As is well known, in his *Aesthetics*—and in the *Phenomenology* as well—for Hegel Greek art represents a supreme moment in his philosophic narrative; if there is any nostalgia in Hegel for the loss of the Hellenic past, it is more than compensated by the future hope that this disappearance is a necessary movement toward the ultimate spiritual appearance of philosophy, which alone has the power to transform the material reality of nature and human history into a spiritual concept. Within Greek art one particularly privileged moment for Hegel is the statuary of Greek gods. The statuary is privileged because in it Greek art succeeds in achieving a *mimetic* moment between spirit and matter, form and content.

This shape assumed obtains its pure form, the form belonging to spirit, by the whole being raised into the sphere of the pure notion. It is not the crystal, belonging as we saw to the level of understanding, a form which housed and covered a lifeless element, or is shown upon externally by a soul. Nor, again, is it that commingling of the forms of nature and thought, which first arose in connexion with plants, thought's activity here being still an imitation. Rather the notion strips off the remnant of root, branches, and leaves, still clinging to the forms, purifies the forms, and makes them into figures in which the crystal's straight lines and surfaces are raised into incommensurable relations, so that the animation of the organic is taken up into the abstract form of understanding, and, at the same time, its essential nature—incommensurability—is preserved for understanding.[12]

Before Greek statuary, art for Hegel has two alternatives. One alternative is a form of imitation that adheres so much to its natural objects as to be incapable of a separation that allows a reflexive identity of form and content. The threat of such art is, of course, that by being too identical with its object it will not create enough of a difference between them to allow philosophy to dialectically sublate that difference.

The other alternative is symbolical art, which, as in the case of the Egyptian pyramids—identified in the *Aesthetics* with natural crystals—can only signify by symbolizing the act of signification—such a symbolization always implying an absence. The problem, of course, is that in the *Encyclopaedia* Hegel identifies poetic language with symbolical representation. For Hegel the poetical image is inseparable qua image from an object upon which it, so to speak, grafts itself. In Hegel's words: "when imagination elevates the internal meaning to an image and intuition, and this is expressed by saying that it gives the former the character of an *existent,* the phrase must not seem surprising that intelligence makes itself *be* as a *thing.*" Then in the *Zusatz* Hegel comments:

This conditioned, only relatively free, activity of intelligence we call *symbolic* imagination. This selects for the expression of its general ideas only that sensuous material whose independent signification corresponds to the specific content of the universal to be symbolized. . . . *poetic* imagination, though it is freer than the plastic arts in its use of materials, may only select such sensuous material as is adequate to the content of the idea to be represented. . . . The sign must be regarded as a great advance on the symbol.[13]

Hegel denies to poetry the abstract proprieties of signs. Symbols remain attached to objects in all their corporeity and materiality, yet since these objects are used to signify, they are not adequate to the reality of the objects, that is, their essence, and hence come to represent the absence of the truth of the objects that they represent; they lack what in another context Hegel calls their "soul," and the poetical language that uses them resists the effort of philosophical sign language to "resurrect" them in the spiritual atemporal form of the concept.

This curious identification between the Egyptian pyramids and poetical language is, then, only paradoxical. In both cases the act of signification is doomed for Hegel because the absence inscribed by symbolical representation is not sublatable, or so to speak, resurrectable into a philosophic concept. In other words—and in the *Encyclopaedia* Hegel's quarrel is with his contemporary lyrical poetical idioms— poetry cannot recuperate into its language the objects it represents, but can only allegorize their loss in representation, their "death" which even philosophy may not be able to resurrect in its own discourse. The privilege of Greek statuary based on a mimetic reflexive identity between form and content over Romantic poetry is understandable. For Hegel such a mimesis can offer philosophical discourse the opportunity to reerase the distance between form and content in the spiritual unity of the concept, a possibility denied by the symbolic nature of poetry.

Let us return to Flaubert. The death of Apollo, more exactly the withdrawal of Apollo, allegorizes the impossibility of any identity between form and content and disrupts any possibility of mimetic recuperation in representation. For Flaubert the artistic act can only assert its necessary failure, but the failed artistic act remains privileged over a hopelessly impossible philosophical discourse. In short, for Flaubert the necessarily failed artistic act points to an epistemological nihilism that would make any philosophical discourse, in the Hegelian sense, impossible. This impossibility is inscribed in the reversal of the Christian redemptive version of the topos of the Death of God as used by Hegel.

Flaubert's version of the Death of God in many ways prefigures Nietzsche's version, which can in fact be read as an extreme radicalization of Flaubert's. For our purposes it would be useful to isolate the form that the topos takes in section 125 of *The Joyful Wisdom*. In spite of its length, the section deserves to be quoted in its entirety, particularly since it is difficult to break its narrative line.

*The Madman.*—Have you ever heard of the madman who on a bright morning lighted a lantern and ran to the market-place calling out unceasingly: "I seek

God! I seek God!"—As there were many people standing about who did not believe in God, he caused a great deal of amusement. Why! is he lost? said one. Has he strayed away like a child? said another. Or does he keep himself hidden? Is he afraid of us? Has he taken a sea-voyage? Has he emigrated?—the people cried out laughingly, all in a hubbub. The insane man jumped into their midst and transfixed them with his glances. "Where is God gone?" he called out. "I mean to tell you! We have killed him,—you and I! We are all his murderers! But how have we done it? How were we able to drink up the sea? Who gave us the sponge to wipe away the whole horizon? What did we do when we loosened this earth from its sun? Whither does it now move? Whither do we move? Away from all suns? Do we not dash unceasingly? Backwards, sideways, forwards, in all directions? Is there still an above and below? Do we not stray, as through infinite nothingness? Does not empty space breathe upon us? Has it not become colder? Does not night come on continually, darker and darker? Shall we not have to light lanterns in the morning? Do we not hear the noise of the grave-diggers who are burying God? Do we not smell the divine putrefaction?—for even Gods putrefy! God is dead! God remains dead! And we have killed him! How shall we console ourselves, the most murderous of all murderers? The holiest and the mightiest that the world has hitherto possessed, has bled to death under our knife,—who will wipe the blood from us? With what water could we cleanse ourselves? What lustrums, what sacred games shall we have to devise? Is not the magnitude of this deed too great for us? Shall we not ourselves have to become Gods, merely to seem worthy of it? There never was a greater event,—and on account of it, all who are born after us belong to a higher history than any history hitherto!"—Here the madman was silent and looked again at his hearers; they also were silent and looked at him in surprise. At last he threw his lantern on the ground, so that it broke in pieces and was extinguished. "I come too early," he then said, "I am not yet at the right time. This prodigious event is still on its way, and is travelling,—it has not yet reached men's ears. Lightning and thunder need time, the light of the stars needs time, deeds need time, even after they are done, to be seen and heard. This deed is as yet further from them than the furthest star,—*and yet they have done it!*"—It is further stated that the madman made his way into different churches on the same day, and there intoned his *Requiem aeternam Deo*. When led out and called to account, he always gave the reply: "What are these churches now, if they are not the tombs and monuments of God?"[14]

Nietzsche's pronouncement that "God is dead" is placed in the context of a narrative that we may describe—following Paul de Man's charac-terization of Nietzsche's *Truth and Illusion in an Extra-Moral Sense*— as a sort of *Conte Philosophique*. The two texts are, in a certain way, related. We must question, first, the necessity of the fable: in what way does section 125 of *The Joyful Wisdom* differ from the simple statement "God is dead" or from the way in which the statement appears a number of times in Nietzsche's work?

I do not intend in this context to analyze the passage in great detail, but simply to question the function and the necessity of the narrative element in the passage.

Section 125 of *The Joyful Wisdom,* in spite of the apparent surface logic of the fable, is a tale about telling tales—a narrative about narrative. The fable tells about the impossible conditions of telling the tale of "The Death of God." The narrative is thus simultaneously a *"mise en abîme"* of narrative, yet a *mise en abîme* that does not simply reflect the table infinitely into itself, but states the impossibility of the reflexive moment; this impossibility constitutes the very temporality of the narrative. In other words, the fable tells a tale, but the tale that is told tells of the impossibility of telling the tale of the Death of God. The event always precedes the narrative moment—"we have killed him"— which states that the understanding of what the narrative tells will always follow it: "This prodigious event is still on its way, and is travelling—it has not yet reached men's ears." The narrative thus unravels its own incapacity to re-present the event it narrates.

The cosmological reference at the center of the text, emblematizing the nonredemptive and nontheological nature of a history into which the impossible narrative of the Death of God is inscribed, echoes the opening paragraphs of *Truth and Illusion in an Extra-Moral Sense.* The two texts are more closely related than one might suspect. *Truth and Illusion* is on the surface a "philosophical" text dealing with the impossibility for re-presentation to be perceptually, linguistically, or conceptually adequate to the object it is meant to represent. In its development, however, *Truth and Illusion* develops a tale which uses a literary narrative form to undermine its status as a philosophical text. In de Man's words:

The wisdom of the text is self-destructive (art is true but truth kills itself), but this self-destruction is infinitely displaced in a series of successive rhetorical reversals, which by the endless repetition of the same figure, keep it suspended between truth and the death of this truth. A threat of immediate destruction stating itself as a figure of speech, thus becomes the permanent repetition of this threat. Since this repetition is a temporal event, it can be narrated sequentially, but what it narrates, the subject matter of the story, is itself a mere figure.[15]

Section 125 of *The Joyful Wisdom* is a philosophical tale that confirms de Man's analysis of *Truth and Illusion*. It is a literary narrative that states the incapacity of narration to represent the event of the Death of God, making of the Death of God the allegory of this incapacity. The "literariness" of Nietzsche's text consists of undercutting its own grounding, thus not allowing philosophical discourse to sublate the Death of God even in a nonredemptive nihilistic history. Nietzsche's Death of God is then doubly a critique of Hegel's version. First by its narrative form it denounces any possibility of a redemptive history, but more important, perhaps, it prevents, by stating the impossibility of representing the event it narrates, the possibility of any philosophical discourse to dialectically sublate it.

Nietzsche in the literary strategy of his tale implicates the reader as well—"Have you ever heard of the madman . . ."; the fable tells the reader of an event in which he is implicated that precedes his awareness of that event. Inasmuch as the reader is implied in the constitution of the signification of the text—its *Bedeutung*—there is no way in which the constitution of such a signification could temporally coincide with the event that generates it. Nor can the reader grasp the meaning of an event that is projected in an indefinite future. The text literally breaks the circle of the "hearing oneself speak" that is at the heart of the Hegelian model of the way language constitutes its significations.[16] At best the text records the memory of an event and constitutes itself into "the tombs and funerary monuments" whose voice is a temporally indefinite *Requiem aeternam Deo!*

Voice is a privileged aspect of language in any recuperative scheme. Voice erases itself in its very utterance, leaving a pure meaning uncontaminated by the materiality of language. Voice in its ideal form of solitary speech gives a perfectly circular form to any utterance: such a circularity is necessary to its erasure, since it does not allow for the intrusion of the otherness of the listener in the constitution of meaning. Nietzsche's narrative succeeds in breaking the circular pattern of speech and remains suspended between the narrator and his readers, the protagonist and his listeners. The breaking of the circularity of voice makes it impossible for the listener to invest any "meaning" in the sayings of the protagonist. The tale thus dramatizes, through its form, the impossibility for "meaning" to become constituted by means of the nondialogue it narrates, hence the relationship of the reader to the narrator of the tale stages the meaninglessness of the utterance "God is Dead." The narrative form of the statement "God is Dead" makes it impossible to invest that statement with any "philosophical meaning"—with any *Bedeutung*. If we were to follow Derrida, who reads in the Otherness introduced in the linguistic sign by any interlocutor a form of "death" inherent to language that resists sublation into a transparent meaning—then Nietzsche's tale allegorizes a form of "death" inherent to language which, in spite of Hegel, is not "resurrectable." The *Requiem aeternam Deo* is also the belated memorialization of the "corpse" of language that resists all metaphysical idealities.

I am aware that my reading runs counter to Heidegger's formidable readings of Nietzsche's saying "God is dead." I cannot in this context analyze in detail Heidegger's reading; however, a few remarks are in order. Heidegger reads, as the title of one of his essays indicates— "Nietzsche's saying 'God is dead' "—all of the instances of Nietzsche's statements "God is dead" as equivalent. This telescoping of the different instances in which the statement appears, the identification of "God" with the Christian God, the realm of values and the supersensible, allow Heidegger to equate Nietzsche's "God is dead" with a critique of metaphysics—and particularly Kantian and Hegelian metaphysics.[17] Nevertheless, it is only by treating Nietzsche's statement "God is dead" as a "philosophical" statement and making it into the emblem of the problematics of nihilism that Heidegger reads Nietzsche's "transvaluation of all values" as a metaphysical reversal of metaphysics and thus makes of Nietzsche the last metaphysical thinker, who reveals and consummates the nihilistic project implicit in Western metaphysics from the beginning. These remarks should suffice to point out that Heidegger's reading, powerful though it may be, in treating Nietzsche's discourse as a philosophical discourse never raises the question that Nietzsche's text may in fact question the possibility of having his text read in a philosophical key or *only* as a philosophical statement.

Heidegger neutralizes completely the "literariness" of Nietzsche's text, or, to say it more technically, Heidegger neutralizes the *Darstellung* of Nietzsche's text: yet in Nietzsche's narrative strategy the *Darstellung* is unavoidable. It may just be, in fact, that the *Darstellung* of section 125 of *The Joyful Wisdom* destabilizes the literary/philosophical opposition, and that the ironic space that it opens makes it impossible for the statement "God is dead" to ground a uniquely philosophical discourse, and that the statement "God is dead" undercuts the very utterance that proclaims it.

It should be clear by now from the reading that I have given of a few examples of the topos of "God is dead" that, at least, in my view the metaphor of the death of God effectively relates the problem of narrative structure to linguistic and literary representation, as inaugurated by the Romantics. I should like now to address that problem in a more specific and direct way.

> *How man became more natural in the nineteenth century . . .—not of "return to nature"—for there has never yet been a natural humanity. The scholasticism of un- and anti-natural values is the rule, is the beginning; man reaches nature only after a long struggle.* Nietzsche

> *Romantic art is only a makeshift substitute for a defective "reality."* Nietzsche

If we were to try to identify the lowest common denominator of the poetics of the major Romantics, we might easily arrive at the conclusion that their preoccupations tend toward two sets of problems. One deals with representation: specifically how can poetical or philosophical language account for nature and object. In Earl R. Wasserman's formulation: "How do subject and object meet in a meaningful relationship? By what means do we have a *significant* awareness of the world?"[18] On the other hand, through the writings of the Romantics runs a constant preoccupation with history—particularly the French Revolution—but this preoccupation itself reflects perhaps a more fundamental concern with the problem of narrative in general. Hegel's *Phenomenology,* Wordsworth's *Prelude,* Keats's "Hyperion" and "The Fall of Hyperion," and even Coleridge's *Biographia Literaria* point to the necessity of a narrative structure to ground the representational structure of the *Lyrical Ballads,* Keats's odes, or the epistemology of the *Logic* or the *Encyclopaedia.* Stated in this form, the question assumes a paradigmatic form in which lyrical representation and narrative structure cannot be isolated or treated independently of each other. Joseph N. Riddel has identified the project of a late Romantic such as Poe in terms of a strategic quest for a pure lyrical moment that would be a spatial moment unaffected by any temporal mode except for the possibility of pure repetition. In Riddel's words: "If one can call the poem an 'emblem' of the origin, it is not a representation, not secondary, but in its way an originary repetition. Pleasure, Poe argues, derives from, or is induced by, an 'identity' of sound and thought, or more accurately, by the intense repetition of a sound (the '*refrain*') that unveils the identity of sound and thought in something that precedes reference, because reference marks the belatedness of language to idea. Only the lyric poem achieves this 'identity.' " Yet, as Riddel correctly points out, such a quest for a "pure lyrical" spatialized moment is bound to fail, and its temporal component is reinscribed in the lyrical moment: "This repetition in Poe has its own aberrational moment, its madness of 'time,' its own bizarre breaking out of space, which therefore causes a perturbation in the circle of its return. . . . The language of Poesque lyric is momentarily out of control before it can return and close, or effect the intensity and brevity that can only come after the word has had its grotesque trial in time."[19] If Riddel is correct, then we may well have to ask whether in the early Romantics a "pure" lyrical moment uncontaminated by a narrative structure was ever possible after all.

For a different statement of the problem let us return to Wasserman's article, which I quoted earlier. Wasserman sees the Romantic dilemma as an epistemological one: in what way can subject and object merge together to produce meaning? At the outset the problem might seem simple; in Coleridge's words: "A Poet's Heart and Intellect should be *combined*, intimately combined and unified with the great appearances in nature"; or, "the object of art is to make the external internal, the internal external, to make Nature thought and thought Nature."[20] The first step, then, for Wasserman is to resolve the problem through perception: "What we might then expect is a system identifying perception with significant cognition and resolving the divorce between subject and object by making perception an act of self-knowledge."[21] The key word here is, of course, "significant." Even granting, for the time being, that the Romantics might have believed in the possibility of immediate perception, the question remains how this perception is transformed into "significant cognition." Wasserman senses that perception per se is not enough and that between perception and poetic representation enters another mechanism, namely that of memory. On this subject Wasserman refers to Wordsworth and adds: "The stuff of the mind . . . is incorporated into memory."[22] He could have quoted Coleridge who, contrasting Philosophy and Poetry with Mathematics, writes: "Philosophy . . . concludes with the definition: it is the result, the compendium, the remembrances of all the preceding facts and inferences."[23] But of course perception and memory are not enough to produce a poetic image. The original perception stored in memory has to be combined with another function, namely imagination. Imagination is often read as sufficient recuperative supplement to memory. In Wasserman's argument memory remains unproblematic and only a necessary step toward the final poetical recuperation in poetry of an original perception. This view may be defensible in reading the way Wasserman does a poem such as "To a Highland Girl:" it may even be defensible in a reading of "Tintern Abbey." Nevertheless, if one locates these poems in relationship to the *Prelude,* the function of memory in relation to poetical representation becomes considerably more complex. Not only does memory inscribe a necessary narrative moment within the lyrical moment, but the function of narrative is to monumentalize elements that do not remain intact as they are translated through memory. The function of narrative is none other than to restitute in representation what of the original experience is lost through memory. In Wordsworth's words:

. . . The days gone by
Return upon me almost from the dawn
Of life: the hiding-places of man's power
Open; I would approach them, but they close.
I see by glimpses now; when age comes on,
May scarcely see at all; and I would give,
While yet we may, as far as words can give,
Substance and life to what I feel, enshrining,
Such is my hope, the spirit of the Past
For future restoration.[24]

(12: 277–86)

Wasserman's argument is centered on the perception/memory/imagination system, and understandably, insofar as his ultimate implicit project is to show that the Romantics epistemologically were successful in recuperating what in another context de Man will call the "Natural Object." De Man's project is, of course, the opposite of Wasserman's. De Man, starting from the premise that a poetical representation is necessarily a linguistic representation, convincingly demonstrates that language cannot representationally recuperate the Natural Object and hence that Romantic poetics are, in fact, centered around the nostalgia for its loss. In his words: "Critics who speak of a 'happy relationship' between matter and consciousness fail to realize that the very fact that the relationship has to be established within the medium of language indicates that it does not exist in actuality"; hence, "The image is inspired by a nostalgia for the natural object. . . . The existence of the poetic image is itself a sign of divine absence, and the conscious use of poetic imagery an admission of this absence."[25]

De Man does not quote Coleridge but he could have, for already Coleridge had sensed some of the problems raised by linguistic representation. In "On Poesy or Art," for example, Coleridge writes:

> Still, however, poetry can only act through the intervention of articulate speech, which is so peculiarly human that in all languages it constitutes the ordinary phrase by which man and nature are contradistinguished.
> . . . As soon as the human mind is intelligibly addressed by an outward image exclusively of articulate speech, so soon does art commence . . . so that not the thing presented, but that which is re-presented by the thing, shall be the source of pleasure.[26]

Coleridge's ultimate gesture might be recuperative, nevertheless his critical strength resides in his recognizing that linguistic representation is necessarily metaphorical and that such a representational system introduces a set of differences irreducible to absolute identity:

> It is sufficient that philosophically we understand that in all imitation two elements must coexist, and not only coexist, but must be perceived as coexisting. These two constituent elements are likeness and unlikeness, or sameness and difference, and in all genuine creations of art there must be a union of these disparates. The artist may take his point of view where he pleases, provided that the desired effect be perceptibly produced,—that there be likeness in the difference, difference in the likeness, and a reconcilement of both in one.[27]

It should be clear by now that what I shall call the "lyric moment" is a metaphorical construct based on representation that goes from the Natural Object to the final linguistic re-presentation via a system that combines perception/memory/imagination. I have tried to show elsewhere the problems raised by each of these terms in Romantic poetry and how in specific texts one can find the allegorization of the way each of these terms fails to maintain the mechanism of identity necessary to "recuperate" the Natural Object and how in fact each of the terms implies a tropological mechanism of re-presentation. I have also tried to show that the canonic form of the paradigm is given to us by Hegel, for whom, allowing for some simplification, the system takes this form: Intuition (Hegel's equivalent for perception)/Representation (*Vorstellung*)/Recollection (*Erinnerung*)/Representation Proper/Imagination/Allegory/Sign/Memory(*Gedächtnis*)/Speech/Concept.  Without analyzing the complete system in detail, I should like to simply underscore a few of the problems raised by some of these terms in particular and by the broader paradigm in general.

To begin with, the immediacy of the object is lost in the first of the terms, namely intuition. Intuition introduces from the beginning a temporal displacement: "In representation mind *has* intuition; the latter is *ideally present* in mind, it has not vanished or merely *passed away*. Therefore, when speaking of an intuition that has been raised to a representation, language is quite correct in saying I *have* seen this." Hegel will predictably dialectically reduce the temporal displacement to a spatial identity. Nevertheless, by translating Hegel into another language we can say a temporal narrative structure is inscribed in the spatial moment of perception. Significantly Hegel will mark this inextricable interrelationship of spatial and temporal elements in representation with the very mark of modernity: "In this use of the word 'have' can be seen a sign of the inwardness of the modern mind, which makes the reflection, not merely that the past in its immediacy has passed away but also that in mind the past is still preserved."[28]

However, the more critical term in Hegel's system is *Erinnerung,* which is more akin to Wordsworth's memory than *Gedächtnis,* which is a linguistic, archival, nonsubjective memory. If *Erinnerung* is central to the Hegelian system of representation, *Erinnerung* is also central to Hegel's concept of history. At the end of the *Phenomenology, Erinnerung* becomes the condition by which history recapitalizes itself and transcends itself into absolute knowledge, that is, philosophical discourse:

The goal, which is Absolute Knowledge or Spirit Knowing itself as Spirit, finds its pathway in the recollection of spiritual forms as they are in themselves and as they accomplish the organization of their spiritual kingdom. Their conservation, looked at from the side of their free existence appearing in the form of contingency, is *History;* looked at from the side of their intellectually comprehended organization, it is the Science of the ways in which Knowledge appears.

And it is no accident that, at this precise point in his argument, Hegel should resort again to the metaphor of the Death of God in its Christian redemptive form:

Both together, or History intellectually comprehended, form at once the recollection and the Golgotha of Absolute Spirit, the reality, the truth, the certainty of its throne, without which it were lifeless, solitary, and alone. Only

The chalice of this realm of spirits
Foams forth to God His own Infinitude.[29]

It is around the concept of *Erinnerung,* then, that narrative and representation become mutually interdependent; the paradigm of one determines the nature of the other. If the function of the Christian metaphor of death and resurrection provides the possibility of a redemptive narrative history, that same redemptive history will make a final recuperative representational system possible. Conversely, the postulation of a nonredemptive scheme for narrative and history will radically question the recuperative possibilities of representation.

It is no accident that in the *Encyclopaedia,* in describing its representational system, Hegel's metaphors associated with *Erinnerung* should be metaphors of burial and entombment. *Erinnerung* transforms intelligence into a "night-like mine or pit" or a "subconscious mine." Hegel concludes his discussion of *Erinnerung* by stating: "No one knows what an infinite host of images of the past slumbers in him; now and then they do indeed accidentally awake, but one cannot as it is said call them to mind."[30] It is interesting to note that Alexandre Kojève, in one of the most important commentaries to the *Phenomenology,* should see in *Erinnerung* the threat of nihilism. What if the recollected should never be brought up to consciousness; what if one should forget what is forgotten or, to borrow Hegel's metaphor, what if what is entombed should never be resurrected?

With Hegel we do not have to fear the threat of nihilism. The same dialectic of sublation that permits him to resurrect history into philosophy will permit him to resurrect the representations buried by *Erinnerung* into symbol and sign, and eventually the sign itself will have to be elevated to the status of philosophical ideality, a concept without body or, rather, having the transparent matter, the free status of a glorified body. In Hegel's terms a philosophical ideality is "the negation of the real which is nevertheless conserved and maintained in a virtual fashion (*virtualiter erhalter*) even if it does not exist."[31]

What one might begin to suspect is that the very model of the Hegelian dialectic is based on the Christian metaphor of death and resurrection. That which is sublated has to first be negated and maintained in its sublated form only as a negation of its original actuality. As Derrida has so forcefully stated, the Hegelian dialectic is a "theory of death," being "the thought that masters corruption and death, the determination of negativity and its conversion in the power of work and of production, the capacity to assume the contradictory and sublation as the very process of the self-conception of Truth and of the Subject." As we said earlier, the dialectical process must not only sublate Nature and History but linguistic representation as well.

To quote Derrida again, for Hegel "natural language bears and affects within itself the sign of its own death; its body is suited for resonating and in so doing for raising its natural corpse to the height of the concept, for universalizing and rationalizing it in the very time of its decomposition."[32]

It should be obvious that to question the redemptive possibility of the metaphor of the Death of God is to question the redemptive possibility of the dialectic in general. Such a critical project, be it in Flaubert or in Derrida, will necessarily consist of showing that any attempt to sublate "the real," "the Natural Object," or "language" always erects their texts as the allegories of funerary monuments that hide the decomposing corpses that lie within them.

Let us return briefly, however, to the problem of Romantic poetics. Hegel's philosophical idealities have an equivalent in a number of statements of the Romantics regarding the function of poetic speech to transform nature into something of a spiritual nature, in Keats's words, "symbol essences," or in Wordsworth's happier expression— "spiritual presences":

. . . by contemplating these Forms [i.e., of Nature]
In his relation which they bear to man
We shall discern, how through the various means
Which silently they yield, are multiplied
The *spiritual* presences of absent things.[33]

The most striking statement about the redemptive function of poetry is Wordsworth's attributing to the imagination of the capacity to transform Nature into the

Characters of the great Apocalypse,
The types and symbols of Eternity,
Of first, and last, and midst, and without end.
(6: 638–40)

Wasserman may be too hasty in identifying Wordsworth's epistemological wishes with Keats's poetical enterprise. If I may digress for a moment, the lines that precede the preceding verses which describe a privileged nature in the Simplon Pass are often read by critics—including de Man—as one of the most successful poetical attempts by Wordsworth to poetically recapture a transcendental nature. Wordsworth's description reads:

> . . . The immeasurable height
> Of woods decaying, never to be decayed,
> The stationary blasts of waterfalls,
> And in the narrow rent at every turn
> Winds thwarting winds, bewildered and forlorn,
> The torrents shooting from the clear blue sky,
> The rocks that muttered close upon our ears,
> Black drizzling crags that spake by the wayside
> As if a voice were in them, the sick sight
> And giddy prospect of the raving stream,
> The unfettered clouds and region of the Heavens,
> Tumult and peace, the darkness and the light—
> Were all like workings of one mind, the features
> Of the same face, blossoms upon one tree; . . .
>
> (6: 624–37)

Leaving aside the fact that the lines are inspired by Milton, Wordsworth's strategy beyond imagination is to place his Nature and his Text into a transcendental voice—"As if a voice were in them";—it is the ideality of the *voice* that guarantees the ultimate identification of Poetical idiom and Nature.[34] Curiously, at the beginning of book 2 of "Hyperion," Keats has a similar passage also inspired by Milton:

> It was a den where no insulting light
> Could glimmer on their tears; where their own groans
> They felt, but heard not, for the solid roar
> Of thunderous waterfalls and torrents hoarse,
> Pouring a constant bulk, uncertain where.
> Crag jutting forth to crag, and rocks that seemed
> Ever as if just rising from a sleep,
> Forehead to forehead held their monstrous horns;
> And thus in thousand hugest fantasies
> Made a fit roofing to this nest of woe.
>
> (2: 5–15)

Keats denies light to his scene and drowns the voice of the Titans in the meaningless *noise* of Nature. The poetical rendition remains then either a vision inadequate to its object or states the incapacity of such a Nature to idealize itself in poetry. In either case, Keats's project can be read as an unintentional rebuttal of Wordsworth's poetic strategy.[35]

Wordsworth, nonetheless, is particularly interesting because, as I said earlier, his poetical enterprise is articulated around the *Lyrical Ballads* and the *Prelude*. The related quests for a lyrical moment and a redemptive narration parallel Hegel's enterprise. Like Hegel, at the end of the *Prelude* Wordsworth will have his version of the ascent of the Golgotha in his climb of Mount Snowdon. It is the climb of Mount Snowdon which, by recollecting past memories, will make the narrative of the *Prelude* possible and ultimately, though retrospectively, ground the *Lyrical Ballads*. It is also during this climb of Mount Snowdon that he discovers Nature's capacity to resurrect itself into a spiritual timeless body:

. . . which Nature thus
To bodily sense exhibits, is the express
Resemblance of that glorious faculty
That higher minds bear with them as their own.
This is the very spirit in which they deal
With the whole compass of the universe:
They from their native selves can send abroad
Kindred mutations; for themselves create
A like existence; and, whene'er it dawns
Created for them, catch it, or are caught
By its inevitable mastery,
Like angels stopped upon the wing by sound
Of harmony from Heaven's remotest spheres.
Them the enduring and the transient both
Serve to exalt; they build up greatest things
From least suggestions; ever on the watch,
Willing to work and to be wrought upon,
They need not extraordinary calls
To rouse them; in a world of life they live,
By sensible impressions not enthralled,
But by their quickening impulse made more prompt
To hold fit converse with the spiritual world,
And with the generations of mankind

Spread over time, past, present, and to come,
Age after age, till Time shall be no more.

(14: 88–111)

Nevertheless, it is worth noticing that even the recuperative lyrical stance generated by a redemptive narrative produces only a "resemblance" and "emblem"—"There I beheld the emblem of a mind"—and not the "object," the "experience," their nature, or their essence.

There is no doubt that Wordsworth strives to be a redemptive poet. Nevertheless, as I said earlier, what makes him interesting is the constant insistence throughout his poetry that the poetic act may fail. Even the climb of Mount Snowdon is not without shadows. The scene takes place at night by the reflected indirect light of the moon in front of a metaphorical abyss—"A fixed abysmal gloomy, breathing-place." It could be argued, in fact, that Wordsworth's constant metaphysical assertions are a necessarily repeated answer to the constant threat of a nonredemptive history. Be that as it may, it will not be long after Wordsworth that Keats will question the status of poetical vision and ask whether the language of poetry belongs to the poet or the visionary. Minimally in "Hyperion" and "The Fall of Hyperion," Keats will dramatically question any possibility of a redemptive history and assert once and for all, "We fall by course of Nature's law."

Before leaving this subject, I should like to return once more to Wasserman's article, "The English Romantics: The Grounds of Knowledge." Wasserman begins his article by invoking Humpty Dumpty's "principle of semantic wages" and, fearing lest we use the word Romanticism (at "a good deal of extra pay"), he rhetorically shies away from it and declares instead his subject to be the epistemologies of Wordsworth, Coleridge, Keats, and Shelley. Since the publication of Wasserman's article in 1964, we have not only learned to be less coy but in fact—after Bloom, Szondi, Nancy, Lacoue-Labarthe, and others—have come to realize the necessity of defining the novelty of Romanticism.

Perhaps instead of invoking Lewis Carroll, Wasserman should have gone further back to the original narrative of the nursery rhyme. If the Romantics inaugurated a new literary problematic, the latter is perhaps related to the belated recognition that the Natural Object, like Humpty Dumpty, "had a great fall" and remains hopelessly shattered in fragments. If Wordsworth might have had the nostalgia for a redemptive history that could put the pieces of Humpty Dumpty together again, Keats, Shelley, and Hölderlin point to such a redemptive history as a theological mirage leaving us with the recognition that "All the King's horses and all the King's men could not put Humpty together again." What we must understand is that the shattering of Humpty Dumpty was the necessary prior condition for his tale to be told and repeated generation after generation. That necessary repetition constitutes *our* belatedness and the most important legacy of our Romantic heritage.

> *[There was] a time when an Egyptian priest was still reproaching Solon that "the Greeks remained forever adolescent"! And we, we more intelligent than all those superb dead, are here having become old men.*   Hölderlin
>
> *How long will this posthumous life of mine last?*   Keats

If one may be allowed a bold generalization, critics have been more generous to Wordsworth, in attempting to read his poetical project by relating the *Prelude* to the rest of his lyrical output, than to Keats. Keats's project seems to have troubled critics who, on the whole, tend to valorize the odes and dismiss the "Hyperion" and "The Fall of Hyperion" fragments as ambitious failures. Wordsworth's and Keats's projects are, curiously, similar. The "Hyperion" fragments—especially if one takes into account their relationship to an early text such as "Sleep and Poetry"—frame Keats's poetical output in the same way that the *Prelude* frames Wordsworth's. The parallel is even more striking, if one considers that in both cases the longer poems are retrospective attempts to ground and justify the rest of the poets' output. The difference is not in the form of the projects but in the fact that the *Prelude*, even though in its own way a "fragment," is a "completed poem," or more exactly a "closed poem," which by a final redemptive gesture provides a genetic narrative for the rest of Wordsworth's works. In the case of Keats, "Hyperion" and "The Fall of Hyperion" not only remain fragments but raise the problem as to whether they can be "closed" in a Wordsworthian sense. Ultimately, it is easy to understand why critics have focused on Wordsworth's poetical project and read it in its intentional unity, since it permitted them to use—in an explicit or implicit fashion—the redemptive scheme of the narrative of the *Prelude* to read in a recuperative key the rest of Wordsworth's poetical output. It is the same critical stance that has forced the division of Keats's canon into two distinct groups of poems, the "successful" odes and the failed "fragments." In this respect and in the context of the problem of the relationship of narrative structure to poetical representation, it would hardly be an exaggeration to say that Keats's odes have been read mainly in the perspective of Wordsworth's poetics.

The more fundamental question that could be raised is why Keats's narrative poems are fragments, and if their failure at narrative closure is accidental or intrinsic to the Keatsian poetical project, and in the latter case, what are the consequences of the impossibility of a redemptive narrative scheme for the poetics of a Keats in particular, and for the later Romantics as well. In other words, the question I wish to raise is to what extent Keats's poetical project constitutes a critical reading of Wordsworth, and more generally, to what extent the narrative exigencies of Romantic poetry rendered vain the hopes for a lyrical idiom that would embody the transparent transfigured presence of the Natural Object.

"Sleep and Poetry" represents Keats's first attempt to provide a narrative ground for his poetical enterprise. The poem contains two long narrative sequences. The first relates the motif that will inspire the young poet from "the realm . . . / Of Flora, and old Pan" (101–2) to the "nobler life / Where I may find agonies, the strife / Of human hearts" (123–24). The second comprises a brief history of poetry in England, where Keats, after assuming the Wordsworthian critique of eighteenth-century English poetical idiom, sees hope for a new poetry: "let me think away those times of woe: / Now 'tis a fairer season; yet have breathed / Rich benedictions o'er us; ye have wreathed / Fresh garlands: for sweet music has been heard / In many places" (220–23). Both narrative sequences define the young poet's belated position; nevertheless, on the surface this belatedness does not seem problematical: "there ever rolls / A vast idea before me, and I glean / Therefrom my liberty; thence too I've seen / The end and aim of Poesy" (240–43). Yet even the youthful optimism of Keats does not lend itself to be read as the assertion of the possibility of a poetic idiom which will somehow generate representations adequate to their objects. At best the poet's words will "echo back the voice of thine [Poesy's] own tongue" (52), and thus become the repeated, secondary copies of an original voice. The image of poetical idiom as echo will naturally lead Keats to treat his poetical enterprise as that of copying from a book in which the natural object is *metaphorically displaced:* "if I can bear / The o'erwhelming sweets, 'twill bring to me the fair / Visions of all places: a bowery nook / Will be elysium—an eternal book / Whence I may copy many a lovely saying" (61–65). The vision of the poetical object is not an "original" one. The poet transcribes a vision which is itself a text, since it is a metaphorical translation of the Natural Object. It is not surprising, then, that the poem should end in a library where the visions are gathered in a portfolio: "Thus I remember all the pleasant flow / Of words at opening a portfolio" (337–38). The poem in the last analysis, then, states the impossibility of grounding poetical language in or on a Natural Object. The language of poetry will only be the translation of a metaphor that is itself a translation. Hence the central theme of the poem is the fact that there is no way for the poet to distinguish between the "visions" he creates and those that come to him in his sleep. The undecidability of the two types of visions will eventually constitute the opening lines of "The Fall of Hyperion."

Let us return for a moment to "Sleep and Poetry." The decisive moment of the failure of the poetic act, besides being thematically stated in the poem, is in fact allegorized in one of the central themes to which we alluded earlier. Keats compares the poetical act with the possibility of identifying with Apollo, himself being a metaphor of an original sun. The failure of the poet will be the failure of Icarus to reach Apollo. Icarus, with whom the poet identifies, fails as the belated son—and here one might complicate the problem further by insisting on the inevitable pun sun/son—attempting his father's impossible project. The poet's genealogical belatedness is redoubled since Apollo, rather than an absolute origin, will be the temporally belated sun/son—replacing an earlier Hyperion in a game of substitutions. Icarus is no more the proper name of the poet than the belated Apollo is the proper name for the sun. Derrida's argument that the sun is a metaphor—the metaphor that states the possibility of metaphor—is well known.[36] The gesture of the poet will be that of attempting to grasp the original metaphorical constitution of poetical language. Such a gesture will, of course, be doomed to failure. The poet like Icarus will be burned by his proximity to the original metaphoricity of metaphor.

Lifted to the white clouds. Therefore should I
Be but the essence of deformity,

A coward, did my very eye-lids wink
At speaking out what I have dared to think.
Ah! rather let me like a madman run
Over some precipice! let the hot sun
Melt my Dedalian wings, and drive me down
Convulsed and headlong! Say! an inward frown
Of conscience bids me be more calm awhile.
An ocean dim, sprinkled with many an isle,
Spreads awfully before me. How much toil!
How many days! what desperate turmoil!
Ere I can have explored its widenesses.
Ah, what a task! upon my bended knees,
I could unsay those—no, impossible!
Impossible!

(300–312)

The possibility of the Keatsian poetical idiom is rooted in this impossibility. The Natural Object will, in fact, be the constructed product that will result from the poet's death as a remembrance of his failed gesture: "If I do fall, at least I will be laid / Beneath the silence of a poplar shade; / And over me the grass shall be smooth-shaven; / And there shall be a kind memorial graven" (277–80).[37] The failure of the poetical act, nevertheless, is more radical than the poet's incapacity to reach Apollo. If Apollo as sun represents the original metaphoricity of metaphor as Derrida reminds us, such an origin never gives itself but leaves at the origin its own death in the belated metaphors of beginnings.

Let us return to the poem. The lengthy description of Apollo/sun appears in a lengthy passage that follows one of the many resolves of Keats to undertake the writing of poetry—"Yes, I must pass them [these joys] for a nobler life" (123). As it is well known after Ian Jack's book on Keats's use of the plastic arts, the passage describing Apollo in fact transcribes Poussin's painting "The Realm of Flora."[38] Apollo/sun then is already a pictorial representation, that is, a textual metaphor. Apollo as poetical origin has already died in a representation that the poet can only transcribe. In this sense the "Hyperion" and "The Fall of Hyperion" fragments are only funerary genealogies of an "always already" dead Apollo—which condemns any poetic idiom to the role of funerary renovation. The poet cannot escape his idiom's being this twice displaced representation of a metaphor, the confrontation of poetical language with "real things" being by definition a representational impossibility.

The visions all are fled—the car is fled
Into the light of heaven, and in their stead
A sense of real things comes doubly strong,
And, like a muddy stream, would bear along
My soul to nothingness.

(155–59)

The "muddy stream" resists being transcribed into the idiom of poetry or, more exactly, the otherness of the muddy stream does not allow for the vision to transform itself into poetical language.

"Sleep and Poetry" had already defined Apollo through a twice displaced metaphor as the origin of poetry and suggested the impossibility of the poet's identifying his idiom with such an origin. "Hyperion" and "The Fall of Hyperion" will radicalize this question by attempting to write the narrative genealogy of Apollo. Such a narrative will be impossible because Apollo will be, rather than an absolute origin, only one name in an infinite series of displacements; but conversely, the infinite series of displacements at the origin will render the closure of narrative impossible.

Inasmuch as the genealogy of Apollo can only be written from the standpoint of his belated appearance, the modern poet's attempt at writing an epic of origins is doomed from the start, and in at least one sense "Hyperion" and "The Fall of Hyperion" are not failures but poems about the necessary failure of a certain type of poetry. And inasmuch as they state above all the impossibility of a certain type of narrative poetry, their fragmentary nature is intrinsic to the poems:

O leave them, Muse! O leave them to their woes;
For thou art weak to sing such tumults dire:
A solitary sorrow best befits
Thy lips, and antheming a lonely grief.
Leave them, O Muse! for thou anon wilt find
Many a fallen old Divinity
Wandering in vain about bewildered shores.

"Hyperion," 3: 3–9

The new belated poetry will be the poetry of the belated God Apollo. Apollo's poetry is inextricably tied to memory–"Mnemosyne! / Thy name is on my tongue" (3: 82–83). Mnemosyne, however, is silent. Apollo's divinity, like his poetry, is based on the possibility of reading the "mute" memories held by Mnemosyne. In other words, the belated poetry of Apollo is the repetition, the rememorization of a dead past that persists representationally only with the ambiguous status of silent memories:

Mute thou remainest—mute! yet I can read
A wondrous lesson in thy silent face:
Knowledge enormous makes a God of me.
Names, deeds, grey legends, dire events, rebellions,
Majesties, sovran voices, agonies,
Creations and destroyings, all at once
Pour into the wide hollows of my brain,
And deify me, as if some blithe wine
Or bright elixir peerless I had drunk,
And so become immortal.

(3: 111–20)

It is thus from the perspective of Apollo that the tale of the earlier god is told. As I suggested, such a tale properly told would be a genealogical narrative of origins and as such an impossible tale to tell. Hence both fragments will begin the fable of the fallen gods with the description of an already fallen Saturn transformed into funerary statuary— "postured motionless, / Like natural sculpture in cathedral caverns" (1: 85–86). The poetical idiom that will describe this "natural sculpture" will be an inadequate translation of the language of mourning for a "death" that necessarily precedes the narrative. "Some mourning words, which in our feeble tongue / Would come in these like accents (O how frail / To that large utterance of the early Gods!)" (1: 49–51).

The poet's attempt at forcing his idiom on such an unrepresentable event can only violently restate his necessarily belated position.

O aching time! O moments big as years!
All as ye pass swell out the monstrous truth,
And press it so upon our weary griefs
That unbelief has not a space to breathe.

Saturn, sleep on—O thoughtless, why did I
Thus violate thy slumbrous solitude?
(1: 64–69)

The nostalgic possibility of a new origin and a final eschatology is raised and then rejected in the *Hyperion*—"Cannot I fashion forth / Another world, another universe" (1: 142–43). "Yes, there must be a golden victory" (1: 126).

The law of the narrative will be stated by Oceanus: "And first, as thou wast not the first of powers, / So art thou not the last; it cannot be: / Thou are not the beginning nor the end" (2: 188–90), thus creating an exigency for a continuous displacement without beginning or end:

. . . For 'tis the eternal law
That first in beauty should be first in might.
Yea, by that law, another race may drive
Our conquerors to mourn as we do now.
(2: 288–31)

The Apollonian moment, then, is not privileged but represents only one instance in a continuous play of substitutions. The unnarratable fall of the gods constitutes thus the impossible present of the text. Appropriately Oceanus, who states the law of the text, will be called a "Sophist and sage." In "The Fall of Hyperion" this law will be stated in a more direct way through the description of the face of Moneta herself being in the later poem the text of memory.

. . . Then saw I a wan face,
Not pined by human sorrows, but bright-blanched
By an immortal sickness which kills not;
It works a constant change, which happy death
Can put no end to; deathwards progressing
To no death was that visage; it had passed
The lily and the snow; and beyond these
I must not think now, though I saw that face.
"The Fall of Hyperion," 1: 256–63

The ambiguity of the text will stem, of course, from the fact that the nonprivilege of the Apollonian moment both stems from and engen-

ders the nonprivilege of the moment of Hyperion which precedes it.
The statement of Hyperion—

The blaze, the splendour, and the symmetry,
I cannot see—but darkness, death and darkness.
Even here, into my centre of repose,
The shady visions come to domineer,
Insult, and blind, and stifle up my pomp.—
Fall!

"Hyperion," 1: 241–46

—will prefigure the purely visionary nature of the belated poet's text.
In a sense "The Fall of Hyperion" is itself a reading of "Hyperion."
If, throughout "Hyperion," Mnemosyne was "straying in the
world," "The Fall of Hyperion" is constituted in great part by the
poetical transcription of Mnemosyne's voice as well as by that of her
belated Latin version, Moneta, "The pale Omega of a withered race."
Significantly, "The Fall of Hyperion" will never reach the Apollonian
moment but end on the ambiguous temporal status of Hyperion.

"The Fall of Hyperion" can be read as a working out of the textual
consequence of "Hyperion"—and of "Sleep and Poetry" as well. If the
impossibility of a redemptive narrative makes it impossible for
the idiom of poetry to be grounded in Nature or History, then what is
the status of the poetical text?

"The Fall of Hyperion" begins with the question, "what if any is the
distinction between mere visions and poetry?" At first there seems to
be a simple answer: poetry is the transcription of visions. Yet the very
nature of this transcription is defined by an impossible mixed metaphor:

. . . Pity these have not
Traced upon vellum or wild Indian leaf
The shadows of melodious utterance.
But bare of laurel they live, dream, and die;
"The Fall of Hyperion," 1: 4–7

Given the definition of poetry as the shadow of melodious utterance, it
is not surprising that the poet should leave open the question of decid-
ing whether "The Fall of Hyperion" is the act of a poet or a visionary.
The poem stages this very ambiguity by transcribing a vision that

takes place during the falling asleep of the narrator within another vision. Representationally, the text is the transcription of a twice displaced nonidentical vision. One could complicate the problem further. If Ian Jack is right in assuming that Keats knew Bellini's *The Feast of the Gods,* then the first vision, describing the narrator eating the leftovers of a divine banquet, might locate that vision in a modified version of Bellini's painting.[39]

It is not surprising, then, that finally the text should denounce itself as vision. Moneta, addressing the poet, states:

What benefit canst thou do, or all thy tribe,
To the great world? Thou art a dreaming thing,
A fever of thyself. . . .
        . . .
. . . Art thou not of the dreamer tribe?
The poet and the dreamer are distinct,
Diverse, sheer opposite, antipodes.
The one pours out a balm upon the world,
The other vexes it.
    "The Fall of Hyperion," 1: 167–69, 198–202

One may well ask who, then, are the poets? The question is insoluble within the context of the "Hyperion" and "The Fall of Hyperion" fragments. What is important, however, is that Keats should follow the preceding verses with an attack on lyrical poets, suggesting the impossibility of a successful lyrical idiom.

        . . . Then shouted I,
Spite of myself, and with a Pythia's spleen,
'Apollo! faded, far-flown Apollo!
Where is thy misty pestilence to creep
Into the dwellings, through the door crannies,
Of all mock lyricists, large self-worshippers
And careless hectorers in proud bad verse.
Though I breathe death with them it will be life
To see them sprawl before me into graves.
        (1: 202–10)

At any rate, the impossibility for the belated poet of grounding his representations, besides being dramatically reenacted through the tale of the falling of the gods, is also thematized in a more direct textual manner. When the narrator in his vision encounters the archaeological remains of Saturn's temple, he is forced to look west:

> Turning from these with awe, once more I raised
> My eyes to fathom the space every way—
> The embossed roof, the silent massy range
> Of columns north and south, ending in mist
> Of nothing, then to eastward, where black gates
> Were shut against the sunrise evermore.
> Then to the west I looked, and saw far off
> An Image.
>
> (1: 81–89)

The belated poet is shut off from the origin of the rising sun and his gaze has to follow the direction of history and of the setting sun.

Hegel in his *Aesthetics* saw in the sound produced at sunrise by the colossi of Memnon the origin of art. Keats will identify his Hyperion with the same statuary and his idiom with the song they produce at dusk:

> . . . Hyperion: a granite peak. . . .
>
> . . .
>
> . . . like the bulk
> Of Memnon's image at the set of sun
> To one who travels from the dusking East:
> Sighs, too, as mournful as that Memnon's harp,
> He uttered, while his hands contemplative
> He pressed together, and in silence stood.
>
> ("Hyperion," 2: 367, 373–78)

The belated poet is forever excluded from the possibility of recuperating a privileged origin. In its stead, always preceding his ungrounded idiom and his interminable narrative, he encounters only the glyphs of a mute, lost, inaccessible original language:

> . . . hieroglyphics old
> Which sages and keen-eyed astrologers
> Then living on the earth, with labouring thought
> Won from the gaze of many centuries—

Now lost, save what we find on remnants huge
Of stone, or marble swart, their import gone,
Their wisdom long since fled.

("Hyperion," 1: 277–83)

Faced with the imperative of belatedness, Keats will renounce the project of writing his version of a redemptive history and instead turn to Apollo and "touch piously the Delphic harp." At this juncture we may well ask whether Keats remembered another famous fragment which stated: "The master to whom the oracle of Delphi belongs, does not speak, does not hide, he makes signs."[40]

## Notes

1. G. W. F. Hegel, *Faith and Knowledge*, trans. Walter Cerf and H. S. Harris (Albany: State University of New York Press, 1977), pp. 190–91. Incidentally Heidegger, in "The Word of Nietzsche: 'God is Dead' "—in *The Question Concerning Technology and Other Essays*, trans. William Lovitt (New York: Harper and Row, 1977), pp. 53–112—will remind the reader that Pascal's statement should belong to the same metaphysical space as Hegel's and Nietzsche's, but for "opposite reasons." He does not, however, analyze what the "opposite reasons" are which presumably connect Pascal to Hegel or Nietzsche.

2. J. C. F. Schiller, "The Gods of Greece," in *The Poems of Schiller*, trans. Edgar A. Browning (London: J. W. Parker, 1880), pp. 74–75.

3. See, for example, Peter Szondi's reading of Hölderlin's hymn "Friedensfeier" in *Hölderlin-Studien mit einem Traktat über philologische Erkenntnis* (Frankfurt: Suhrkamp, 1977).

4. Nerval, of course, knew Jean-Paul's text directly and quoted it in the series of poems entitled "Le Christ aux Oliviers." For a brief summary of the influence of Jean-Paul on French Romanticism, see Jeanine Moulin's appendix to her edition of Nerval's *Les Chimères* (Geneva: Droz, 1969).

Nerval's version is interesting inasmuch as, by problematizing the temporal sequence of the news of God's death in relationship to the event, he prefigures Nietzsche's version of the topos:

[the Lord] . . .
. . . started shouting, "God does not exist!"

They slept. "*The change*, friends—can you see it now?
I've touched the eternal firmament with my brow;
I've suffered many days, bleeding, broken!

Brothers, I cheated you: Abyss, abyss!
God's missing from my altar of sacrifice . . .
There is no God! No God now!" They slept on.

[(le Seigneur) . . .
. . . se prit à crier: "Non, Dieu n'existe pas!"

Ils dormaient. "Mes amis, savez-vous *la nouvelle?*
J'ai touché de mon front à la voûte éternelle;
Je suis sanglant, brisé, souffrant pour bien des jours!

Frères, je vous trompais: Abîme! abîme! abîme!
Le dieu manque à l'autel, où je suis la victime . . .
Dieu n'est pas! Dieu n'est plus!" Mais ils dormaient toujours!

Gérard de Nerval, *Les Chimères/The Chimeras,* trans.
Peter Jay (London: Anvil Press, 1984), pp. 26–27

5. Thomas Carlyle, *Critical and Miscellaneous Essays* (Boston: Brown and Taggart, 1884), 2: 133–34.

6. Gustave Flaubert, *The Temptation of Saint Anthony,* trans. Lafcadio Hearn (New York: Williams, Belasco and Meyers, 1930), p. 121.

7. Ibid., pp. 137–38.

8. Ibid., p. 143.

9. Ibid.

10. Ibid., p. 148.

11. Ibid., p. 156.

12. G. W. F. Hegel, *The Phenomenology of Mind,* trans. J. B. Baillie (New York: Harper and Row, 1967), pp. 713–14.

13. G. W. F. Hegel, *Philosophy of Mind,* vol. 3 of *The Encyclopaedia of the Philosophical Sciences,* trans. William Wallace (Oxford: Clarendon Press, 1971), pp. 211–12.

14. Friedrich Nietzsche, *The Joyful Wisdom,* trans. Thomas Common (1909–11; rpt. New York: Russell and Russell, 1964), pp. 167–68.

15. Paul de Man, *Allegories of Reading* (New Haven: Yale University Press, 1979), pp. 115–16.

16. I am, of course, referring to Derrida's analysis of the constitution of *Bedeutung* in Hegel in his "The Pit and the Pyramid: Introduction to Hegel's Semiology," in *Margins of Philosophy,* trans. Alan Bass (Chicago: University of Chicago Press, 1982), pp. 69–108.

17. For example, in the chapter on "European Nihilism," in his *Nietzsche,* Heidegger will write: "For that nihilism the saying 'God is Dead' signifies the powerlessness not only of the Christian God but for anything suprasensible to which man could or would wish to submit himself. This powerlessness consummates the ruin of the order that had prevailed until then." I will just quote

one more example, among many, that shows clearly Heidegger's strategy in reading Nietzsche:

Nietzsche speaks about "European Nihilism." He does not mean the positivism that arose in the mid-nineteenth century and spread throughout Europe. "European" has a historical significance here, and means as much as "Western" in the sense of Western history. Nietzsche uses *nihilism* as the name for the historical movement that he was the first to recognize and that already governed the previous century while defining the century to come, the movement whose essential interpretation he concentrates in the terse sentence: "God is Dead." That is to say, the "Christian God" has lost His power over beings and over the determination of man. (Martin Heidegger, *Nihilism*, vol. 4 of his *Nietzsche*, trans. Frank A. Capuzzi, ed. David Farrell Krell, New York: Harper and Row, 1982, p. 4).

On the difficult problems raised by Heidegger's reading of Nietzsche and particularly concerning the problem of Heidegger's neutralization of Nietzsche's *Darstellung*, see the works of Philippe Lacoue-Labarthe, in particular his "Typographie" in *Mimesis des articulations*, ed. Sylviane Agacinski (Paris: Aubier-Flammarion, 1975), pp. 165–270.

18. Earl R. Wasserman, "The English Romantics: The Grounds of Knowledge," in *Romanticism: Points of View*, ed. Robert F. Gleckner and Gerald E. Enscoe (Princeton: Princeton University Press, 1962), p. 335.

19. Joseph N. Riddel, "A Somewhat Polemical Introduction: The Elliptical Poem," *Genre* 11:4 (1978): 460, 463–64.

20. Quoted by Wasserman, "The English Romantics," p. 339.

21. Ibid., p. 334.

22. Ibid., p. 337.

23. Samuel Taylor Coleridge, "On the Principles of Genial Criticism," in *Biographia Literaria*, ed. J. Shawcross (Oxford: Clarendon Press, 1907), 2: 223.

24. All references to *The Prelude* will be to the 1850 version (New York: Norton, 1979).

25. Paul de Man, "Intentional Structure of the Romantic Image," in *The Rhetoric of Romanticism* (New York: Columbia University Press, 1984), pp. 6, 8.

26. Coleridge, *Biographia Literaria*, 2: 254.

27. Ibid., 2: 256.

28. Hegel, *Philosophy of Mind*, p. 201.

29. Hegel, *Phenomenology of Mind*, p. 808.

30. Hegel, *Philosophy of Mind*, p. 205.

31. Quoted by Derrida in "The Pit and the Pyramid," p. 90.

32. Jacques Derrida, *Glas*, trans. John P. Leavey, Jr., and Richard Rand (Lincoln: University of Nebraska Press, 1986), p. 10.

33. Quoted by Wasserman, "The English Romantics," p. 338.

34. Derrida's comment on the privilege of *voice* in Hegel is particularly significant in this context:

... objectivity and interiority ... are only apparently opposed, since idealization has as its meaning (from Plato to Husserl) the simultaneous confirmation of objectivity one by the other. ...
According to a metaphor well coordinated with the entire system of metaphysics, only hearing, which preserves both objectivity *and* interiority, can be called fully ideal and theoretical. Therefore in its eminence it is designated by optical language (*idea, theōria*) .... (Derrida, "The Pit and the Pyramid," p. 93n)

This teleological concept of sound as the movement of idealization, the *Aufhebung* of natural exteriority, the *relève* of the visible into the audible, is, along with the entire philosophy of nature, the fundamental presupposition of the Hegelian interpretation of language, notably of the so-called material part of language, lexicology. (Derrida, "The Pit and the Pyramid," pp. 93–94)

35. The opposition voice/noise will appear again in "The Fall of Hyperion." Nature may have a voice, but such a voice is the belated "legend-laden" voice of a past history. Nature's voice, then, is memory, yet even this voice is only "barren noise" to the nonpoets. The function of the poet is to "humanize" the memorial voice of nature by "making comparisons," i.e., creating metaphors, and it is only *through* these metaphors that the voice of nature acquires the semblance of a memorial narrative:

Mortal, that thou mayst understand aright,
I humanize my sayings to thine ear,
Making comparisons of earthly things;
Or thou mightst better listen to the wind,
Whose language is to thee a barren noise,
Though it blows legend-laden through the trees—
In melancholy realms big tears are shed,
More sorrow-like to this, and such-like woe,
Too huge for mortal tongue, or pen or scribe.
　　　"The Fall of Hyperion," 2: 1–9

All references to the poems of Keats are to *The Complete Poems*, 2nd ed., ed. John Barnard (Harmondsworth: Penguin, 1973).

36. In Derrida's words (from "White Mythology," in *Margins of Philosophy*, p. 251):

Each time that there is a metaphor, there is doubtless a sun somewhere; but each time that there is sun, metaphor has begun. If the sun is metaphorical always, already, it is no longer completely natural. It is always, already a luster, a chandelier, one might say an *artificial* construction, if one could still give credence to this signification when nature has disappeared.

37. These lines will be echoed in some of the last words spoken by Keats on his deathbed to his friend Severn:

Four days previous to his death—the change in him was so great that I passed each moment in dread—not knowing what the next would have—he was calm and firm at its approaches—to a most astonishing degree—he told [me] not to tremble for he did not think that he should be convulsed—he said—"did you ever see any one die" no—"well then I pity you poor Severn—what trouble and danger you have got into for me—now you must be firm for it will not last long—I shall soon be laid in the quiet grave—thank God for the quiet grave—O! I can feel the cold earth upon me—the daisies growing over me—O for this quiet—it will be my first." (*The Letters of John Keats*, ed. Hyder E. Rollins, Cambridge: Cambridge University Press, 1958, 2: 378.)

38. Ian Jack, *Keats and the Mirror of Art* (Oxford: Clarendon Press, 1967), particularly pp. 176–90.

39. Ibid., p. 127.

40. *The Fragments of the Work of Heraclitus of Ephesus on Nature*, trans. G. T. W. Patrick (Baltimore: Murray, 1889), fragment 93.

# 8 The Ruins of Memory: Archaeological Fragments and Textual Artifacts

*Tout être vivant est* aussi *un fossile.*
Jacques Monod

*Nature is not an origin but a run down trope.*   Joseph Riddel

*Le signe, monument-de-la-vie-dans-la-mort, monument-de-la-mort-dans-la-vie, le sépulture d'un souffle ou le corps propre embaumé, l'altitude conservant en sa profondeur l'hégémonie de l'âme et résistant à la durée, le dur texte de pierres couvertes d'inscriptions, c'est la* pyramide.   Jacques Derrida

Freud more than once compared the task of the analyst to that of an archaeologist. In his article "Construction in Analysis," for example, he writes:

His [the analyst's] work of construction, or, if it is preferred, of reconstruction, resembles to a great extent an archeologist's excavation of some dwelling-place that has been destroyed and buried or of some ancient edifice. The two processes are in fact identical, except that the analyst works under better conditions. . . . Just as the archeologist builds up the walls of the building from the foundations that have remained standing . . . so does the analyst proceed when he draws his inferences from the fragments of memories.[1]

Consciousness, then, is continuous with itself neither temporally nor spatially. The past of an individual does not allow itself to be apprehended as simple, immediate, transparent, or total presence. The past as memory remains buried and ruined, a well inhabited by fragments incapable of presenting themselves to the light of memory without the elaborate machinery of linguistic constructions and representations.

Furthermore, elements buried in the past of memory are of a different nature than the belated representations they may engender. As archaeological fragments they will always remain distinct and discontinuous from their perceptual or linguistic reconstructions. Even if one were to assume that the archaeological fragments buried in the past are themselves nothing but representations, the order of what lies ruined in memory is different from the order of later reconstructions. The identities and continuities generated by the repetitive mechanism of recollection, reconstruction, or re-presentation, in fact, hide an unresolvable difference between the elements buried in the past of memory and their belated rememoration in the present of representation.

The psychoanalytic unconscious is as much the space in which the fragments of memory lie as it is the product of a memory which does not offer itself immediately to perception and which, literally, ruins the objects or representations that come to inhabit it. Memory is not a simple past that can be willed to presence, nor are its objects ordinary objects which are perceptually identifiable. They need to be reconstructed so as to become objects of ordinary perception; they will then, and only then, exist as linguistic or pictorial representations. Freud's gesture in assigning such an ambiguous status to memory was not novel, but continued instead in a well-established tradition, bringing to its logical conclusion a process that permeates all of eighteenth-century epistemology.

In the following notes I should like to examine, somewhat sketchily, some of the configurations assumed by the problems of memory, and to note some of its implications for the problems of representation in general, and of literary representation in particular.

The analytics of representation which have become a dominant concern in contemporary literary criticism have problematized the relationship between the literary "object" and its linguistic representation, and have thereby destabilized the central position that the subject held, acting as "intention" or as the locus of perception, in maintaining their identity. In this article we face the task of minimally reexamining that section of our literary canon which, at the origin or at the end of literary discourse, presumably either postulated the identity of "object" and representation, or assigned to literary discourse the function of being the testimonial of such an experience of adequation.

It is to such a new critical context that we owe a great deal of the renewed interest in the Romantics, for it would be difficult to name any other literary canon that is as motivated by, or approaches in as systematic a way, the problem of literary representation and the problematic role the "object" plays in relation to it.

Because of its scope, influence, and succinctness, Paul de Man's article "Intentional Structure of the Romantic Image"[2] might provide us with a useful point of departure. After briefly characterizing the linguistic peculiarities of Romantic poetry as "an abundant imagery coinciding with an equally abundant quantity of natural objects, the theme of imagination linked closely to the theme of nature," and concluding that "such is the fundamental ambiguity that characterizes the poetics of Romanticism" (RR, 2), de Man goes on to raise the question of the status of the Natural Object in particular and of Nature in general in Romantic poetry. After assuming that "the image is inspired by a nostalgia for the natural object, expanding to become nostalgia for the origin of this object" (RR, 6), de Man continues: "Such a nostalgia can only exist when the transcendental presence is forgotten. . . . The existence of the poetic image is itself a sign of divine absence" (RR, 6). In consequence, for de Man, "the nostalgia for the object has become a nostalgia for an entity that could never, by its very nature, become a particularized presence" (RR, 15).

This very nostalgia is what for de Man creates, in some cases, the illusion of an immediacy with the Natural Object. To quote de Man again: "At times Romantic thought and Romantic poetry seem to come so close to giving in completely to the nostalgia for the object that it becomes difficult to distinguish between object and image, between imagination and perception, between an expressive or constitutive and a mimetic or literal language" (RR, 7). Accordingly, de Man warns against "critics who speak of a 'happy relationship' between matter and consciousness," for they "fail to realize that the very fact that the relationship has to be established within the medium of language indicates that it does not exist in actuality" (RR, 8). He concludes that the Romantics are "the first modern writers to have put into question, in the language of poetry, the ontological priority of the sensory object" (RR, 16).

If I have quoted so extensively from de Man's article, it is because it clearly delineates a number of themes which have become quite prevalent in contemporary criticism. The representation of the Natural Object constitutes the ontological murder of that same Object; the nostalgia for the Object is first and foremost the poetic allegorization of that same murder; finally—and this perhaps constitutes de Man's implicit underpinning, rather than his explicit argument—if language is essentially responsible for the impossibility of a relationship that would maintain the object as transcendental presence, such a relationship does not exist even in a privileged perception which might later be nostalgically recaptured in a linguistic representation.

If the first proposition—that language renders a "happy relationship" between matter and consciousness impossible—is now, after Derrida, something of a commonplace, the second, which is in fact implicit in the first—that the "ontological priority of the sensory object" can be put into question—is perhaps more problematic. True enough, here again we could rely on the authority of Derrida when, for example, he writes:

In affirming that *perception does not exist* or that what is called perception is not primordial, that somehow everything "begins" by "re-presentation" (a proposition which can only be maintained by the elimination of these last two concepts: it means that there is no "beginning" and that the "representation" we were talking about is not the modification of a "re-" that has *befallen* a primordial presentation) and by reintroducing the difference involved in "signs" at the core of what is "primordial," we do not retreat from the level of transcendental phenomenology toward either an "empiricism" or a "Kantian" critique of the claim of having primordial intuition.[3]

Using the crucial distinction introduced by Edward Said, we may rephrase the preceding proposition to say that, for Derrida, perception is a beginning and not an origin. Derrida's argument is based on a deconstructive reading of Husserl and it is minimally questionable whether or not the argument can be transposed, without a new strategy of reading, to Romantic texts which, at least on the surface, often seem to valorize the perceptual moment of experience, even if this same perceptual moment is often treated as distinct and distant from the writing instance which commemorates it.

Let us briefly return to a well-known text such as Wordsworth's *Tintern Abbey* in the hope not of offering a new reading of the poem but of situating the problem. *Tintern Abbey* at first does not seem to problematize the perceptual component of the poem in relation to its linguistic inscription. The poet revisits a spot which he had visited in the past and reexperiences perceptually as well as emotionally the impact of the natural scene before him:

> . . . Once again
> Do I behold these steep and lofty cliffs,
> That on a wild secluded scene impress
> Thought of more deep seclusion; and connect
> The landscape with the quiet of the sky.
>
> (4–8)

Nevertheless, the temporal scheme in which the preceding verses and the ensuing description are framed is far from simple. The description is triggered not by an original vision or a first impression but by a second repeated visit to a place which the poet had once visited:

> Five years have past, five summers, with the length
> Of five long winters! and again I hear
> These waters, welling from their mountain-springs
> With a soft inland murmur.
>
> (1–4)

On his second visit, however, the poet cannot recapture his original experience. His present self being temporally discontinuous with his earlier self, he cannot recapture his earlier self or his original perception which, in its immediacy, was not contaminated by reflection:

> . . . I cannot paint
> What then I was. The sounding cataract
> Haunted me like a passion; the tall rock,
> The mountain, and the deep and gloomy wood
> Their colours and their forms, were then to me
> An appetite; a feeling and a love,
> That had no need of a remoter charm,
> By thought supplied, nor any interest
> Unborrowed from the eye.—That time is past,
> And all its aching joys are now no more,
> And all its dizzy raptures.
>
> (75–85)

This earlier perception, indescribable or unrepresentable though it may be, nevertheless maintains itself as a representation that can be recuperated at will through the mechanism of memory. Memory thus offers a means to inscribe a representation of an original unrepresentable perception and creates a semblance of temporal continuity.

When the poet revisits the banks of the Wye, he confronts his belated mnemonic representational perception—which will in turn allow for a linguistic representation—and not his original vision or perception. The poem is made possible by an image inscribed in memory: "The picture of the mind revives again" (61). Should the poet disappear, it is memory again and not its poem that will guarantee a future to that same representation through the same mechanism of mnemonic inscription, since that same representation will continue to exist through his sister's memory: "Thy memory be as a dwelling place / For all sweet sounds and harmonies" (141–42).

These cursory references to *Tintern Abbey* are not meant to offer a sketchy scheme for the reading of the poem, nor are they an attempt to elucidate Wordsworth's complex metaphysics of nature. I simply wish to suggest, by choosing one example among many, that for the Romantics the problematics of perception and representation are inextricably connected to those of memory. If representation excludes presence or if the epiphany of the Natural Object forbids representations, then it is through memory that perception maintains that Object in a suspended temporal state. Such a representation can then be recaptured by recollection or rememoration in the idiom of poetic language.

I would now like to turn briefly to Hegel, for it is in Hegel that we find the most systematic elaboration of the function of memory in relation to perception and representation.

*Geist,* which Hegel describes as "the truth of soul and consciousness,"[4] covers a great number of Romantic sins in its generality. Nevertheless—and this is what interests me here—without consciousness and thus without perception, it cannot acquire an objective content. *Geist* will have to discover itself objectively by representationally displacing the data of perception: "*Geist* is just this elevation above nature and physical modes, and above the complication with an internal object" (PM, 179).

We can already see the two problems, one explicit, one implicit, which Hegel will have to overcome with the help of his dialectical machine. In the first place, what consciousness and perception will provide him with are fragmentary, disconnected elements. Perception is by definition metonymic and synecdochal. The content of perception in its immediacy will allow the realization neither of a total self nor of a total nature. In the second place, the immediacy of perception will have to be representationally displaced, for otherwise immediacy will not allow for a cognitive grasp of either the subject or the object. These two problems are, in fact, at the bottom of the whole Romantic epistemology of the Natural Object. Romantic poetry is constantly preoccupied with the problems of how to pass from the fragmentation of perception to a totality, and how to arrive at the nature of the Object without losing the privilege of the immediacy of perception.

But let us return to Hegel. Hegel calls "intuition" (*Anschauung*) what would seem to be the first immediate perception of the object by a subject: "When intelligence reaches a concrete unity of the two factors, that is to say, when it is at once self-collected in this externally existing material, and yet in this self-collectedness sunk in the out-of-selfness, it is *Intuition* or Mental Vision" (PM, 155). Yet this "intuition" is more than a simple perception; it is a privileged perception that appropriates the essence of its object, a perception that does not stop at the mere externality of the object but succeeds in grasping the essence of the object hidden behind its appearances. It is thus "intuition," and not simple perception, which is necessary for both philosophy and poetry.[5]

This "intuition," however, is immediately displaced upon a representation which will then be stored in memory:

. . . mind posits intuition as its own, pervades it, makes it into something inward, recollects (inwardizes) itself in it, becomes present to itself in it, and hence free. By this withdrawal into itself, intelligence raises itself to the stage of mental representation. In representation, mind *has* intuition; the latter is *ideally present* in mind, it has not *vanished* or merely *passed away.* Therefore, when speaking of an intuition that has been raised to a representation, language is quite correct in saying: I *have* seen this. By this is expressed no mere past, but also in fact *presence;* here the past is purely *relative* and exists only in the *comparison* of *immediate* intuition with what we now have in representation. But the word "have," employed in the perfect tense has quite peculiarly the meaning of presence; what I have seen is something not merely that I *had,* but still *have,* something, therefore, that is present in me. In this use of the word "have" can be seen a general sign of the inwardness of the modern mind, which makes the reflection, not merely that the past in its immediacy has passed away, but also that in the mind the past is still present. (PM, 201)

The "intuition," then, is only "ideally present" because it is relegated to a nonrecuperable past— "I have seen this"—by a first representation of the object as an image. In spite of Hegel's desire to salvage some form of presence for intuition from his argument, it is clear that intuition is always buried in a past that cannot be immediately present. Representation usurps the presence of the intuition and relegates it to the nonrecuperable past of memory. The first image, the first representation, in spite of Hegel, constitutes the "murder" of the Natural Object. The Natural Object is only an absence inscribed in an image or a representation.

Images and representations constitute the storehouse of memory. These objects of memory are curious entities inasmuch as they neither have an ontological status— "representation cannot as it stands be said to *be*" (PM, 201)—nor do they mimetically succeed in maintaining the illusion of the presence of the object: "what is imaged gains this imperishableness only at the expense of the clarity and freshness of the immediate individuality of what is intuitively perceived in all its firmly determined aspects; the intuition, in becoming an image, is obscured and obliterated" (PM, 203).

This accumulation of images is described by Hegel as constituting a curious dark pit temporally and spatially cut off from consciousness but which is nevertheless essential for the comprehension of the later representation of the object in consciousness or language:

The image when thus kept in mind is no longer existent, but stored up out of consciousness. . . . Intelligence as this night-like mine or pit . . . is to be conceived as this subconscious mine. . . . No one knows what an infinite host of images of the past slumbers in him; now and then they do indeed accidentally awake, but one cannot, as it is said, call them to mind. (PM, 204–5)

It is from this curious dark pit inhabited by shadowy images that intelligence will constitute, through a second displacement, another set of representations that Hegel will consider to be "proper" representations: "the image is at once rendered distinguishable from the intuition and separable from the blank night in which it was originally submerged. Intelligence is thus the force which can give forth its property, and dispense with external intuition for its existence in it. This 'synthesis' of the internal image with the recollected existence is *representation* proper" (PM, 205).

The "proper" representations are not only at least twice removed from the Object, but constitute themselves only through a double mechanism of repetition. On the one hand, they are conscious recollections of unconscious recollections; on the other hand, for an intuition to be recalled, it has itself to be repeated: "If, therefore, I am to *retain* something in my memory, I must have repeated intuitions of it" (PM, 205). Without this second recollection, there is no guarantee that I should ever be able to read what was stored in memory. If I can recollect, it is because a second intuition permits me to read what until now was perhaps inscribed but remained unreadable. It is only by one's possible recovery of an intuition through a mechanism of repetition that one is ever certain that a given intuition was there at the beginning.

The function of giving a form to these representations is assigned by Hegel to imagination: "the intelligence which is active in this possession [of the representation] is the *reproductive imagination,* where the images issue from the inward world belonging to the ego, which is now the power over them" (PM, 206). Imagination finally succeeds in creating a stable image which leaves behind it the shadowy images of intuition or the ghastly representations of recollection. One must never lose sight, however, that for Hegel the representations created by imagination, which will in turn become the first signifying representations by constituting themselves as symbols (which are for Hegel the stuff of poetry), are originally subtended by an abysmal structure.

I need not proceed any further in Hegel's analysis of how representations become symbols and signs, and how for him the distinction between the two—symbols constituting the privileged language of poetry, and signs the privileged language of philosophy—is as necessary as it is untenable. Derrida, in his essay "The Pit and the Pyramid," has given us as precise an analysis as could be hoped for of Hegel's semiological machine.[6]

For my own purposes, I should simply like to add two remarks. First, after having constructed his realm of images, Hegel proceeds to create a world of language constituted by signs as opposed to symbols. Signs, for Hegel, constitute a system where the relationship between representation and object represented is arbitrary. Language is thus metaphorically once more removed from the Natural Objects which it represents. To use an older vocabulary, we may say that where image representations are motivated metaphors, language is constituted by a set of unmotivated metaphors. Hegel, in a curious metaphor—dramatized in Derrida's title—compares the linguistic sign to a pyramid: "The sign is some immediate intuition, representing a totally different import from what naturally belongs to it; it is the pyramid into which a foreign soul has been conveyed, and where it is conserved" (PM, 213). We have Hegel's own comment in his *Aesthetics* to the effect that what is inscribed and maintained in the pyramid is death itself. The pyramid is in fact a symbol of the death of the Natural Object in the sign. In the final analysis, Hegel's secondary memory created by language (*Gedächtnis*), is nothing but an archaeological cemetery populated by funerary monuments. I have tried to show in the previous chapter how this metaphor is in fact an allegorical emblem for the mode of signification of the Romantic literary text in general.

Second, the image representation created by imagination is a tropological construct. The image is constructed by a synecdoche which has been metonymically displaced onto a metaphorical representation. To this extent, Hegel's epistemology is a critical epistemology. Hegel, like all the Romantics, attempted to overcome, through philosophical and metaphysical considerations, the limitations of that epistemology. Nevertheless, for us the interest of Hegel's "philosophical mythology"—to use an expression borrowed from Nietzsche—and that of the poetic practice of the Romantics resides in their having radicalized the questions raised by their epistemology, rather than simply dismissing them, as their metaphysical and aesthetic beliefs might have authorized them to do.

Parenthetically, I would like at this point to briefly introduce a text which, though marginal to our concerns, might help us focus upon the Romantics' problem of the representation of the Natural Object. Locke, in the tenth chapter of the second book of the *Essay Concerning Human Understanding*, writes:

The memory of some men, it is true, is very tenacious, even to a miracle; but yet there seem to be a constant decay of all our *ideas,* even of those which are struck deepest, and in minds the most retentive; so that if they be not sometimes renewed by repeated exercise of the senses, or reflection on those kinds of objects which at first occasioned them, the print wears out, and at last there remains nothing to be seen. Thus the ideas, as well as children, of our youth often die before us; and our minds represent to us those tombs to which we are approaching; where, though the brass and marble remain, yet the inscriptions are effaced by time, and the imagery moulders away.[7]

This passage could be read as a direct rebuttal (before the fact) to Hegel's analysis of recollection and memory. Memory as a system cannot maintain itself as a global totality, nor do we have any guaran-

tee that under the pressure of time or history any one individual element of the system will remain intact. The elements of memory become
themselves funerary allegories of the inevitable erasure of the whole
representational system. Locke is, of course, talking of an individual memory. Yet inasmuch
as the Romantics needed a system of memory to salvage the status of
the Natural Object in spite of representation, they had to stabilize the
system of memory. The strategy is reasonably constant and consists in
attributing memory—or its equivalent, perception—to a transcendental subject. Hegel names his transcendental, historically total subject
*Geist*. Coleridge, on the other hand, ascribes a privileged perception to
a transcendental subject: "The IMAGINATION then I consider either as
primary, or secondary. The primary IMAGINATION I hold to be the
living Power and prime Agent of all human Perception, and as a repetition in the finite mind of the eternal act of creation in the infinite I
AM." Coleridge then makes the individual perception, in his words,
"an echo of the former." Without a transcendental subject, again in
Coleridge's words, "all objects (*as* objects) are essentially fixed and
dead."[8] But it is not these individual strategies that need to concern us
here, as much as the common and constant need to stabilize the representational systems which threaten the privileged status of the Natural
Object, which, in spite of all possible metaphysical guarantees, comes
to be metaphorized as memory or emblematized as a dark pit or
funerary monument.

Let us return to de Man's article, from which we began. In the second
half of the article de Man argues, by quoting texts of Rousseau, Hölderlin, and Wordsworth, that the Romantic loss of the privilege of the
Natural Object with respect to literary representation manifests itself
through a nostalgia for another, different nature. In his words, "the
nostalgia for the object has become a nostalgia for an entity that could
never by its very nature become a particularized presence" (RR, 15).
The insight into this entity is provided by imagination. But, adds de
Man, "this 'imagination' has little in common with the faculty that
produces natural images. . . . It marks instead a possibility for consciousness to exist entirely by and for itself, independently of all relationship with the outside world" (RR, 16).
    Without completely disagreeing with de Man, I would like to sug-
gest, through a brief examination of the texts by Wordsworth which he
cites, that in fact there is a spatial displacement of the Natural Object
which corresponds to the temporal one effected by representation.

Confronted with this double loss of an entity which can never be *here* and *now,* the poet does indeed yearn for a transcendental presence, but all that imagination can offer him is a representational fiction:

> . . . words for things
> The self-created sustenance of a mind
> Debarred from Nature's living images,
> Compelled to be a life unto herself
> And unrelentingly possessed by thirst
> Of greatness, love, and beauty.[9]
>
> (300–305)

Along with a passage from *La Nouvelle Héloïse* and one from Hölderlin's "Heim Kunft," de Man quotes the well-known passage from the sixth book of *The Prelude,* describing a valley in the Simplon Pass:

> . . . The immeasurable height
> Of woods-decaying, never to be decayed,
> The stationary blasts of waterfalls,
> And in the narrow rent at every turn
> Winds thwarting winds, bewildered and forlorn,
> The torrents shooting from the clear blue sky,
> The rocks that muttered close upon our ears,
> Black drizzling crags that spake by the wayside
> As if a voice were in them, the sick sight
> And giddy prospect of the raving stream,
> The unfettered clouds and region of the Heavens,
> Tumult and peace, the darkness and the light—
> Were all like workings of one mind, the features
> Of the same face, blossoms upon one tree;
> Characters of the great Apocalypse,
> The types and symbols of Eternity,
> Of first, and last, and midst, and without end.
>
> (6: 624–40)

The Nature described in the passage does in fact stand out as unique, contradictory, and privileged. Its temporal marker indicates its special Nature. This is not a Nature submitted to the temporality of representation. It stands in absolute immediacy because it is temporally immutable, invariable, always present.

Nevertheless, this passage is not without a number of problems.

Before discussing them, though, I would like to make a commonplace generalization. All the texts quoted by de Man refer to the same geographical area and deal with mountains and altitude. The fact is significant for, beginning with the Romantics and throughout the nineteenth century, altitude is the spatial emblem of difference and distance from an absolute origin. Thus, for example, a privileged original Nature or Natural Object is often placed at an unreachable height in relationship to the representationally temporalized Nature in the valleys. Immediacy and epiphany are often postulated in the mountains. Height becomes a familiar metaphor for difference from an origin.

Wordsworth's description of the crossing of the Alps in book 6 of *The Prelude* is then particularly significant since, in a way, it allegorizes the poetic quest for the Natural Object. At the outset, let us again state the obvious. The description of the Alps is part of a poem created by memory. The passage about the crossing of the Alps, like the rest of the poem, is constructed out of fragments of a memory. The passage does not, in fact, pretend to reconstruct a narrative continuity, but is simply an enumeration of specific, distinct moments valorized by memory: the view of Mont Blanc, the valley of Chamonix, the Simplon Pass, the lakes.

The first scene consists of Wordsworth's view of Mont Blanc. Inasmuch as Mont Blanc stands for the highest elevation, it also defines the possibility of the greatest representational difference. It is not surprising, then, that Mont Blanc should remain beyond the reach of language and, in a way, not even bestow a full perception.

The image of the highest summit of the Alps, placed at the beginning of the episode, is allegorized by Wordsworth as not quite a perceptual representation. As "soulless image," the original perception—the perception of the original difference—is "dead"; or rather, death is necessarily inscribed in the original perception of the origin, making it impossible for this first image to be displaced into perception, let alone into linguistic representation. This inscription of death into the original image will prevent it from being recuperable:

> That very day
> From a bare ridge we also first beheld
> Unveiled the summit of Mont Blanc, and grieved
> To have a soulless image on the eye
> That had usurped upon a living thought
> That never more could be.
>
> (6: 523–28)

Mont Blanc is thus not an origin that can ground perception or representation, but instead dispels any hope that the poet might have had to reach an origin through perception and representation. Deprived of beholding the mountain, the poet consoles himself by looking at the valley, which instead of offering itself as an absolute vision, offers itself as a textual representational construct.

> The wondrous Vale
> Of Chamouny stretched far below. . . .
> . . .
> . . . With such a book
> Before our eyes, we could not choose but read
> Lessons of genuine brotherhood, the plain
> And universal reason of mankind,
> The truths of young and old.
>
> (6: 528–29, 543–47)

The poet, however, does not resign himself to the textual space localized as a place of low altitude which is at the greatest possible distance from the original height of the summit of Mont Blanc whence the passage began. Wordsworth will not narrate his crossing the Alps at the Simplon Pass. If the episode marks an important moment in the narrative, then the metaphorics of altitude connected with the episode are also significant. A pass is, from a topographical standpoint, a curious space; higher than the valley it leaves below, it nevertheless remains lower than the highest elevation. It offers, therefore, the possibility of strategically substituting a secondary high point for the original unreachable highest point, which did not lend itself to an immediate perceptual or textual representation.

The episode is well known: the poet is eager to capture the moment when he will be at the summit of the pass, but he crosses the top of the pass without realizing it. The moment of awareness coincides with the belated realization that the highest point of the pass is in the past and that it has escaped the poet's perception.

> We must descend. . . .
> . . .
> . . . our future course, all plain to sight,
> Was downwards, with the current of the stream.
> Loth to believe what we so grieved to hear,
> For still we had hopes that pointed to the clouds,

We questioned him again, and yet again;
But every word that from the peasant's lips
Came to reply, translated by our feelings,
Ended in this,—*that we had crossed the Alps.*

(6: 581–91)

It is impossible for the poet to localize temporally or spatially the moment and place of highest altitude, which will remain perceptually and representationally indescribable. It is in the face of this failure that Wordsworth discovers, or has recourse to, Imagination, which, as we have seen, supplies a substitute secondary image for what was originally perceptually unattainable:

Imagination—here the Power so called
Through sad incompetence of human speech,
That awful Power rose from the mind's abyss
Like an unfathered vapor that enwraps,
At once, some lonely traveller. I was lost;
Halted without an effort to break through;
But to my conscious soul I now can say—
"I recognise thy glory": in such strength
Of usurpation, when the light of sense
Goes out.

(6: 592–601)

Imagination then usurps the function of that which is denied to the poet.

Having discovered the power of Imagination, the poet can thereby literally imagine the description of the impossible Nature hidden in the valley of the Simplon Pass. Again it is important that the extraordinary vision be in a valley where the poet can—to quote from a different passage—"be lost within himself / In trepidation, from the blank abyss / . . . [and] look with bodily eyes" (6: 469–71). Imagination, substituting itself for a privileged perception, creates an image of an original Natural Object which is no more spatially than it was temporally available.

The moment of the Imagination is a perceptual moment and not a textual one: The latter will come only after a complete descent upon reaching the shores of a lake "where Tones of Nature smoothed by learned Art / May flow in lasting current" (6: 674–75). In the 1805 version Wordsworth significantly had written, "Where tones of learned Art and Nature / May frame enduring language" (6: 604–5). The whole episode of the crossing of the Alps can thus be read as an allegory of Wordsworth's poetical development which is triggered by his spatial as well as temporal inability to capture an original Natural Object in its immediacy. The spatial problematic is of course subordinated to the temporal one: in other words, if space sends us back to the abyss in which we may recognize a variant of the dark pit of memory, in the last analysis it is the temporal pit of memory which determines the production of the text in which the spatial abyss appears.

Before returning to the problem of the "pit of memory," it might be of interest to juxtapose Shelley's *Mont Blanc* with Wordsworth's treatment of the crossing of the Alps in *The Prelude,* though without pretending to give a reading of the totality of the Shelley poem. Like Wordsworth, Shelley weaves the themes of representation and poetic diction in with his treatment of the natural scenery. Unlike Wordsworth, however, Shelley begins with a description of a ravine, before considering the mountains. The imagery is strangely similar to Wordsworth's, and would easily qualify as that specific imagery which de Man attributes to the Romantic poets in their attempts to render a privileged Natural Object. The poetic text is generated by the gaze of the poet upon the scene. What the perception generates, though, is a private and distinct subjective representation:

> . . . When I gaze on thee
> I seem as in a trance sublime and strange
> To muse on my own separate phantasy,
> My own, my human mind, which passively
> Now renders and receives fast influencings.
> (34–38)

Shelley's gaze is, of course, a privileged form of perception. Nevertheless, even in this privileged perception the Natural Object will remain absent from its poetic linguistic representations; for, despite the "thou art there," the Natural Object cannot be present in a linguistic representation which, at best, is only a ghostly image:

> Where that or thou art no unbidden guest,
> In the still care of the witch Poesy,
> Seeking among the shadows that pass by

Ghosts of all things that are, some shade of thee
Some phantom, some faint image; till the breast
From which they fled recalls them, thou art there.

(43–48)

Mont Blanc, where the valley originates, stands behind and above it,
and is representationally even more unreachable than the valley. All the
images associated with the mountain— "unearthly forms," "frozen
floods," "unfathomable deeps"—are in fact images that systematically
signify the impossibility of finding images representationally adequate
to the mountain. In front of the mountain the poet can only interpret,
and this through an act of faith:

The wilderness has a mysterious tongue
Which teaches awful doubt, or faith. . . .
                        . . .
Thou hast a voice, great Mountain . . .
                        . . .
                        . . . not understood
By all, but which the wise, and great, and good
Interpret.

(76–83)

After the texts of Hegel, we should not be surprised that Mont
Blanc, as an original Natural Object, should generate a "city of death"
inhabited by pyramids, themselves the symbol of death in the Natural
Object in representation:

                        . . . The glaciers creep
Like snakes that watch their prey, from their far fountains,
Slow rolling on; there, many a precipice,
Frost and the Sun in scorn of mortal power
Have piled: dome, pyramid, and pinnacle,
A city of death, distinct with many a tower
And wall impregnable of beaming ice.
Yet not a city, but a flood of ruin
Is there, that from the boundaries of the sky
Rolls its perpetual stream; vast pines are strewing
Its destined path, or in the mangled soil
Branchless and shattered stand: the rocks, drawn down

From yon remotest waste, have overthrown
The limits of the dead and living world,
Never to be reclaimed.

(100–114)

What the mountain has in fact generated is the ravine described at the beginning of the poem. If representations belong to the domain of the living, Natural Objects belong to the realm of the dead.

Flaubert is in many respects a writer symptomatic of the problems of memory. His aesthetics were based upon the search for an unmediated vision of what he called the Idea, which could ontologically ground the work of art. With his lucid irony he nevertheless had to admit the impossibility of the task. For Flaubert, the modern writer with his imagination could only construct ungrounded linguistic artifacts: "What a feat of engineering the natural is! And what a load of ruses one must employ in order to be true."[10]

To describe the futility of the task, Flaubert also resorts to the image of the mountain:

Is not the artist's life, or rather the work of art to be achieved, like a great mountain to be scaled? A difficult passage, one which requires a tenacious will. First, you glimpse a peak from below. Up in the heavens, it sparkles in its purity; its height is frightening but it beckons you for this very reason. You set out. Yet with each leveling of the path, the summit grows larger, the horizon recedes and one proceeds through precipices, vertigo and discouragements. It is cold and the eternal hurricane of the mountainous areas lifts you up and slices through to your last scrap of clothing. The Earth is lost forever, and the end will likely never be attained. This is when you assess your weariness, when you look upon the *cracks in your skin* with horror. You are left with nothing but an indomitable desire to climb still higher, to be done with it, to die. . . . Let us die in the snow, perish in the white agony of our desire, in the murmur of the torrents of Spirit [*l'Esprit*], our faces turned toward the sun! (C, 3: 342–343)

Of course this failure expressed here by Flaubert in spatial terms has its temporal equivalent. For example, in a letter to his niece Caroline he writes: "The Present is everything that is least important, for it is very short, elusive. The true is the Past, and the Future" (C, 7: 363). In a letter to Bouilhet he writes: "The future torments us and the past holds us back. No wonder the present is slipping from our grasp" (C, 2:

279). Since the future holds no hopes, the only refuge left for the writer is the past, with its store of memories: "I find it impossible to do anything. I spend my time bringing the past back to life" (C, 6: 166). The writer's present is inhabited by fragments of representations from memory. The same memory stands between himself and a non-representationally mediated nature, yet the barrier that memory puts between the self and Nature prevents the writer from living in an immediate relation with himself through the perception of a Natural Object. In a desperate attempt to salvage Self, Nature, and Presence, Flaubert would like to break off from memory. The task, however, is impossible. In a particularly significant letter to Bouilhet, he writes:

I've been daydreaming a lot about the theater of my passions. I've taken leave of them and forever, I hope. Here I am halfway through life. It is time to bid farewell to juvenile despairs. I make no attempt to hide, however, the fact that for the last three weeks they've been coming at me in torrents. I spent two or three good afternoons alone on the sand in the bright sunshine, sadly discovering something other than broken seashells. . . . Is nature ever insolent! What a brazen, mischievous face it turns to us! We rack our brains trying to understand the abyss which separates it from us. But there is something more comical still: the abyss that separates us from ourselves. It astounds me to think that right here in this place, while looking at this green-trimmed white wall I fell prey to heart palpitations while full of "Poh-etry": I can't make sense of it, and I become as dizzy as if I had suddenly come upon a two-thousand foot vertical cliff just below my feet. (C, 3: 316–18)

Memory, then, is an abyss inhabited by representations which invade the writer's present, cut him off from Nature, separate him from himself. Not surprisingly, in another striking passage, Flaubert describes the abyss of memory as a catacomb inhabited by an interminable series of corpses which constitute a history that inhabits the present of the writer—a present which the writer is forbidden to inhabit:

I went over everything again, like a man visiting the catacombs, looking slowly from side to side at endless rows of corpses. Going by the number of years, I wasn't born that long ago, but I have so many memories I feel overwhelmed, just as old men feel overwhelmed by all of the days they've lived. Sometimes it seems to me that I've lived for centuries and that my being contains the debris of a thousand past existences.[11]

Baudelaire's poem "J'ai plus de souvenirs que si j'avais mille ans (Spleen II)" is simultaneously the allegorizing and the apex of the problematics of memory inaugurated by the Romantics. For convenience, I shall quote it in its entirety:

Souvenirs?
More than if I had lived a thousand years!

No chest of drawers crammed with documents,
love-letters, wedding-invitations, wills,
a lock of someone's hair rolled up in a deed,
hides so many secrets as my brain.
This branching catacombs, this pyramid
contains more corpses than the potter's field:
I am a graveyard that the moon abhors,
where long worms like regrets come out to feed
most ravenously on my dearest dead.
I am an old boudoir where a rack of gowns,
perfumed by withered roses, rots to dust;
where only faint pastels and pale Bouchers
inhale the scent of long-unstoppered flasks.

Nothing is slower than the limping days
when under the heavy weather of the years
Boredom, the fruit of glum indifference,
gains the dimension of eternity . . .
Hereafter, mortal clay, you are no more
than a rock encircled by a nameless dread,
an ancient sphinx omitted from the map,
forgotten by the world, and whose fierce moods
sing only to the rays of setting suns.[12]

The poet is thus constituted by an accumulation of memories, an archaeological museum of fragments of the past, haphazardly juxtaposed, each a synecdochal textual representation ordered by the metonymic accident of proximity—"vers," "billets doux," "procès," "romances." The collection of memories, however, counts less than their emblem, the pyramid, which we are now in a position to read as the symbol of linguistic representation itself. Memory as representation is the funerary monument containing the corpse of the Natural Object. The poet, then, being nothing more than a set of representations, is reduced to a cemetery containing nothing but funerary monuments.

Nature itself *is* no more, it exists only as representation, that is, as funerary monument: "Hereafter, mortal clay, you are no more / than a rock encircled by a nameless dread, / an ancient sphinx omitted from the map, / forgotten by the world." The only way Nature can signify is through another representation, through a chant. But the chant can only take place in the light of a setting sun. Since Hegel, we also know that the setting sun is the emblem of the end of History. It is in the belated moment of a history that has run its course and exists only as an archaeological memory that Nature speaks in the sepulchral voice brought forth by, and as, the representation of textual funerary monuments.

It is not surprising then that Nietzsche, in quest of a new origin, demands an active forgetfulness, a capacity to actively forget the past, and that he remembers to erase, in a willful gesture, the temporal bondage of temporality. But that is perhaps another story and certainly another History.

## Notes

1. Sigmund Freud, *Standard Edition of the Complete Works of Sigmund Freud,* trans. James Strachey (London: Hogarth Press, 1953–73), 23: 259.

2. Paul de Man, "Intentional Structure of the Romantic Image," in *The Rhetoric of Romanticism* (New York: Columbia University Press, 1984), pp. 1–17. All subsequent references will be identified in the text by the letters "RR" followed by the page number.

3. Jacques Derrida, *Speech and Phenomena,* trans. David B. Allison (Evanston, Ill.: Northwestern University Press, 1973), pp. 45–46n. It is of interest to note that the original version of de Man's article was published in 1960 and thus predates the works of Derrida. This might suggest that the recent interest in the works of Derrida is not due to a fashionable importation of a foreign critical idiom, but that there is a close affinity, yet to be studied, between recent, post-New Critical developments of Anglo-American criticism and continental philosophy.

4. G. W. F. Hegel, *Philosophy of Mind,* vol. 3 of *The Encyclopaedia of the Philosophical Sciences,* trans. William Wallace (Oxford: Clarendon Press, 1971), p. 179; all subsequent references to this work will be indicated in the text by the letters "PM" followed by the page number. In quoting Hegel I shall not distinguish between the main text and the *Zusätze* but treat them both as a single text. I have retained the German word *Geist* rather than translate it, as does Wallace, as "mind."

5. In the *Zusatz* of section 449, for example, Hegel writes:

In general, it is the educated man who has an intuition free from a mass of contingent detail and equipped with a wealth of rational insights. An intelligent, educated man, even though he does not philosophize, can grasp the essentials, the core of the subject-matter in its simple qualitative nature. Reflection is, however, always necessary to achieve this. People often imagine that the poet, like the artist in general, must go to work purely intuitively. This is absolutely not the case. On the contrary, a genuine poet, before and during the execution of his work, must meditate and reflect. (PM, 200)

6. Jacques Derrida, "The Pit and the Pyramid: Introduction to Hegel's Semiology," in *Margins of Philosophy*, trans. Alan Bass (Chicago: University of Chicago Press, 1982), pp. 69–108.

7. John Locke, *An Essay Concerning Human Understanding*, ed. John W. Yolton (New York: Dutton, 1961), 1: 119.

8. Samuel Taylor Coleridge, *Biographia Literaria*, vols. 7 and 8 of *The Collected Works of Samuel Taylor Coleridge* (Princeton: Princeton University Press, 1983), 7: 304.

9. All references to *The Prelude* will be to the 1850 edition (New York: Norton, 1979).

10. Gustave Flaubert, *Correspondance* (Paris: Louis Conard, 1926–37), 3: 155. All subsequent references to this edition will be indicated in the text by the letter "C" followed by the volume and page number.

11. Gustave Flaubert, *Oeuvres complètes* (Paris: Editions du Seuil, 1964), p. 248.

12. Charles Baudelaire, *Les Fleurs du Mal*, trans. Richard Howard (Boston: David R. Godine, 1982), p. 75. The French text reads:

J'ai plus de souvenirs que si j'avais mille ans.

Un gros meuble à tiroirs encombré de bilans,
De vers, de billets doux, de procès, de romances,
Avec de lourds cheveux roulés dans des quittances,
Cache moins de secrets que mon triste cerveau.
C'est une pyramide, un immense caveau,
Qui contient plus de morts que la fosse commune.
—Je suis un cimetière abhorré de la lune,
Où comme des remords se traînent de longs vers
Qui s'acharnent toujours sur mes morts les plus chers.
Je suis un vieux boudoir plein de roses fanées,
Où gît tout un fouillis de modes surannées,
Où les pastels plaintifs et les pâles Boucher,
Seuls, respirent l'odeur d'un flacon débouché.

Rien n'égale en longueur les boiteuses journées,
Quand sous les lourds flocons des neigeuses années

L'ennui, fruit de la morne incuriosité,
Prend les proportions de l'immortalité.
—Desormais tu n'es plus, ô matière vivante!
Qu'un granit entouré d'une vague épouvante,
Assoupi dans le fond d'un Sahara brumeux;
Un vieux sphinx ignoré du monde insoucieux,
Oublié sur la carte, et dont l'humeur farouche
Ne chante qu'aux rayons du soleil qui se couche.

# 9  Bodies: On the Limits of Representation in Romantic Poetics

> *A living death was in each gush of sounds.*  John Keats
>
> *Words are not permanent unless the graphite be scraped up and put into a tube or the ink lifted. Words progress into the ground. . . . Words are the flesh of yesterday.*  William Carlos Williams
>
> *Un livre est un grand cimetière où sur la plupart des tombes on ne peut plus lire les noms effacés.*  Marcel Proust
>
> *. . . a theory is not something objective which might be adequate to nature; a theory is only an image of phenomena and corresponds to them as a sign does to the thing that is signified.*  Ludwig Boltzmann

A series of incongruous epigraphs, assuming that such a statement is not in itself redundant. If epigraphs are "inscriptions on stone, statue, coin, etc." (Oxford English Dictionary), then, as inscriptions, repeated copies of inscriptions, or graphic representations, they stand apparently detached from the absent surface that is supposed to support them. If epigraphs partake of a space of writing, then as epigraphs they are always incongruous, that is, out of place. They inhabit the margins of texts and monuments: the indefinite border which frames them. Yet as textual fragments, as master quotes, they transform the margins into the blank center that all texts or monuments attempt to circumscribe. The ambiguity of epigraphs is the figure of the undecidable borderline of all textual representations.

Again, if figuratively epigraphs are texts in the margin of other texts, as figures they problematize the space between texts. Is a text written upon the blank space of epigraphs (can one always find one or more epigraphs for a given text?), or are epigraphs written on texts (are texts an attempt to mark the empty space of epigraphs?)? If epigraphs are incongruous, so are the texts with which they are associated.

If, as epigraphs, these textual fragments suggest anything, it is in turn their own incongruity as representations: the incongruity of all forms of representation—sound, word, book, self, theory—to something else whose absence is marked by a figure: "living death," "flesh of yesterday," "cemetery," "nature." As epigraphs they stand as figures for epigraphs. The incongruity of texts and epigraphs is perhaps nothing but the incongruity of all figuration and representation. Figuration as the absent space of texts; texts as the absent space of figures.

It might have been more appropriate to have begun with the descriptive statement: "A series of incongruous metaphors or, in the vocabulary of traditional rhetoric, a series of improper or unmotivated metaphors." But then, according to what criteria would we differentiate between proper and improper metaphors? The disquieting tenor of the metaphors that I began by enumerating does violence to any everyday, "proper" definition of voice, word, book, self, or theory. And without a proper definition of voice, word, book, self, or theory, we must renounce any hope of distinguishing a proper figure from an improper figure. The difficulty, of course, resides in attempting to characterize, in no matter how phantasmatic a way, that which determines the impropriety of any figuration.

Let me, at the risk of beginning again from a false starting point, attempt a brief gloss of the series of incongruous metaphors with which I began.

*A living death was in each gush of sounds.*

A sound ideally—or, more exactly, as ideality—should mean, express, indicate, represent, but never contain any otherness within itself. If a sound could contain within itself anything other than itself, then that heterogeneous element which would inhabit sound would threaten its very ideality. The statement that sound might be marked by such an otherness cannot be a simple statement but is rather a metaphor compounding an oxymoron: a figure as heterogeneity, or heterogeneity as figure. The interest of the compounded metaphor is, of course, to subordinate sound to the oxymoron of a living death. A metaphor connecting life and sound would have seen a metaphysical platitude, whereas one connecting death with sound could be read in a Hegelian key as a nostalgic evocation of the loss of the object in representation. The oxymoron, on the other hand, suggests the independent life of that which dies in sound, as well as the strangely dead property of that which metaphorically might be said to live in representation. Let us, however, postpone the question as to what can be rendered as "living death," and why the oxymoron resists being reduced to a noun or an ordinary proposition.

> *Words are not permanent unless the graphite be*
> *scraped up and put in a tube or the ink lifted.*
> *Words progress into the ground. . . . Words are the*
> *flesh of yesterday.*

That words—or, for that matter, any representations—should be marked temporally in addition to their apparent spatial relations, is something which, after Derrida, does not need to be elaborated. What is worth underscoring is Williams's claim that the temporality of words breaks their spatial stability. If words are always the flesh of yesterday and if they progress into the ground, then their function is to reenact repeatedly and forever a process of entombment. Reversing the proposition, we may be tempted to say that words are the apparently innocent yet enigmatic surface which suggests yet occults a process of burial which, by its very temporality—always yesterday, always progressing—can never become present.

> *Un livre est un grand cimetière où sur la plupart*
> *des tombes on ne peut plus lire les noms effacés.*

If a book can be figuratively called a cemetery, it is because within it, reflexively, is produced another figure: the tombstone. The important thing, however, is not this reflexive allegorization of the figure. What is more significant is the fact that this repeated figuration depends on the absolute alterity and heterogeneity of the bodies that lie beneath the tombstones. The master figure of this otherness of figuration—namely, the name—is absent; the relation of bodies to representation escapes the ordinary logic of representation. The names of the bodies which lie in the cemetery of the book and which constitute it by their effacement always already precede the book and cannot be represented by it or in it.

> . . . a theory is not something objective which
> might be adequate to nature; a theory is only an
> image of phenomena and corresponds to them as a
> sign does to the thing that is signified.

From the outset we might have to renounce the project of elaborating a proper theory for the scenario that I am trying to suggest. Theory belongs to figuration or, more precisely, is the reflexive redoubling of figuration: "a theory is only an image of phenomena." As such, a theory does not have any immediate hold over the alterity of figuration which Boltzmann calls "nature." It does not stand to the latter in a privileged relationship any more than figuration does. Theory, like figuration and signification, belongs to the belated realm of representation.

Without hoping to erect a proper theory of the relationship of representation to an alterity that can only be hinted at as "invisible bodies" or "erased names," but simply in an attempt to proceed more systematically, let me begin again and take my point of departure from a number of established critical positions.

In attempting to describe the mechanisms of noncontinuity, nonidentity, nonadequation, and nonpresence which govern the production of systems of signification, poetical figuration, or narrative development, we must recognize that these systems—in their derived secondary and belated quest for identity, presence, immanence, or poetical epiphany—attempt to occult their generative mechanism by a polished surface of meaning, image, and plot. The analytical critique of representation which constitutes the theoretical nucleus of a considerable body of recent literary theory has generated a distinct metaphorical field which, implicitly or explicitly, appears to be governed by expressions organized around the motifs of Death, Absence, and Nostalgia.

From the outset it should be made clear that these metaphorical motifs cannot be reduced to nouns or concepts. Expressions such as "death," "absence," and "nostalgia" are metaphorical representations which suggest the impossibility for representation to sustain presence. Death, absence, or nostalgia as terms introduce from the outset modes of spatial and temporal discontinuity between themselves and the terms they invoke which resist the reduction of the representational machine to simple concepts, stable meanings, or poetical epiphanies. De Man's early article "Intentional Structure of the Romantic Image" provides a useful illustration of the critical use of these metaphors. Discussing the general problem of the Romantic Image through a close analysis of Hölderlin's "Brot und Wein," and commenting on the lines "nun aber nennt er sein Liebstes / Nun, nun mussen dafür Worte, wie Blumen entstehn," de Man writes:

. . . the intent of the poetic word is to originate like the flower . . . it strives to banish all metaphor, to become entirely literal.

We can understand origin only in terms of difference: the source springs up because of the need to be somewhere or something else than what is now here. The word "entstehn," with its distancing prefix, equates origin with negation and difference. But the natural object, safe in its immediate being, seems to have no beginning and no end. Its permanence is carried by the stability of its being, whereas a beginning implies a negation of permanence, the discontinuity of a death in which an entity relinquishes its specificity and leaves it behind, like an empty shell.[1]

Generalizing his analysis, de Man continues:

The image is inspired by a nostalgia for the natural object, expanding to become nostalgia for the origin of this object. . . . The existence of the poetic image is itself a sign of divine absence, and the conscious use of poetic imagery an admission of this absence. (RR, 6)

De Man goes on to conclude that "the nostalgia for the object has become a nostalgia for an entity that could never, by its very nature, become a particularized presence" (RR, 15).

The metaphors used by the critic reduplicate the poetical figuration which is itself the result of the incapacity of poetic language to name an original entity. The original spatial and temporal displacements posited by the poem reinscribe themselves in the critic's idiom, thus preventing a conceptual closure.

In a more philosophical vein, Derrida, in his early work *Of Grammatology*, shies away from the metaphor—and the ethos—of nostalgia

and instead strategically employs the metaphors of "trace" and "differance," "arche-writing" and "gramme" to provide an analysis of the
mechanisms at play in representation. He writes: "The trace is in fact
the absolute origin of sense in general. Which amounts to saying once
again that there is no absolute origin of sense in general. The trace is
the differance which opens appearance [*l'apparaître*] and signification."[2] And: "Arche-writing as spacing cannot occur *as such* within the
phenomenological experience of a *presence*. It marks *the dead time*
within the presence of the living present, within the general form of all
presence. The dead time is at work" (OG, 68). And again: "Becoming
is the constitution of subjectivity. On all levels of life's organization,
that is to say, of *the economy of death*. All graphemes are of a testa-
mentary essence. And the original absence of the subject of writing is
also the absence of the thing or the referent" (OG, 69). To quote one
final example:

> The outside, "spatial" and "objective" exteriority which we believe we know
> as the most familiar thing in the world, as familiarity itself, would not appear
> without the gramme, without difference as temporalization, without the non-
> presence of the other inscribed within the sense of the present, without the
> relationship with death as the concrete structure of the living present. (OG,
> 70–71)

"Trace," "writing," and "gramme" are therefore makeshift metaphors to allow for the possibility of a critical discourse on representation. Nevertheless, all of them remain in complicity with the master
metaphor of Death. What is explicit in Derrida is the spatial and
temporal divide which necessarily entails the recourse to the metaphor
of Death: "the original absence of the subject of writing is also the
absence of the thing or the referent" (OG, 69). In Derrida's brilliant
lapidary formula: "What can look at itself is not one; and the law of
the addition of the origin to its representation, of the thing to its image,
is that one plus one makes at least three" (OG, 36).

It is clear, I hope, that the purpose of these remarks is not to give a
quick overview of de Man's or Derrida's thought, but to point to the
importance of certain metaphors for our understanding of the problems raised by representation and to hint at the relation that these
metaphors maintain with those of a Romantic poetics.

At the beginning of "The Fall of Hyperion," Keats defines the poetical act as one of tracing "the shadows of melodious utterance" (l. 6).
This compounded metaphor might serve in this context as an excellent
emblem for Romantic figuration. The poetical text traces—it delin-

eates, copies, or represents—a shadow; the shadow is itself the reflection of a presumed absence—unavailable, inaudible, "melodious utterance." The poetical image is thus a metaphorically thrice-removed representation of an absent original saying. Yet each metaphorical level does not simply displace a preceding one. The image is not the single symbol of a symbol. The metaphors, in fact, attempt the impossible gesture of bridging domains which are radically heterogeneous. The final text is not simply the distant echo of an original utterance. The poetical act paradoxically mimics the circular path of an original meaning returning to itself. That is to say, the poetical act parodies a metaphysical economy of representation, yet in its pseudocirculation it succeeds in inscribing within itself two representationally heterogeneous moments, vision and voice, each incapable of rendering the original dead or absent word. After all, "The Fall of Hyperion" is a myth about the origin of poetic diction.

Yet can we simply and unequivocally reduce to such a model a passage like the following from "Sleep and Poetry"?

Will not some say that I presumptuously
Have spoken? that from hastening disgrace
'Twere better far to hide my foolish face?
That whining boyhood should with reverence bow
Ere the dread thunderbolt could reach? How!
If I do hide myself, it sure shall be
In the very fane, the light of Poesy:
If I do fall, at least I will be laid
Beneath the silence of a poplar shade;
And over me the grass shall be smooth-shaven;
And there shall be a kind memorial graven.
(270–80)

The passage considers the possibility of poetic failure. In fact, failure is not a possibility but a certainty, for to identify with "poesy" in Keats's poem is to identify with the sun Hyperion/Apollo, that is, to face certain annihilation.

Ah! rather let me like a madman run
Over some precipice! let the hot sun
Melt my Dedalian wings, and drive me down
Convulsed and headlong!
(301–4)

Eventually the possibility of the poetic act will require a movement away from the incandescent divine origin, "Deep in the shady sadness of a vale / Far sunken from the healthy breath of morn / Far from the fiery noon" ("Hyperion," 1–3), to the realm of the half-dead, de-throned original god, Saturn. Be that as it may, Keats's poetical enterprise is from the beginning a necessarily failed enterprise. Yet the failure of a successful poetical act is the very condition for the existence of poetry, the function of poetry's idiom being that of stating its impossibility or its own inevitable failure. This much perhaps we already knew. What is different in the passage I quoted is not so much a metaphorical relation between death and poetical representation as the phantasmatic scenario through which this metaphorical death is staged. The poet's failure will not lead him to an abstract and conceptual realization of his death, but to his burial. His body will be covered with a pastoral scene which in turn will contain a "memorial graven."

In one sense, then, we know what the poetical act generates: an engraving on a memorial stone. The poetical text will thus stand as a belated testimonial to the poem's failure to achieve its representational end. The nature of the text at this level is that of a testimonial metaphorically inscribing a death which is the repetition of an earlier one.

Read in this way, the interest of Keats's passage resides more in its particular treatment of a Romantic topos than in any particularly novel conception of the status of poetry's idiom. Keats's "memorial graven"—as opposed to, say, Wordsworth's (I am thinking here of his "Essays on Epitaphs")—is solitary and does not bind a community through a process of commemorative continuity. That is to say, Keats does not offer an ethical or theological avenue by which to salvage the necessary idiom of poetry.

More interesting, perhaps, we might ask the question as to what is engraved on the memorial. The poem does not spell it out. However, the concerns of Keats's friend Severn about Keats's actual tomb may provide us with a clue to this funerary puzzle. Keats had asked Severn to place the inscription "Here lies one whose name was writ in water" on his tomb. The inscription is itself a reduplication of an earlier erased tracing. What the erasure of the earlier tracing dissolves is a name with all the identities that it might sustain: self, intention, essence, and so on. The erasure of the name forces the metaphoricity of the later engraving which reduplicates the heterogeneous metaphorical relation between that which is written on water and that which is written on stone. We may also legitimately ask, on the one hand,

"Who is it that writes 'Here lies one whose name was writ in water'?" and on the other, "Who writes on water?" The two inscriptions are radically, temporally, and spatially divided from each other. Even if one can identify the author of the inscription with the author of the poem, one still cannot identify the latter with the hand that writes on water. The closest one can come to recognizing he who writes on water in the Keatsian canon is to see him as the one who asks, "How long will this posthumous life of mine last?"—that is to say as a corpse, the corpse lying beneath the grave on which is written "Here lies . . . ," or the corpse which, in the poem, is buried underneath the pastoral scene that contains a "memorial graven."

Yet here we have to face something different from a representation symbolizing its own funerary nature. If there is a strict textual and figurative relation between the poem and the "memorial graven," the relation that binds the corpse to the text—as well as to the figurative scene it generates—is, strictly speaking, unutterable. The corpse is a poetical condition for the possibility of the apparently innocent pastoral scene which occults it and which constitutes the poetical image, as well as the absent object to which the engraved memorial refers. It may be useful to remember that the "living corpse" that asks, "How long will this posthumous life of mine last?" will also say "thank God for the quiet grave—O! I can feel the cold earth upon me—the daisies growing over me—O for this quiet—it will be my first."[3] Yet again, there is no representational scheme which will permit the inscription of the corpse in the text, nor will there be any critical idiom which will succeed in characterizing it in any way whatsoever.

The corpse, a necessary condition for the logic of any representational system, will itself always remain in a relationship of absolute Otherness to such a system. Using the syntactical facility of French, all we can say is, "il y a du cadavre" ("there is corpse"). What we cannot say is that "le cadavre est," for if we were to say "a corpse is," or "a corpse is there and then," we would have to ask "there where?" and "then when?" and "is where?" and "is when?" But, as we have seen, what the corpse does is to cleave spatial and temporal identities so as to make the questions "where?" and "when?" highly problematic. In Blanchot's happier formulations:

Death suspends the relation to place, even though the deceased rests heavily in his spot as if upon the only basis that is left to him. To be precise, this basis lacks, the place is missing, the corpse is not in its place. What is it? It is not here, and yet it is not anywhere else. Nowhere? But then nowhere is here. The cadaverous presence establishes a relation between here and nowhere. . . . The corpse is here, but here in its turn becomes a corpse.[4]

No matter how calmly the corpse has been laid out upon its bed for final viewing, it is also everywhere in the room, all over the house. At every instant it can be elsewhere than where it is. It is where we are apart from it, where there is nothing; it is an invading presence, an obscure and vain abundance. (SL, 259)

It is the corpse, then, and not a recollected, nostalgic evocation or conceptual idealization, that problematizes the temporal and spatial markers of representation. The relationship of death to representation is, strictly speaking, dialectical, whereas the corpse destabilizes all the oppositions necessary to maintain the economy of the dialectical operation, the economy of the negated object and the sublated idealized representation, or the economy between object and sign, the function of the latter being to restore the object to the position of an idealized conceptual entity. At least since Hegel, we know that death partakes of dialectics; Blanchot's remark, on the other hand, underscores the subversive role of the corpse in relation to any operation that aims at recapturing the lost object in a belated rememoration.

The corpse cleaves the "here and now" which constitutes the space of visibility and presence. By never being in its proper place and by never having a proper place to be in, as Blanchot would have it, the corpse establishes a relationship between a "here" and an elsewhere which is, in fact, nowhere. The corpse inhabits this uncanny space, which assumes the properties of the corpse that inhabits it. Blanchot's meditation on the corpse is in fact a meditation on the poetical image and the peculiar representational space it generates and inhabits. In Blanchot's words: "the cadaver's strangeness is perhaps also that of the image" (SL, 256).

Images are woven in the web of a representational system. Yet if images give us the mirage of the presence of the object, and if images can be read or allegorized to nostalgically evoke the absence of the Object (or, in Blanchot's Heideggerian vocabulary, of the Thing), it is only because the very possibility of the image depends on the Thing/Corpse. Having become image,

instantly it has become that which no one can grasp, the unreal, the impossible. It is not the same thing at a distance but the thing as distance, present in its absence, graspable because ungraspable, appearing as disappeared. It is the return of what does not come back, the strange heart of remoteness as the life and the sole heart of the thing. (SL, 255–56)

Whether we try to read in the image the plenitude of the Object, or rather see in it a nostalgic evocation of the loss or the absence of the Object, speculation always follows figuration. What "precedes" figuration—the corpse of the Object which conditions and pervades the image—remains invisible and unattainable. Any attempt to speculate on the corpse of the Thing/Object which subtends figuration can only have the status of a mythopoetic speculation on the absent Origin of representation.

In a brilliant analysis Paul de Man, referring to the illustrations and graphic figurations on the blank pages which follow Shelley's *Triumph of Life*, writes:

The poem is sheltered from the performance of disfiguration by the power of its negative knowledge. But this knowledge is powerless to prevent what now functions as the decisive textual articulation: its reduction to the status of a fragment brought about by the actual death and subsequent disfigurement of Shelley's body, burned after his boat capsized and he drowned off the cost of Lerici. This defaced body is present in the margin of the last manuscript page and has become an inseparable part of the poem. At this point, figuration and cognition are actually interrupted by an event which shapes the text but which is not present in its represented or articulated meaning. It may seem a freak of chance to have a text thus molded by an actual occurrence, yet the reading of *The Triumph of Life* establishes that this mutilated textual model exposes the wound of a fracture that lies hidden in all texts. (RR, 120)

For de Man, then, Shelley's text is doubly emblematic. On the one hand it constitutes itself by representationally staging its "negative knowledge." In this particular configuration, the poem is "readable" even if the critic will eventually reveal the impossibility of constituting an ultimate meaning, and even if the poem's textual function is to undo the possibility of a "meaningful reading." On the other hand, the poem is framed by a margin that is inhabited but also constituted by a corpse which cannot be represented in or by the text but which, ultimately, conditions the ontological status of the text.

With all the necessary qualifications implicit in the preceding remarks regarding the possibility of a "Theory" that could account for the status of the Corpse/Thing in relation to representation, I should like to briefly refer to one such theory, if for no other reason than that it has been the pretext for an important development by Derrida. Nicolas Abraham and Maria Torok, in a number of studies now collected under the title *L'Ecorce et le noyau*, have attempted to reinstate the concept of introjection as originally introduced by Ferenczi.[5] There they argue for the necessity of distinguishing introjection from both incorporation and the closely related notion of interiorization.

Ferenczi's definition of introjection— "taking into the ego as large as possible a part of the outer world, making it the object of unconscious phantasies"[6]—differs little, as Laplanche and Pontalis have pointed out, from the Freudian notion of incorporation, which they define as "a process by which the subject, more or less on the level of phantasy, has an object penetrate his body and keeps it 'inside' his body."[7]

I will not attempt to summarize Abraham and Torok's argument as to the difference between these two notions. Rather, and despite the necessary distortions entailed by such a way of proceeding, I shall simply attempt to subordinate the distinction to my interests and ask the question: "What does one do when faced with a corpse?"

Within a psychoanalytic framework, the simplest and "normal" answer is, of course, that one considers the corpse as dead and goes through the "work of mourning" which consists in detaching one's libidinal investments from the lost object. In one sense a normal mourning consists in forgetting the dead or, as Daniel Lagache, barely paraphrasing Freud, puts it, in "killing death."[8] Psychoanalysis does not say it, but it is not too difficult to infer that at the end of a "normal" work of mourning one should be left with, at most, a nostalgic memory of the lost object.

Of course the work of mourning might fail and take a pathological aspect. The failure of a "normal" mourning is a failure to "kill the dead"; such mourning is replaced by an attempt to incorporate the dead. In Freud's words: "The ego wants to incorporate this object into itself, and, in accordance with the oral or cannibalistic phase of libidinal development in which it is, it wants to do so by devouring it."[9] Or, as Laplanche and Pontalis put it, incorporation has three meanings: "it means to obtain pleasure by making an object penetrate oneself; it means to destroy this object; and it means, by keeping it within oneself, to appropriate the object's qualities."[10] These three meanings, far from being contradictory, taken together constitute a coherent dialectical mechanism not unrelated to the Hegelian process of sublation. The object is destroyed to allow it to remain ideally present while inseparable from the subject in whom the operation takes place. The process of incorporation leads thus to a representational idealization of the object. As such, the dead object is eliminated yet maintained within a representational scheme. The incorporated object will eventually allow a further secondary elaboration in a psychoanalytic context through which it is exorcised and speculatively transformed into a theoretical object. Psychoanalysis thus buries the corpse and "reads" the dead in much the same way that, according to de Man, we read the dead in Romantic poetry:

For what we have done with the dead Shelley, and with all the other dead bodies that appear in romantic literature . . . is simply to bury them, to bury them in their own texts made into epitaphs and monumental graves. They have been made into statues for the benefit of future archeologists. (RR, 121)

Following Abraham and Torok, a third alternative when one is faced with a corpse would thus be to introject it, maintaining it intact as the living dead, enshrining it in a mausoleum, allowing it to maintain its words, its utterances, its language, allowing it to hide its name in a foreign crypt that inhabits the Ego. The incorporated corpse thus becomes an otherness which is absolutely close yet absolutely distant from the representational veil that surrounds it. Yet the operation of introjection is exceedingly fragile. The name, the body, and the text of the introjected corpse have to remain occulted and should resist any form of analytical or theoretical elaboration. Abraham and Torok insist on the difficulty of analyzing patients who have introjected the corpse of an object, desire, or person. Clinically they claim to have accidentally stumbled upon this enshrined and occulted object through the analytical process of "working through." Without questioning their clinical good faith, we may nevertheless question their undertaking in the name of their own theoretical suggestions. In other words, we may legitimately ask what the relationship is between an introjected object and an incorporated one, or between a corpse and the representational machine of reading.

To illustrate the problem, let me refer back to two letters I quoted in an earlier chapter, letters in which Flaubert describes his sister Caroline's wake and that of his close friend Alfred le Poittevin. What can we deduce from these two extraordinary scenes? Recall, first, that it is in the presence of his sister's corpse that Flaubert discovers the necessary relationship between writing and corpses and thus comes to realize the unique nature of his aesthetics. In an earlier chapter we saw how

Caroline's corpse leads to the birth of a certain type of literary representation. This becomes even clearer in the scenario Flaubert constructs upon the death of Alfred le Poittevin. In a long letter to Maxime du Camp describing the wake of his friend, Flaubert writes:

Alfred died on Monday night at midnight. I buried him yesterday, and I am now back. . . . I buried him in his shroud, I gave him the kiss of farewell, and saw his coffin being sealed. I spent two very full days there. While watching over him I read Creuzer's *Religions of Antiquity*. . . .
The last night I read *Les Feuilles d'automne*. I kept coming across pieces that he liked best or that for me had some relation to the present situation. From time to time I got up and went to lift the veil that they had placed on his face, and looked at him. I was myself bundled up in a coat that belonged to my father and that he had worn only once, the day of Caroline's wedding. . . .
There, my dear friend, you have what I have lived through since Tuesday night. I have had unheard-of perceptions and flashes of untranslatable ideas. Many things have been coming back to me with choirs of music and whiffs of perfume. . . . I feel the need to say incomprehensible things.[11]

Here again we are faced with a scenario that stages the presumed origin of literary representation. Flaubert himself gives us a clue as to the relationship between this scene and that of his sister's wake, when he recalls that he was wearing the coat that his father wore at Caroline's wedding, that is, on the day on which she wore the dress that was to become her shroud. Alfred le Poittevin is also covered with a shroud, like a Christ about to be entombed, to be resurrected not in body but as vision, text, music, and perfume—that is, as representation.

More important, however, Flaubert will problematize the representational machine triggered by Alfred le Poittevin's corpse. What he sees, hears, and understands is, strictly speaking, unrepresentable, and the statements describing the unrepresentable will be "meaningless" oxymorons: "unheard-of perceptions," "flashes of untranslatable ideas." His final wish will be to say "incomprehensible things," and it is the need to utter "incomprehensible things" which will be the foundation of his literary career. In the last analysis, Flaubert's literary output will necessarily refer to another text which, by definition, will remain as unreadable as it is unalterable.

As I suggested earlier, like Keats, Flaubert provides us with a mythopoetic staging of the generation of a representational system. Unlike in the case of Keats, however, the corpse that governs the scene is the corpse of another—another corpse—and the representational quest, rather than being a quest for writing, is in Flaubert a quest for reading. If such a discrimination is important in characterizing Flaubert's text—or any text, for that matter, as de Man's reading of Shelley's *The Triumph of Life* attests—even if such a distinction is only practical, it may nevertheless serve to remind us that the critic and the analyst are in no way privileged. Neither the critic nor the analyst will ever succeed in grounding a theory of the relation of the corpse to representation. In their "reading" they will never know *who* reads. The knowledge of the dead which we, perhaps, carry in us will have to remain every bit as occult as the corpses that lie hidden in the texts we read. For can we be so certain that Abraham and Torok's theory allows them to exorcise the corpses hidden in the crypts of their patients?

We might never have felt the need to ask that question, had it not been for Derrida's essay entitled "Fors."[12] On the surface, "Fors" is not a problematic text. As an introduction to the work of Abraham and Torok, particularly to their reading of Freud's famous case history of the "Wolf Man," "Fors" seemingly seeks to underscore their most important contribution to psychoanalytic theory: namely, their elaboration of the notions of introjection, of a dead/live body maintained within a Crypt contained within the Ego from which it is relatively independent.

Let us briefly attempt to characterize Derrida's elaboration of the notion of the crypt. A crypt is the phantasmatic and hermetically sealed space which surrounds, encloses, hides, and maintains a corpse introjected by the Ego. The inhabitant of the crypt is always "a living dead, a dead entity we are perfectly willing to keep alive, but *as* dead, one we are willing to keep, as long as we keep it, within us, intact in any way save as living" (F, xxi). The phantasmatic space of the crypt is a linguistic space as well. As such it encloses an occulted name through the elaboration of a cryptic code whose function is to displace, by misreading it, every symbol or sign which attempts to penetrate the crypt or read the name that it hides.

Since the crypt escapes its inscription in any representational system, whether perceptual or verbal, "no crypt presents itself. The grounds [*lieux*] are so disposed as to disguise and to hide: something, always a body in some way. But also to disguise the act of hiding and to hide the disguise: the crypt hides as it holds" (F, xiv). Hence it cannot, strictly speaking, be temporally or spatially located: "the crypt keeps an undiscoverable place" (F, xii).

Following Derrida's argument, one might be tempted to say that a crypt is by its singular nature undecipherable, its language untranslatable, and the name it conceals unreadable, that any attempt to read a crypt not only reduces an introjection to an incorporation, the crypt to a funerary monument, and the noun to a metaphor, but also that such a reading—more precisely (and literally), such a *translation*—is itself an *effect* of the Crypt. Derrida himself suggests, on the one hand, that Abraham and Torok's attempt to read the crypt of the Wolf Man is such a reduction: "What is to take place here—I'm speaking of both an *event* and a *monument*—will first of all be *analogous* to an archeological decoding."[13] But on the other hand, such an attempt "reads like a novel, a poem, a myth, a drama, the whole thing in plural translation" (F, xxv). That is to say, it reads like literature; thus Abraham and Torok's theoretical undertaking is itself a scenario for the birth of literature.

One suspects, however, that Derrida's ultimate aim is not simply to provide a sympathetic, though problematical, introduction to the work of Abraham and Torok. In a gesture that is strictly his, Derrida—in an obvious reference to Heidegger—relates the Crypt to the Thing: "what, originally, is a Thing? What is called Thinking? . . . The Thing is to be thought out *starting from* the Crypt, the Thing as a 'crypt effect'" (F, xiii).

The elaboration of this Heideggarian reference is better left to Derrida. Let us simply note that it is in this context that Derrida reveals the ultimate aim of his essay. After elaborating on the literary forms to which Abraham and Torok must recur in their attempt to "decrypt" the Wolf Man, Derrida points to the incapacity of these very forms to recuperate the Thing buried in the Crypt. Derrida concludes:

> But if this description is still insufficient, it is because it does not explain the necessity of this recourse to all these "forms." That necessity, it seems to me, springs in the final analysis from the *cryptic* structure of the ultimate "referent." The referent is constructed in such a way as never to present itself "in person," not even as the object of a theoretical discourse within the traditional norms. The Thing is encrypted. Not *within* the crypt (the Self's safe) but *by* the crypt and *in* the Unconscious. The "narrated" event, reconstituted by a novelistic, mytho-dramatico-poetic genesis, never appears. (F, xxvi)

Representation, then, and thus literature as well, is the effect of the occultation of the "ultimate referent," which can only be evoked as the "Thing" lying buried in the crypt. Ultimately the thrust of Derrida's textual operation points to Hegel. For the postulation of the inevitably cryptic nature of the Thing confirms the breakdown, at the origin, of the Hegelian dialectic—the original incapacity for dialectics to recuperate the Thing—and posits dialectics as an aftereffect of the originally cryptic nature of the Thing. As Derrida would have it, the crypt maintains and suppresses without any possible synthesis. What the crypt commemorates is "not the object itself, but its exclusion" (F, xvii).

Derrida's "Fors" acts, then, as a generative scenario for both writing and reading, and serves to interpret his earlier assertions regarding death and representation, pointing to the necessary Hegelian tenor of his earlier formulation. But if "Fors" reads at all, it reads by pointing to the limits of reading, inserting itself as a theoretical crypt within Derrida's philosophical corpus, infinitely problematizing his signature.

To conclude, the critic—like the writer and the analyst—reads, writes, translates and, in the course of accomplishing his task, manipulates a number of representational systems, contemplates images without body, and speculatively generates abstract and transparent idealities. Nevertheless, ultimately the bodies, names, or things which generate these representations are occulted by them. We may all share a necrophilic desire to "follow the path back to the tomb, then violate a sepulcher," yet we must also recognize the impossibility of the task and the necessary failure of our *undertaking*.

If as readers and writers we name and we sign, we may have to resign ourselves to the fact that we may never know to whom the signature properly belongs, because, to quote Flaubert one last time, "with the exception of idiots, one almost always dies uncertain of one's proper name."

## Notes

1. Paul de Man, "Intentional Structure of the Romantic Image," in *The Rhetoric of Romanticism* (New York: Columbia University Press, 1984), p. 4. All subsequent references to this book will be indicated in the text by the letters "RR" followed by the page number.

2. Jacques Derrida, *Of Grammatology*, trans. Gayatri Chakravorty Spivak (Baltimore: Johns Hopkins University Press, 1974), p. 65. All subsequent references will be indicated in the text by the letters "OG" followed by the page number.

3. John Keats, *The Letters of John Keats*, ed. Hyder E. Rollins (Cambridge: Cambridge University Press, 1958), 2: 378.

4. Maurice Blanchot, *The Space of Literature,* trans. Ann Smock (Lincoln: University of Nebraska Press, 1982), p. 256. All subsequent references will be indicated in the text by the letters "SL" followed by the page number.

5. Nicolas Abraham and Maria Torok, *L'Ecorce et le noyau* (Paris: Aubier-Flammarion, 1978).

6. Sandor Ferenczi, *First Contributions to Psycho-Analysis,* trans. Ernest Jones (London: Hogarth Press, 1952), p. 47.

7. Jean Laplanche and J. B. Pontalis, *The Language of Psychoanalysis,* trans. Donald Nicholson-Smith (New York: W. W. Norton, 1973), p. 211.

8. Daniel Lagache, "Le Travail du deuil," *Revue Française de Psychanalyse* 10:4 (1938): 695.

9. Sigmund Freud, *Standard Edition of the Complete Works of Sigmund Freud,* trans. James Strachey (London: Hogarth Press, 1953–73), 14: 249–50.

10. Laplanche and Pontalis, *Language,* p. 212.

11. Gustave Flaubert, *Correspondance,* ed. Jean Bruneau (Paris: Gallimard, 1973, 1980), 1: 493–95.

12. Jacques Derrida, "Fors," trans. Barbara Johnson, foreword to Nicolas Abraham and Maria Torok, *The Wolf Man's Magic Word: A Cryptonymy,* trans. Nicholas Rand (Minneapolis: University of Minnesota Press, 1986). All subsequent references will be identified in the text by the letter "F" followed by the page number.

13. From a short text by Derrida printed on the unbound flyleaf (and left untranslated in the English edition, *The Wolf Man's Magic Word*) included in Nicolas Abraham and Maria Torok, *Cryptonymie: le verbier de l'homme aux loups* (Paris: Aubier-Flammarion, 1976).